MW01152100

CRUISING COAST TO COAST THROUGH THE PANAMA CANAL 2020-21

A GUIDE ON WHAT TO EXPECT

CONTENTS

The majority of maps used in this book are courtesy of Open Street Maps. For enlargements or further detail visit on line to *www.openstreetmap.org* .

The majority of photos are from my vast collection taken during my various travels through Central and South America. Where a photo is used that is not from my personal collection, credit is given below the photograph.

INTRODUCTION

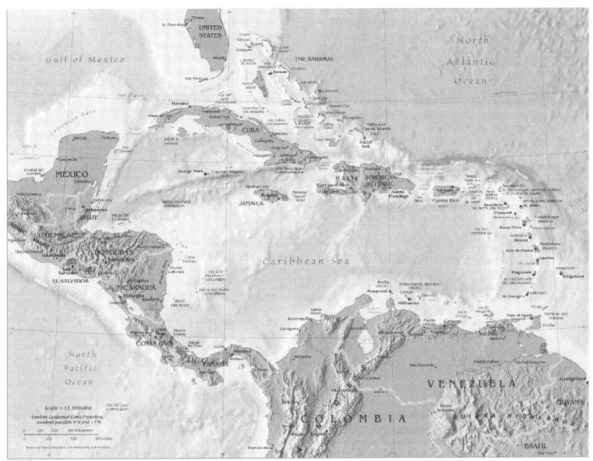

A map of the Caribbean Sea (CIA)

One of the most popular cruise itineraries is the transit of the Panama Canal on a journey between Los Angeles or San Francisco, California and either Miami or Fort Lauderdale, Florida. For many a transit through the Panama Canal fulfills a lifetime dream, as there is no other canal on earth as famous or that symbolizes as much as does this manmade wonder, opened in 1914. Other cruise itineraries include a transit through the canal, especially on the route between the west coast of South America and Florida or as part of an around the world cruise. Some cruise lines also offer an end of season repositioning cruise between Vancouver, Canada and Florida at the start of the fall season to prepare for the Caribbean itineraries or in mid spring to be ready for the Alaska cruise experience. More details regarding itineraries will be presented in the next chapter.

A CRUISE THROUGH THE CANAL: Today the standard cruise between Florida and California takes around two weeks to 16 days depending upon the specific itinerary. And for the majority of passengers the highlight or crown jewel of the voyage is the actual transit of the Panama Canal. It takes anywhere from seven to nine hours to cross between the two oceans, and for cruise ships it is always a daylight passage so that passengers can enjoy the experience. However, if you are on one of the mega cruise ships, your transit will be through the new, modern set of large locks, which do not have the same majesty as the older and more historic canal locks that the majority of ships still use. As the old expression states, newer and bigger is not always better.

The best time of the year to book a Panama Canal cruise is between late November and the end of April, with January and February being the choice months. Even during this period, the weather is difficult to predict, but at least there are no hurricanes occurring in that timeframe. In the tropical reaches of Northern Hemisphere during winter high temperatures are in the mid 20's Celsius or mid 80's Fahrenheit. And the humidity is lower than other times of the year, as this is technically the dry season. But there are still many days during which some rain will fall. During the Northern Hemisphere summer, both temperature and humidity levels increase to a degree that it is not comfortable for most visitors and from June into November there is the danger of hurricanes in both the Caribbean and Pacific waters.

Passing through the third Gatun Lock in the early morning

When you look at a map of the Americas, the North American continent narrows to only 100 kilometers or 60 miles at the Isthmus of Panama, yet building the canal was a monumental undertaking in the late 19th or early 20th centuries. Tropical conditions, rough topography and the threat of disease made such an effort almost Herculean at the time, yet we humans prevailed and in 1914 the Panama Canal opened to traffic.

Prior to the building of the canal the only other alternative in traveling between the two oceans was a 12,875 kilometer or 8,000 mile journey around the bottom of South America. And this journey was fraught with many dangers, especially traversing the Drake Passage at the bottom of South America. Even today a visit by cruise ship to Cape Horn, which is Land's End for the Americas, can never be guaranteed. I have felt winds in excess of 160 kilometers or 100 miles per hour and have been in seas greater than 12 meters or 35 feet and believe me when I say it is not a comfortable experience. If you have ever read an account of the HMS Bounty and captain Bligh's attempt to traverse the Drake Passage from east to west, you can appreciate how perilous a journey it was. In the end, after a month of trying to make it through, he had to turn his battered ship around, cross the Atlantic, put into Cape Town for repairs and then continue across the Indian Ocean and through the Indonesian Islands to ultimately reach his destination of Tahiti, a journey nearly three quarters of the way around the globe because the shortest distance around South America proved to be impossible. Today's great American aircraft carriers utilize the calm waters of the Straits of Magellan when doing a transit between the two oceans to avoid the perils of the Drake Passage because even with the new added locks to the Panama Canal there are still many supersized ships that are too large to make the transit.

I have organized this book to explain in detail the transit of the Panama Canal in three separate sections. I will take you on a virtual transit from the Caribbean Sea westbound to the Pacific Ocean, eastbound from the Pacific to the Caribbean and then present you with a glimpse of the transits through the larger new locks. Most of you will travel through the old Panama Canal locks, as the new ones are reserved only for ships too large to utilize the original route. Although the new locks are quite elegant to view, they lack the majesty of the old Panama Canal, which even today is an engineering marvel considering when and how they were constructed.

I trust that this personalized guide will be beneficial in helping you to become acquainted with the landscapes, history and cultures of the countries to be visited on your Panama Canal cruise. Through my book you will come to gain an understanding of the building of the canal and its significance in today's global economy. In this totally revised edition, I have added very specific recommendations as to dining and shopping in the various ports of call you will visit. My recommendations are based upon presenting you with the highest quality establishments given that the levels of health and sanitation in many of the ports of call fall below what most travelers expect. It is always best to be careful rather than sorry when it comes to dining. And in this edition it has also become necessary for me to provide expanded information on the topic of crime and your personal safety. It is best that you are forewarned and know what to expect. This is not a typical guidebook such as the mass market publications such as Fyodor's or Frommer's. You will find geographic and historic detail to give you a good picture of each country and port of call. And my recommendations for what to see, where to dine and shop are based upon my years of travel experience in this area.

Lew Deitch
June 2019

**Visit my web site for other publications
and a beautiful around the world slide show**
http://www.doctorlew.com

PREPARING TO CRUISE

A dramatic Caribbean sunset

For those of us living in North America or Europe there is a certain mystique about the Panama Canal. The actual transit occupies the better part of one day, thus most cruises include ports of call on either side of the canal to generate an itinerary that entices people to book. There is essentially one route, the possibility for varied ports of call is extensive. The majority of the Panama Canal cruises are between southern Florida and the Pacific Coast of California. During the middle of spring and in early fall there are a few repositioning cruises between Vancouver and Montréal that offer a cruise of approximately 30-days. And in the period of mid-December through March there are a few rather lengthy cruises between southern Florida and either Valparaiso (San Antonio) or Buenos Aires.

The following list (starting on the Atlantic side) presents the major ports of call that can be included in the majority of the cruises between southern Florida and California:
* Santa Marta, Colombia
* Cartagena, Colombia
* Puerto Limón, Costa Rica
* San Blas Islands, Panama
* Colón, Panama
* PANAMA CANAL TRANSIT
* Panama City, Panama
* Punta Arenas, Costa Rica
* Puerto Quetzal, Guatemala

* **Puerto Chiapas, México**
* **Acapulco, México**
* **Ixtapa-Zihuatanejo, México**
* **Manzanillo, México**
* **Puerto Vallarta, México**
* **Cabo San Lucas, México**
* **San Diego, California**

This travel guide is based upon these ports of call shown above and is not aimed at the far smaller cruise audience planning a cruise between South America and Florida or one of the Vancouver-Montréal repositioning cruises.

PREPARING TO CRUISE: What do you need to do to prepare for your cruise and what are some of the general questions you may have on your mind? There are many questions people have regarding documentation, flights, packing, currency, health issues and crime. I attempt to answer most of those questions in the material that follows. If you have a specific and personalized question that is not answered by this chapter, you can send me an email through my web page, which is *www.doctorlew.com* and I will be happy to answer.

* **DOCUMENTATION:** All passengers on cruises through the Panama Canal will absolutely need to carry a valid passport. Normally the ship's purser will collect and hold the passports, distributing them only if needed for any face to face immigration inspections or for going ashore. For citizens holding American, Canadian or European Union passports, no visas are required for the ports of call. If, however, you are planning to leave the ship in México, you will need to first obtain a tourist card. Check the requirements for tourist cards at the following website, *www.mexicotouristcard.com* for full details. For holders of passports from countries not noted above, please check with your cruise line to see if any visas may be required for your journey.

* **FLIGHTS TO AND FROM THE SHIP:** For those of you living in North America, flights to or from Miami, Fort Lauderdale or Los Angeles are numerous. All three cities have direct or single connection flights to most major airports within the United States and Canada. If you are sailing on one of the Canadian repositioning cruises, Vancouver and Montréal are connected by air to most cities in the United States and a great number of foreign airports. For European or Asian guests, Miami and Los Angeles are among the largest international airports in the United States. For overseas flights, I highly recommend booking into Business Class for the added comfort. Some cruise itineraries may include Business Class air fare.

* **WEATHER:** For Panama Canal sailings, you will be in tropical waters most of the time. The daily weather will be warm and humid. Temperatures will be in the mid 20's Celsius or 80's Fahrenheit. Humidity levels can be anywhere from 70 to as high as 90 percent, especially in Panama. Rainfall is variable, but during the December to February period late morning or afternoon thundershowers are common. It is less common to have a full day of rain during this time period. If you are doing an eastbound repositioning cruise in September there is the chance of either a Pacific or Caribbean hurricane, but the ship's captain keeps a close eye on conditions and will never put the ship in danger.

* WHAT TO PACK: You are advised to pack light clothes, preferably in light colors, as dark clothing absorbs the sun's energy and makes you feel warm. Cotton does breathe easier and is cooler in tropical conditions. If you are prone to any adverse reaction from the sun you should wear a hat and sun glasses. If you are going on any rainforest tours, insect repellant is recommended.

Depending upon you cruise line, you may need formal or smart casual dress for evening on board. This varies with each cruise operator. And attending such evening events is always optional.

On deck a light sweater or windbreaker is advisable once the ship enters more temperate latitudes. The California coast can be quite cool during winter. And if you are on a repositioning cruise between Canadian ports in the autumn a warmer sweater or jacket will be necessary. A raincoat or poncho is also recommended if you will be doing any tours into the tropical rainforest.

* CURRENCY: In most ports of call the majority of local merchants or restaurants will accept major credit cards. However, street vendors and small merchants will not generally accept American or Canadian Dollars, Pounds or Euro. Only change money if you plan to go off on your own, as you could face a situation where local currency is needed such as hiring a local taxi. If your plans call for more independent sightseeing, you can have your local bank order small amounts of currency for Colombia, Costa Rica, Guatemala and México. Panama does use the United States dollar as its currency.

* POSTAGE: If you wish to send post cards or letters you will need local currency. But keep in mind that the postal services in all countries along the route except Costa Rica are unreliable. There is a fifty percent chance your mail will néver reach its destination.

* FOOD AND WATER: Countries in Central America have a notorious reputation for being places in which it is easy to become ill from contaminated water and food. It is always better to safe than sorry, as some water borne or food bacteria can cause you long term serious problems such as hepatitis. México has the worst reputation for what is euphemistically called "Montezuma's Revenge." If you eat in reputable restaurants and stay away from raw foods you lessen the odds of becoming sick by a significant factor.

Always drink bottled water, preferably taken with you from the ship. If you buy bottled water ashore make certain that the bottle is properly sealed. Do not indulge in salads or fruit unless you are in a major five-star restaurant where your chances of contracting a water borne or food illness is greatly reduced. Frankly I advise you to stay away from any uncooked foods. If you buy fresh fruit and peal it yourself after carefully washing it in bottled water with soap is the safest way to minimize any contamination. Remember that the local inhabitants have been raised with the local bacteria and have a natural immunity, which you do not have.

Of all the countries on your itinerary Costa Rica maintains the best overall health and food safety standards. The exception to this statement is the Caribbean port of Puerto Limón, which is not as prosperous as the rest of the nation.

It is a good idea to have your doctor give you a prescription for Cipro and Lomotil to have with you as a precaution.

On a quiet street in Antigua, Guatemala, a relatively safe city to tour on your own

* OVERALL HEALTH ISSUES: There are no special vaccinations required for the ports on the Panama Canal cruise. Although mosquitos can be pesky at times in the rainforest, there is little to no danger of the transmission of malaria or yellow fever in places you will be visiting.

Always take out traveler's health insurance before leaving home, as foreign countries will not accept your health coverage from your home country. Air evacuation is an important part of such a policy in the event you do need to be airlifted home.

CRIME: Street crime is a problem in some of the ports of call, especially purse snatching and pickpockets. Just observe the normal precautions you would in many parts of the world. Do not wear expensive jewelry or watches. Do not flash large sums of money when making a transaction. These are wise precautions.

You no doubt have read about extreme drug violence in Colombia, Guatemala and México. In Colombia the police have curbed violence to where it is no longer a major threat. Santa

Marta and Cartagena are one among the safest ports you will visit. Despite the drug violence in Guatemala, it rarely impacts tourists, especially in Antigua or Tikal, the two most visited sites. México is, however, still plagued with a lot of drug violence. Acapulco is one of the most notorious ports. It is best in México to be part of a tour group. If you do go out with a local driver or taxi, make certain of their credentials before getting in. If you do speak Spanish, it will be a great benefit in your overall relations with locals. I speak it very well and as a result I have been out on my own and have always been comfortable. But I do observe my surroundings and do not take chances.

Costa Rica until recently did not experience any drug violence that spilled out into the streets. Unfortunately this is changing, but it is still the safest of the countries in Central America, especially in the tourist oriented locales.

If you go out with a car and driver or a taxi, keep to major streets and do not wander off onto back roads just as an added precaution.

FINAL NOTES: I trust these details have been helpful. Throughout my book it is my intent to provide you with material based in good measure upon my own personal experiences and long standing expertise in the travel industry. When you are armed with the necessary information your cruise is bound to be far more successful and enjoyable.

ATLANTIC CARIBBEAN PORTS

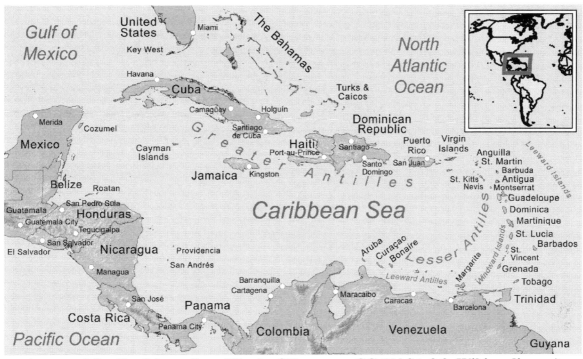

A map of the Caribbean Sea, (Work of Kmusser, CC BY SA 3.0, Wikimedia.org)

There are few ports of call on the Atlantic or Caribbean side of the continent that are included in Panama Canal cruises. With the vast number of Caribbean itineraries offered by all of the major cruise lines, it would be redundant and add unnecessary time to a Panama Canal cruise if many Caribbean ports were included. In stark contrast, the Pacific Coast has very few itineraries outside of those along the Mexican coast that are confined to just the Pacific region south of the United States. Thus the Panama Canal cruise itineraries are also heavily oriented toward visiting ports of call in Costa Rica and Guatemala as well as some of the lesser ports in México.

On the Caribbean side of the canal, Santa Marta and Cartagena, Colombia are the most commonly visited ports of call, as these are not included in Caribbean cruise itineraries and they are fascinating places to visit. There are a few itineraries that follow a more westerly direction, passing between the United States and Cuba and then stopping in Puerto Limón, Costa Rica. A few of the smaller, upmarket cruise ships in the five-star category also stop for a day in the San Blas Islands, Panama, home to indigenous people that are most welcoming. And an even fewer number of cruise itineraries include the Caribbean port of Colón, Panama as a port of call. Personally I do not understand the value in such a stop, as unfortunately Colón has so little of interest to offer.

Likewise, there are a few mixed Western Caribbean-Panama Canal cruises that visit Jamaica and the Cayman Islands and then enter the Gatun Locks and turn around and backtrack into the Caribbean and continue onward. I do not consider those to be true Panama Canal cruises.

The San Blas Islands are an indigenous reserve and quite primitive, yet captivating

Essentially the Caribbean side of the continent does not figure prominently into the majority of Panama Canal cruises. If your cruise will visit either Santa Marta, Cartagena or the San Blas Islands you will find any one or all of these ports of call quite memorable. For many guests a visit to Santa Marta or Cartagena may be their first and possibly only visit to a port of call on the South American continent.

COSTA RICA'S FORGOTTEN COAST

A map of Costa Rica (CIA)

Costa Rica is the most prosperous and stable of the countries of what is called Central America. In essence the concept of Central America has come about to identify those nations south of México that have a Latin history and culture but are still a part of the North American continent geographically. Only Belize has a British colonial origin, but the majority of its people are culturally similar to those of its neighbor Guatemala despite the former colonial history.

THE LANDSCAPE: The Caribbean shore of Central America is totally the opposite of the Pacific coast. On the Caribbean side of the continent the land is essentially flat, lying close to the sea. It has a rather smooth coast with few significant natural harbors and in many places the shoreline is protected by sandy offshore bars that make navigation difficult.

The Caribbean side of Central America is quite hot, especially humid and receives heavy amounts of rainfall, as well as being subject to frequent hurricane strikes. The high mountains and plateaus that are home to the majority of the population in Guatemala, Honduras, Nicaragua and Costa Rica are well to the interior and there is little direct road or river access. These low lying areas were and still essentially are far less desirable than the highlands or Pacific Coast. Swampy land and disease made them quite unattractive. The nickname for the Caribbean coast of Nicaragua, even showing up on maps, has been The Mosquito Coast. Thus this side of each country has been essentially forgotten and become a cultural and economic backwater.

There is some natural beauty on the Caribbean shore of Costa Rica, (Work of Haakon S. Krohn, CC BY SA 3.0, Wikimedia.org)

There are few coastal ports and apart from Roatan Island in Honduras, which has been developed as a vacation destination, the only other port of call visited by cruise ships is Puerto Limón in Costa Rica.

A BRIEF HISTORY: If you have ever heard the term Banana Republic and have not been sure what it refers to, it developed at the turn of the 20th century when United Fruit Company and other smaller entities invested in the raising of bananas on the Caribbean coast from Guatemala south into Costa Rica. And United Fruit Company became quite dominant in the political lives of these countries, but less so in Costa Rica. Essentially the governments of Guatemala, Honduras and Nicaragua were dependent upon income derived from the banana trade with the United States and became subservient to the growers. And that is the origin of banana republics.

The Caribbean coast, and Puerto Limón in particular do not represent the true flavor of Costa Rica. Fortunately Panama Canal cruises regularly stop in Puntarenas on the Pacific Coast and this port of call enables visitors to reach the rainforests, volcanic regions and other highlights of Costa Rica, including the capital city of San José.

Costa Rica is a small country occupying 50,901 square kilometers or 19,653 square miles, about the size of the Baltic Sea nation of Estonia. Its population is just over 5,100,000, mainly found in the high plateaus closest to the Pacific Coast. It was settled by the Spanish during the mid 17th century, primarily by colonists seeking more independence from the Spanish crown, not looking for mineral wealth. There were few native inhabitants, thus Costa Rica to this day has a predominantly European population that is very well educated and has more of a middle class way of life.

Puerto Limón is a new city that was founded in 1854, serving as a port for the banana plantations and it was to be the base of a railroad to the interior capital of San José. The population is not typical of Costa Rica, as it has a mix of descendants of Jamaicans and Chinese who came because of what at that time was more highly paid jobs. In the 19th and early 20th centuries, the Costa Rican government imposed a travel ban upon Puerto Limón, not allowing non-European residents to move into the interior heartland of the country.

The city has a ramshackle look about it and is not in any way attractive or representative of the interior of the country. In recent years it has also become an unfortunate victim of the drug trade, which in neighboring Nicaragua and Honduras is quite rampant.

To the present day, Costa Ricans have little interest in visiting the Caribbean coast, and even dating back to Spanish colonial times, the government found it hard to entice people to settle despite offers to give land to citizens. Those few who did take land started small plantations raising primarily cocoa as a cash crop and using imported labor in their fields.

WHAT TO SEE AND DO: Quite frankly there is little to interest visitors in Puerto Limón as a city. If you cruise itinerary does include Puerto Limón, I highly recommend that you take one of the tours out into the rainforest, as they have a strong ecological base since this is the focus of tourism throughout Costa Rica. This is the nation that essentially invented ecotourism and has been very successful in bringing the entire global tourist industry to the recognition that the natural environment should be both protected and then shown to visitors as a great natural resource.

Staying in Puerto Limón for the time the ship is in port would be a day wasted. The city has virtually nothing to offer in the way of any venues of interest.

A look at downtown Puerto Limón, (Work of Balou46, CC BY SA 4.0, Wikimedia.org)

The coastal plain has become recognized today by the ecological community for its unique and dramatic vegetation and animal life, so get out and enjoy the landscape by taking one of the tours offered by your cruise line.

I do not recommend attempting to hire a local taxi or even renting a car and driving on your own. You are much better off being part of a group and having a professional guide who will show you the landscape. In Costa Rica guides are highly trained and have a great degree of knowledge to impart to visitors.

Here are the four major ecological sites that are the focus of organized tours from the port of Puerto Limón shown alphabetically:

* Cahuita National Park – This park is located a short distance south of Puerto Limón. It is along the coast where plant and animal species of both the wetland shoreline and rainforest intermingle. Guided tours are quite fascinating and very informative. The park is open from

* Foundation Jaguar Rescue Center – This is a major rescue and rehabilitation center for the endangered jaguar, which is the major predatory species in the rainforests of Central America. By African standards, the jaguar is a relatively small carnivore similar in size to

the cheetah, but far more elusive. Seeing one up close in the wind is exceptionally difficult, but at this center you can get close to this endangered and rare species. The park is located just outside of Puerto Limón and is open from 9 AM to 2:30 PM Monday thru Saturday.

* Tortugero National Park – This park offers a beautiful mix of coastal and rainforest landscapes blended together by nature. It is a beautiful place for a nature walk and is often seen as the easiest option of the tours offered. The fresh water estuaries are quite fascinating and are home to many distinctive species, especially among turtles. The park is open only from 8 AM to 4 PM. Visits by cruise passengers are usually in the morning hours when it is cooler.

* Veragua Rainforest Park – Located close to the city, this park gives you a very good look at a tropical rainforest through interpretative guides who walk with you through the trees. You will learn the difference between what is often perceived as jungle, but is actually rainforest. The park is open Tuesday thru Sunday from 8 AM to 3 PM.

Tropical rainforest in Veragua Rainforest Park

DINING OUT: If you are on a longer tour that lasts the better part of the day, lunch will be included, usually at one of the ecological lodges at a restaurant in or adjacent to the reserve you will be visiting. I will not recommend any since you will not be given a choice, but can be assured that your cruise line will have chosen well.

If you are on a half day tour or are staying in Puerto Limón my recommendation is to return to the ship for lunch. Puerto Limón is a somewhat scruffy community and it does not represent the standards of cleanliness that typify the core of Costa Rica. Apart from the national park and reserve lodges where food and water safety are guaranteed, there is absolutely no restaurant in Puerto Limón that I would feel comfortable recommending. I am sorry to find it necessary to be so negative, but I never wish to send my readers anywhere I would not feel comfortable visiting or dining at myself.

SHOPPING: Costa Rica is noted for its fine woodcarvings, painted wood miniature ox carts, woven wares and leather. But the best shopping is found in the central highlands or along the Pacific coast where tourism is a major part of the economy.

In Puerto Limón there is the Mercado Municipal located in the heart of town at Calle 3 # 2. It is a typical Caribbean and quasi Latin American marketplace. You will find some craft items here. No hours are given for the Mercado, but it is generally open all day when a ship is in port. The majority of nice shops selling local crafts are located in or adjacent to the national parks or reserves. If you are on a tour, hopefully your motor coach will stop at one of these venues to give you some time to shop.

FINAL WORDS: Take advantage of any opportunity in Costa Rica to maximize your time and see as much of the landscape as possible. Remember this is a country in which ecotourism is a major component of visiting. As for the city of Puerto Limón, just accept it for what it is and do not think of it as being typically Costa Rican.

In the Veragua Rainforest Park

COLOMBIA AS A NATION

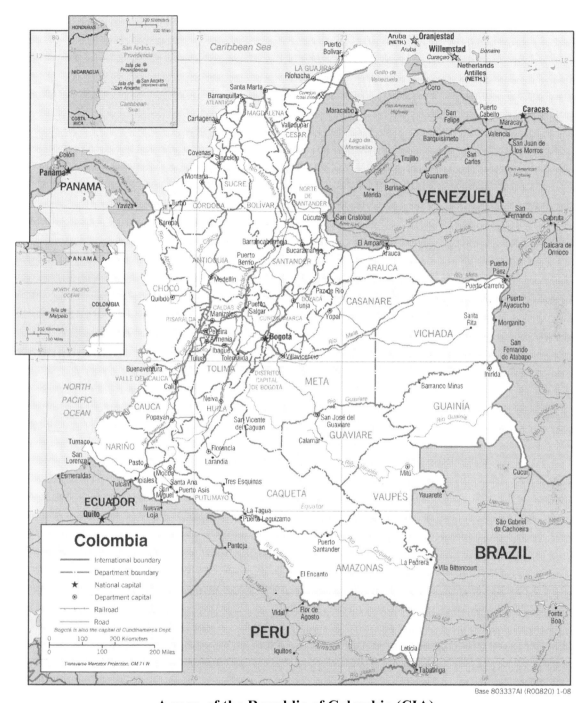

A map of the Republic of Colombia (CIA)

Colombia is a relatively large country occupying 1,141,666 square kilometers or 440,800 square miles making it about the size of France. Its current population is estimated at being just over 48,000,000. It is located at the northwest corner of South America and the only country on the continent to have two coastlines. Because the Isthmus of Panama is attached to Colombia, the country has both a Pacific and Caribbean shore. Santa Marta and

Cartagena are both on the Caribbean coast of Colombia. The coastal plains are relatively narrow and have a relatively hot, humid climate with pockets of very thick and diverse tropical rainforest vegetation mixed with drier landscapes where the onshore trade winds are blocked by mountain spurs.

The romantic fishing village of Tagana east of Santa Marta

There are many ribs of the high Andes Mountains with high altitude intervening valleys that comprise the core of Colombia and it is in these areas that the majority of people live. Valleys are as high as 2,450 meters or over 8,000 feet and peaks extend as high as 4,900 meters or over 16,000 feet. Bogotá, the nation's capital is the highest city at over 2,640 meters or 8,660 feet. Colombia's mountain regions are prone to severe earthquakes and there are numerous active volcanoes. But Santa Marta and Cartagena are in the coastal plain that is benign and does not experience these conditions.

Beyond to the mountains the eastern part of Colombia is a part of the vast Amazon Basin and contains thick and sparsely settled tropical rainforest. The population is heaviest in the mountains because of the more equitable climate, this despite the earthquake and volcanic dangers. The mountain areas are very productive and coffee is the country's most famous export. Unfortunately cocaine derived from the coca plant is the country's most infamous export.

Fortunately for Santa Marta and Cartagena the hurricanes of the Caribbean do not penetrate this far south, developing in the open waters of the Atlantic Ocean and tracking across the Caribbean Sea to the north of the Colombian coast.

The Spanish first arrived in Colombia in 1499, conquering or killing the majority of the native peoples and creating the Viceroyalty of New Granada. During the colonial era, there was much exploitation of those natives that survived. Through inbreeding the bulk of the population today claims both native and Spanish blood. Spain was more concerned with gold, silver and emeralds than it was with converting the people. However, it did establish a branch of the Inquisition in Cartagena to root out pagan and heretical beliefs.

The people of Colombia ultimately rebelled against Spain and gained independence in 1819. Initially Gran Colombia included Venezuela and Ecuador, but they went their own way by 1830. After internal strife, corruption and autocratic rule, modern Colombia emerged in 1896 as a republic and it has been relatively successful in maintaining democratic ideals to the present.

In the late 20th century, the drug cartels created a period of great brutality in Colombia, assassinating government leaders, terrorizing whole communities and making its cities among the most dangerous in all of Latin America. At the same time, a rebel group based in the interior rainforest also terrorized much of the rural population, attempting to sew discontent against the government. Finally in the first decades of the 21st century the government has been able to settle its differences with FARC, known as Fuerzas Armadas Revolucionarias de Colombia, the revolutionary army, as it was known, and an uneasy peace finally has occurred. Drug violence is still a problem, but nowhere to the degree it was a few decades back. Visitors to Colombia today no longer need to fear becoming caught in the crossfire between the military and either FARC or the drug cartels.

Colombia wears its ethnic diversity quite proudly with pure Spanish, mestizo, indigenous and African roots intertwined and living side by side. More recent immigration from Europe and the Middle East has added to the diversity. The country is still quite agrarian with coffee and sugar cane being the two great legal cash crops and coca still adding to the illicit side of the economy. Gold and emeralds are still mined and add greatly to the overall economic picture. And in the major cities there are various manufacturing and industrial enterprises.

SANTA MARTA

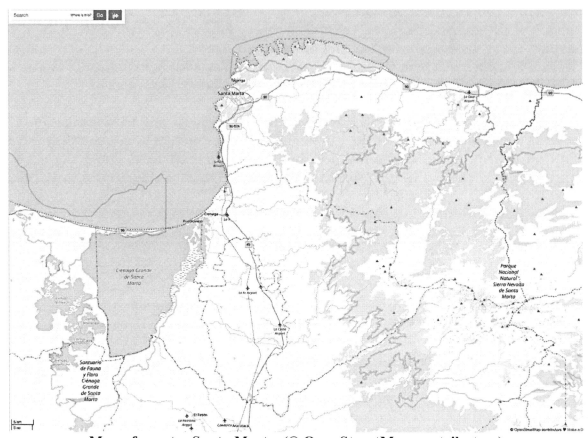

Map of greater Santa Marta, (© OpenStreetMap contributors)

For most of you who are reading this book there is little likelihood that your cruise will visit Santa Marta. And that is a shame. I have been there four times and found it to be a very enjoyable experience. It is an attractive city, has a rich history, especially important in the colonial era and again during the revolutionary period in the mid 19th century. If you happen to book your cruise on one of the smaller ships in the five-star category such as Silversea, Seabourn or Regent you will be more apt to have Santa Marta in your itinerary. And you will find it a most enjoyable experience.

THE LANDSCAPE: ;Santa Marta is in the northeastern corner of Colombia, built around a small bay of the same name and backed up by an isolated mountain mass that is stands geologically alone, separated from the northernmost Andes Mountains. The Sierra Nevada de Santa Marta present a superb backdrop for the city, rising to their highest altitude of 5,700 meters or 18,700 feet and their base is just a bit over 40 kilometers or 25 miles from the shore. They are the tallest independent mountain mass on earth so close to the coast that are not a part of a mountain chain, making them geologically quite distinct. The outer suburbs of Santa Marta almost reach the base of the mountains. These mountains are geologically quite ancient and formed independently of the Andes, their core being over one billion years old. As the ancient supercontinent was breaking up, the Sierra Nevada de

Santa Marta were propelled northeastward from their original location in Peru. They have experienced both tectonic and volcanic activity during their long period of development.

The mountain mass helps to force moist air coming in off of the Caribbean Sea propelled by the Northeast Trade Winds to rise and drop copious amounts of rainfall. Snow regularly drapes the tops of the highest peaks. In the more moderate middle and warmer lower slopes there are thick forests, much of which today is national park and has a potential for the development of ecotourism. Some cruise lines may offer a tour into a portion of the lower Sierra Nevada de Santa Marta, which for anyone wanting to enjoy the natural environment will be a real treat.

The shoreline of Santa Marta with the high Sierra Nevada de Santa Marta rising in the background, usually draped in clouds.

The city of Santa Marta has a moderate tropical climate because of both the sea and the cooling breezes that often blow down from the high mountains. The vegetation surrounding the city is composed more of scrub woodland but with pockets of rainforest tucked into the narrow folded valleys or coves along the coast. The rainfall does make it possible for the growth of tropical trees and flowers in the city that add to its overall feeling of being a lush paradise.

A BRIEF HISTORY: There is a long indigenous history that predates the coming of the Spanish. One of the groups known as the Tayrona were a very sophisticated people and had reached a pinnacle of development centuries before the colonial era, the ruins of their

long ago civilization now being appreciated by Colombians and visitors alike. But as with so many civilizations in the Western Hemisphere they fell to Spanish conquest and to diseases brought by the European plunderers.

Docking in Santa Marta – A view of the beach

The city of Santa Marta is the oldest Spanish settlements in all of the Americas, having first been established in 1525 b Rodrigo de Bastidas. The focus of Santa Marta's growth was the knowledge that the Tayrona had been mining gold in the Sierra Nevada de Santa Marta, as evidenced by the many golden artifacts their towns possessed. The Spanish ultimately defeated the Tayrona in a series of bloody campaigns, plundered their wealth and set about to mine gold themselves. To the present day, gold has been a part of the Santa Marta economy and its gold museum is one of the absolute must see venues for visitors.

It was from Santa Marta that the earliest exploration of the interior pressed through the river valleys and up into the high valleys and led to the founding of Bogotá in 1538, the city that would become the capital of colonial Gran Colombia and is today the capital of the modern nation. Santa Marta grew in size and wealth because of the exploitation of gold, the development of sugar and later coffee plantations and it also became the major port for the interior, especially for Bogotá. Today it has an urban population of approximately 450,000, making it one of the four largest coastal cities in the nation. But it could never match the importance of Cartagena when it came to the role of trade.

During the long colonial era, Santa Marta was also subjected to pirate attacks and raids by both France and Britain. But given that Cartagena was the principal target, Santa Marta did not experience the full brunt of constantly being threatened with invasion.

During the struggle for independence from Spain, Simón Bolivar was the predominant figure in securing the autonomy of Bolivia, Peru, Ecuador, Colombia and Venezuela. The great revolutionary general died at the plantation of Quinta de San Pedro Alejandrino just south of the main city of Santa Marta on December 17, 1830. He was initially buried in the Cathedral of Santa Marta, but later his body was removed to the Cathedral in Caracas, Venezuela. But today the plantation is a national shrine and the great monument to Bolivar has made this essentially a shrine not only for Colombia, but for all the northern countries he liberated and set on the path to independence.

A magnificent colonial building on Parque Simón Bolivar

One event that is considered a major element of modern Colombian history is the so called Banana Massacre that took place in December 1928 outside of Santa Marta. A strike by banana workers for United Fruit Company, the corporate entity often referred to in Central America as having pandered to corrupt governments leading to the creation of "Banana Republics," ended in violence. The Colombian Army was sent to keep order at the request of the United States government under threat of a Marine invasion. The Colombian forces brutally put down the uprising, not sparing even women and children, killing as many as 3,000 people. This action ultimately set off a decade long period of internal violence between the main political factions in Colombia.

In more recent decades, Santa Marta and its surrounding countryside has seen its share of drug related violence and that of the rebel group FARC, but today those days are now considered to be part of history. The city is quite safe for visitors and it is developing a tourist infrastructure based upon both foreign and domestic guests. Rodadero Beach just to the west of Santa Marta is one of Colombia's most popular resorts with many wealthy Bogotá residents spending holiday time on the Caribbean coast.

Statue of Simón Bolivar at Quinta de San Pedro Alajandrino

VISITING SANTA MARTA: Those of you fortunate enough to visit Santa Marta will most likely take one of the escorted tours offered by your cruise line. This city does not yet have any tourist infrastructure such as hop on hop off bus service or an abundance of taxi drivers versed in other languages. For those who do not take one of the guided motor coach or coach and walking combination tours, most cruise lines will at least offer a shuttle into the city center.

Cruise shore excursion desks can also arrange for a private car and driver/guide, which is what I have always done in Santa Marta. In this way you have the freedom and flexibility to explore more of the city, drive over to Rodadero Beach and to visit Quinta de San Pedro Alajandrino since both are a bit out of the city.

Yes you can feel safe walking around the city and trying to take in those major venues listed below that are within walking distance of the shuttle drop off. There will be some taxis waiting at the dock, but few drivers are fluent in English. If you choose to use a local taxi, be certain the driver understands what it is you want to do and make certain to set a price in advance and shake hands on it to seal the deal. If you do go out by taxi, be sure and include your driver in your lunch plans, as it cements good relations.

Santa Marta is a relatively prosperous community. Its economy is diverse and includes the role of its port, its fishing fleet and it serves as the market center for the surrounding plantations that raise bananas, tropical fruits and some sugar cane. In the highlands of the Sierra Madre de Santa Marta there are coffee plantations raising fine quality product. And Santa Marta is the center of these activities as the major trade, financial and educational hub.

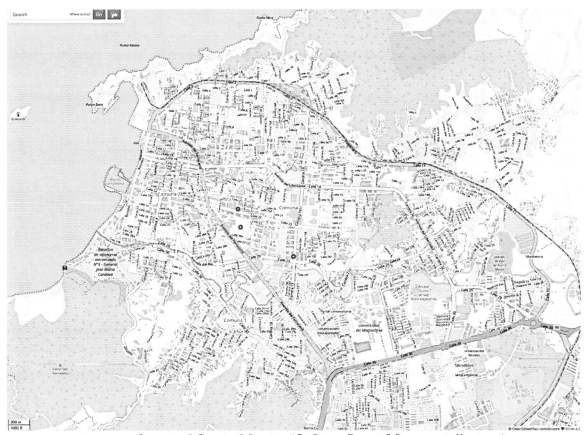

A map of central Santa Marta, (© OpenStreetMap contributors)

* MAJOR SIGHTS TO SEE: I have listed what I consider to be the must see venues within greater Santa Marta. Many, if not most, will be on the ship sponsored motor coach tours. And if you have arranged for private touring, you can choose only those that suit your taste. I have listed them in alphabetical order so as not to present any personal bias:

** Catedral de Santa Marta – Located in the heart of the Old City, it is a beautiful building with baroque style. It is where Simón Bolivar was initially buried until Venezuela demanded his body be brought to Caracas. The cathedral is open during daylight hours. Most walking tours do include a visit.

** Centro Historico de Santa Marta – Essentially the Old City is intermingled with the newer and more modern buildings of the commercial district. But the main plaza opposite the gold museum is located. It is the focal heart of the central city.

** Ciudad Perdida – This is an important archaeological site located in the lower Sierra Madre de Santa Marta. It is quite an old city and was once a center of commerce under the Tairona. Local tribes have known about it but never let European know it existed. It was not until 1972 that it was discovered by archaerologists. At first it suffered from looting until the government and Global Heritage Fund stepped in to protect the site. You may find that your cruise line will offer a special tour or include a brief visit as part of an overall excursion to the mountains.

** Museo del Oro Tairona – Located in the historic old Custom's Building facing Parque Simón Bolivar, this is an incredible museum for its collection of artifacts mainly from the Tairona. And much of the collection consists of beautifully handcrafted gold objects. The museum should be a must. It is open Monday thru Saturday from 9 AM to 5 PM and on Sunday from 10 AM to 3 PM.

The Museo del Oro Tairona

** Parque de los Novios – This is one of the oldest and without question the most beautiful of the many plazas in Santa Marta. It was once the site of the city's public marketplace. It is also surrounded by many restaurants, nightclubs and on one side it fronts on the Palace of Justice. The park is never closed.

** Plaza Parque Simón Bolivar – This is most important public square in the city, located in the very heart of Santa Marta. The Museo del Oro Tairona and numerous other grand colonial buildings line the three sides of the park while its northern edge faces the bay.

** Quinta de San Pedro Alejandrino – This was once the main residence of a great plantation. It happens to be the palatial home where the great liberator Simón Bolivar died. Today the house has become essentially a memorial to the great man and there is also a shrine on the property as well. This to Colombians is sacred ground, as well as being important to visitors from Venezuela, Ecuador, Peru and Bolivia, all countries that Bolivar helped liberate. The site is open daily from 9 AM to 4:30 PM. It is the absolute must see venue when visiting Santa Marta, situated on the southern edge of the city.

One of the historic Old City streets

** Rodadero Beach – This is essentially a separate community, but politically incorporated into Santa Marta. It is the most famous beach resort on Colombia's Caribbean coast, especially for wealthy residents of Cali and Bogotá. Not all tours will include this resort community, but with your own private car or taxi be sure to visit.

** Rodadero Sea Aquarium and Museum – Located in Inca Cove, this is a public aquarium and sea museum that highlights the marine life of the Caribbean. It is well presented and enjoyed by visitors and Colombians alike, especially popular with children and young adults. It is open daily from 10 AM to 6 PM.

DINING OUT: If you have booked an all day tour, lunch will no doubt be included, but the cruise line will have already made all arrangements. If you are touring by either a private car or taxi, I offer several recommendations for top restaurants. And if you are simply taking the ship shuttle into the city center, you can avail yourself of those restaurants on my list that are in the downtown area. My recommendations are based upon personal knowledge and you can trust that these will be among the best for lunch and reservations are not necessary and thus no phone numbers are given. I list the few excellent choices that I feel comfortable about alphabetically to avoid personal bias:

On the white sand of Rodadero Beach

* Carambolo – Located at Calle 19 # 3-105, this is a popular Mediterranean fusion restaurant that features very fresh seafood prepared with a mix of traditional and modern touches. By fusion the restaurant is attempting to present recipes from the Mediterranean with those of the Middle East and also from Colombia, leading to a very tasty menu. Service is daily from 8 AM to 11 PM.

* Carmesi, Cocina Fusion – This restaurant blends together the flavors of the Caribbean with those of the Mediterranean to create a very tasty array of menu choices. They are located at Calle 17 # 2-73 in the historic city center near Parque Simón Bolivar. They serve Tuesday thru Sunday from Noon to 3 PM for lunch and from 6:30 to 11 PM for dinner.

* Lulo – Located at Carreta 3 # 16-34 Callejon del Correo,
in the heart of the historic Old City, this is a very nice restaurant with both indoor and patio dining in comfortable surroundings. The restaurant features a mix of Colombian and overall Caribbean dishes with a heavy emphasis upon very fresh seafood. They also accommodate vegetarian and vegan diners with appetizing menu items. They serve weekdays from 8 AM to 11 PM and weekends from 9 AM to 11 PM.

* Restaurante Lamart – Found at Carrera 3a # 16-36, this is a great place to sample not only Colombian and Caribbean cuisine but also dishes representing much of northern South America. Seafood of course figures prominently and all dishes are artfully prepared using the finest ingredients. They are open Tuesday thru Thursday from 9 AM to 11:15 PM, remaining open Friday to 11:30 PM. Saturday hours are from 10 AM to 11:30 PM and Sunday they serve from 4 to 11:30 PM.

* Soul Food – You cannot get more Colombian or Caribbean than this restaurant with its eclectic mix of flavors. This is a very popular restaurant with locals and visitors alike, known for its freshness and traditional menu choices. It is found in the historic center at Carrera 20 #3-511 and open Wednesday thru Sunday from Noon to 3 PM for lunch and nightly from 6 to 10 PM for dinner.

SHOPPING: The historic city center does offer several shopping venues. Many of the more tourist oriented shops are not really worthy of mention. But there are two nice shopping centers that you may wish to visit.

A very friendly group of local school boys enjoying an afternoon outing

* Centro Comercial Arrecife – This rather modern and stylish is found on Carrera 4 at # 11A-119 in Rodadero. It is more oriented toward clothing, some of it made in Colombia or elsewhere in South America. It is open daily from 8 AM to 10 PM, but you will need a taxi or have a private car and driver to get to the mall.

* **Centro Comercial Buenavista** – This is a large and modern shopping mall located at 2 9a # 9A-14 in the suburb of Mamata, and offers a great variety of stores selling a broad range of merchandise. If nothing else, it gives you a good understanding of the wide array of merchandise available to Colombians in all price categories. There is a large movie theater and several restaurants within the mall. The mall is open daily from 11 AM to 10 PM but extends closing to 11 PM on Friday and Saturday evenings.

FINAL WORDS: I personally like the laid back and friendly atmosphere of Santa Marta and the fact that it is a smaller city and easier to get around. The Sierra Nevada de Santa Marta form a magnificent landscape backdrop and the surrounding countryside is easier to access than from Cartagena. But to fully appreciate the city and its surroundings you should have access to a private car and driver.

The main house at the Quinta San Pedro Alajandrino estate

The main house at the Quinta San Pedro Alajandrino estate

The lush tropical gardens at Quinta San Pedro Alajandrino

Remember Juan Valdez and Colombian coffee? He is a popular coffee bar at the Buenavista Mall

Entering Rodadero Beach from Santa Marta

CARTAGENA

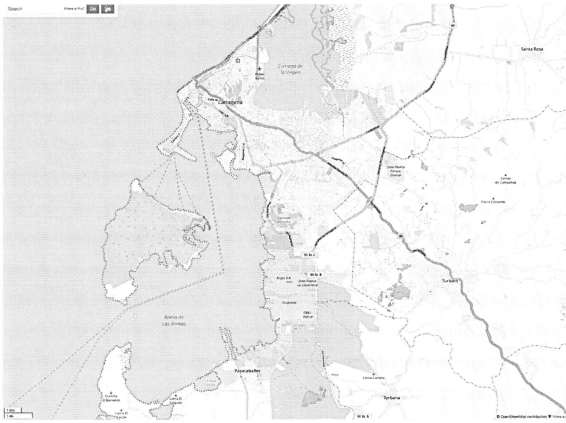

A map of greater Cartagena, (© OpenStreetMap contributors)

Cartagena de Indias, Colombia is the largest city and port on the country's Caribbean Coast. This is a major port of call for nearly all Panama Canal cruises. The city is also a very important and historic city within Colombia. Today's greater Cartagena population is in excess of 1,300,000 residents. It is a very old and historic city as well as having an ultra-modern and very dynamic skyline because of being a popular resort with wealthy Colombians who live in the interior of the country.

THE LANDSCAPE: The Caribbean coast of Colombia is well within tropical latitudes. The coastal plain around Cartagena is quite flat, as the mountains are a significant distance to the south and southeast unlike the landscape around Santa Marta. The climatic patterns give this area warm to sometimes hot days with temperatures well into the 20's Celsius or upper 80's Fahrenheit. And the humidity is generally quite high. Some visitors find it a bit uncomfortable under normal conditions. But the old historic and beachfront districts of the city are located on a large bulging peninsula that has the Caribbean Sea to the north and Bahia de las Aninas to the south, giving the heart of the city the effect of cooling breezes. Most cruise ships visit during the period of late November to mid-April when conditions are at their most favorable.

The surrounding countryside is covered in thick woodland with a few pockets of old growth rainforest. Given its high population, the hinterland around Cartagena is well populated with farms and plantations raising a great variety of tropical fruits for both the local market and export. Coffee, for which Colombia is so famous, is raised in the interior highlands, as the coastal margins are not favorable.

THE ARRIVAL INTO PORT: It will take your ship well over an hour to sail into the port of Cartagena even though you will see a large opening in the bay know as Boca Grande adjacent to the city. Despite meaning wide mouth in Spanish, during early colonial times a subsurface wall of stone was laid across to keep enemy ships from easy access to the inner harbor. Thus all ships were and still are required to enter through the smaller southern gap known as Boca Chica where Bateria San José and Fuerte San Fernando could open a hail of cross fire to destroy any would be invader. It is impressive today to sail past these now quiet historic fortresses, then through the clear blue waters of the bay and watch the dramatic skyline of modern Cartagena emerge.

The magnificent skyline of the Boca Grande shoreline of Caragena

A RICH HISTORY: Native settlement can be dated as far back as 9,000 years ago, showing that this rich coastal plain has a long history of occupation. Spanish history begins when Pedro de Heredia founded the port of Cartagena de Indias in 1533, named after the city of Cartagena on the Mediterranean coast of Spain. It soon became an important trade center with discoveries of gold in the interior and the raising of sugar cane along the coast.

French and British pirates pillaged the port in 1544 and 1563, followed by a British privateer's attempt to capture the city in 1568.

The famous British seaman Sir Francis Drake managed to capture and plunder Cartagena in 1574. He extracted a hefty ransom from the Spanish crown in order to get him to leave the city. These repeated attacks forced Spain to heavily fortify the fort in the early 17th century, and this included the building of the subterranean wall across Boca Grande. The ultimate achievement was the building of the huge Castillo San Felipe de Barajas on a hill overlooking the city where it still sits brooding in the tropical heat. Today the Castillo and the two forts at the entry to Boca Chica along with other sites are all under protection as UNESCO World Heritage Sites.

The once thought to be impregnable walls of Castillo San Felipe

Despite the fortifications, raids upon Cartagena were relentless. In 1697, the French were successful in capturing the city and destroying much of its infrastructure. By 1711, with the end of the War of the Spanish Succession and the restoration of military control, the Castillo was greatly strengthened since it had fallen to the French in 1697.

The most audacious attach came in 1741 when British Admiral Edward Vernon mounted a land invasion to attack the city. Spanish forces did repel his invasion and the city did not fall. One interesting side note to this event was the fact that George Washington's half-brother served with Admiral Vernon and was so impressed with his bravery that this prompted the future American president to name his plantation in Virginia Mount Vernon to honor the admiral.

During the 18th century, Cartagena reached its pinnacle of wealth, being the major center for the export of gold, silver, emeralds, sugar and coffee. During this period many of the magnificent churches, palatial homes and public buildings were erected inside the protective walls. And this today is what is the most visited site in Cartagena, as the entire historic Old City is an historic gem.

On the grand and lively streets of Old Cartagena today

There is a dark side to Cartagena. It became home to the Palace of the Inquisition Holy Office Court in 1610 to root out infidels and those unfaithful to the Catholic church. The inquisition office came complete with instruments of torture that are still on display when you visit today. The Palace of the Inquisition functioned until 1811 when Cartagena declared its independence from Spanish rule. For three centuries, this palace was one of the three centers for the inquisition in the Spanish Americas.

The revolutionary war that followed the declaration of independence from Spain nearly destroyed Cartagena when a Spanish expeditionary force captured the city in 1816. But in 1821 patriots recaptured the city following a 159 day siege, but it left much of the city in ruin and Cartagena's importance began to wane. This was followed by famine and cholera. The road to recovery after Colombian independence was slow, but by the early 20th century the city once again became an important and prosperous port.

CARTAGENA TODAY: Today tourism plays a major role in the economy, as does shipping and industry. Cartagena is a major container port for the major inland cities. It is also a center for chemical and petroleum production. There are several tax free incentive zones that have further increased manufacturing.

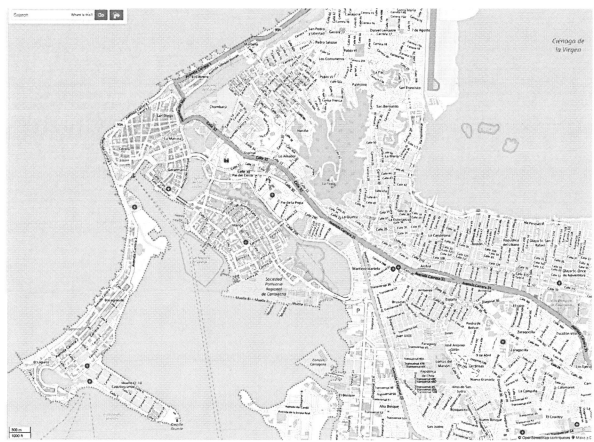

A map of Old Cartagena and Boca Grande, (© OpenStreetMap contributors)

Tourism has had the greatest impact. Many wealthy Colombians have built lavish homes or purchased elegant high-rise condominiums along the narrow strip of land known as Boca Grande. The strip is manmade and results from the dredging of the bay. This is the first sight you see when your ship sails into the port. The strip is about three kilometers or two miles long and is essentially wall-to-wall high rises of impressive height. Strong winds, however, have precluded anything over 40 stories. This zone of beautiful modern architecture is immediately adjacent to the historic old city.

SIGHTSEEING IN CARTAGENA: What is there to see or do in Cartagena? Most cruise passengers choose one of the tours of the city offered by their cruise line. It may be a motor coach or walking tour, or a combination of both. Remember that this is a large city of over one million people. But most of the historic sites of interest are in and around the Old City or on that strip of land known as Boca Grande. Some cruise companies offer a shuttle bus that normally drops off passengers at the famous Clock Tower along the wall of the Old City where there is a large entry gate.

Modern Boca Grande skyline

Is it safe to go off on your own and walk around the Old City if not on a tour? The answer is yes. The government considers Cartagena to be a showplace and is proud of its developing tourist industry. Police maintain a strong presence in and around the Old City, and thus visitors can feel quite safe. However, keep in mind that not all locals speak English. You are on the northern shore of South America far from the United States or Canada and thus English is not as widely spoken as you might expect. If you have a working knowledge of Spanish you can navigate around the Old City with greater confidence. This is why I strongly urge passengers to sign up for one of the ship tours. You will see the highlights of Cartagena in the company of a guide and will therefore learn more about the city's rich past, the architecture you will be seeing and the overall experience will be richer.

If you have an adventurous nature such as I do, and if you have a working knowledge of Spanish you can then either hire a taxi or you can arrange for a private car and driver through the ship's tour desk. I have toured around every quarter of Cartagena and have found it very interesting. There is a massive open air market district that covers many blocks selling food, clothing, furniture and just about anything people with limited incomes need. It is very crowded, which for some visitors might be a bit intimidating. Farther south into the main residential heart of the city there are middle income and more affluent districts where both single-family homes and apartment blocks are interspersed with local parks and sports fields. Once again it is safe to stop your car, get out and take a walk to capture the local flavor of daily urban life. You can visit one of the massive Exito stores, a Colombian version of Walmart, which is an interesting experience.

On the northern bay that faces the International Airport there are some very depressed barrios where the poorest people live. It is sad to see that segment of the population lives in makeshift houses built out of whatever scrap material can be salvaged. These barrios have no running water, electricity or sewage disposal. If you do visit, it is best to remain in your car and simply observe. Photography in such areas is risky, so only take pictures from inside the car, preferably with a telephoto lens.

* THE MAJOR HIGHLIGHTS OF CARTAGENA: I have listed what I consider to be the must see venues in the city. Many of these sites will be included on the tours offered by your cruise line, but not all. All of the sites I list below are generally open during daylight hours. My list is presented in alphabetical order as to avoid any prejudicial view. Addresses are not given, as so many streets are unsigned and building numbers either hard to find or absent. It is best to have a driver or taxi, but if walking, just mention the name of the site you want to visit and someone will point you in the right direction.

** Boca Grande – Here you find the narrow strip of reclaimed land that is home to a string of beautiful, modern high rise apartments interspersed with shops and cafes. This is a very upscale beachfront district that is quite safe to walk in.

** Castillo San Felipe de Barajas – This massive fortress overlooking the Old City is the true highlight of Cartagena. Its thick walls and battlements are especially impressive, as are the views from the top of the walls. It is open during daylight hours.

* Catedral de San Pedro de Claver – This important cathedral in the Old City is dedicated to the memory of an early priest whose mission was to the slaves that served the government and nobility in the early centuries of the city. It is open during daylight hours.

* Cerro la Popa and Convento de la Popa – The best vantage point for a sweeping view over the entire city is had from the mountaintop convent. The convent is most historic and quite beautiful. You will need to be on a tour or have a private taxi or car. The vantagepoint is open during daylight hours.

** Getsemani – This is an old and somewhat ramshackle neighborhood outside of the walls of the Old City. It is filled with many cafes, a few good restaurants and many nightclubs. It is best to visit only if you have a private car and driver who can accompany you to either take a walk or have a drink.

** Museo Naval de Caribe – You will find this a fascinating museum on the role of the Colombian Navy and of military life over the past centuries. It also offers many historic exhibits on life in Cartagena in general. The museum is open daily from 9 AM to 5 PM.

** Palacio de la Inquision – This is one of the most important sites to visit because it brings to life the story of the Spanish Inquisition and the horrors of the tortures used to force people to confess even if innocent. A guided tour is quite an experience. It is open from 9 AM to 6 PM Monday thru Saturday and from 10 AM to 4 PM on Sunday.

A view from atop Cerero la Popa with Boca Grande in the distance

** Plaza Bolivar – This small and well-shaded plaza is in the very heart of the Old City. It is quite a popular meeting spot for locals. Sit down on a bench for a few minutes and just soak in the local color. The large statue honors Simon Bolivar, the great liberator of the northern countries of South America from the oppression of Spain in the early 19th century.

*** Plaza Santo Domingo – This is the main historic plaza in the center of the Old City. It is surrounded by many cafes and filled with colorful street vendors. Do not purchase any unbottled drinks or fruit from local vendors, as the level of sanitation is questionable.

** Saint Catherine of Alexander Cathedral – Located in the Old City, this is one of the most beautiful of the many baroque churches in Cartagena. It is open during daylight hours.

** Teatro Heredia – In the Old City this is the opera house built in the 19th century with all the grandeur of a European opera house. You may be fortunate enough to have a special performance of folk dancing if your cruise line has arranged it. Otherwise the building is only open for organized walking tours.

** Walled Old City – This is the heart of any visit to Cartagena and most walking tours will give you the best of the historic Old City. It is quite extensive and if you are on your own, ask your driver or personal guide to take you to the most important venues.

A view of Plaza Bolivar from the Palacio de la Inquisicion

These are the major highlights of sights to see in Cartagena. With only a short time to visit, if you manage to see half of the sites listed above you will have done quite well. Cartagena is the type of city that many visitors wish to return to, as it is filled with beautiful architecture and exudes an inviting and romantic image of what an old Spanish colonial city should look like. I have visited numerous times and have enjoyed exploring not only the Old City but also some of districts well outside of the historic center. But of course this cannot be done during a one-day port call, so you must decide what will be of most interest to you.

DINING OUT: If you are on a full day tour from your cruise line, it will include lunch. Usually the cruise lines pick a nice restaurant in the Old City. But if you are out on your own either with a taxi or private car, lunch is your responsibility. There are numerous restaurants in the Old City, in Centro, which is downtown, and out in the suburban areas. I have chosen restaurants I feel meet the highest sanitation standards and that serve quality meals with a definite Colombian touch. In any dining experience, even restaurants I recommend, it is best not to have salad or raw fruits since you cannot be assured as to how vegetables and fruits were washed. My choices listed below are in alphabetical order to avoid any personal bias:

* Caff Lunatico – At Calle Espiritu Santo #29-184, this is a rather off beat looking café that has excellent food with a genuine Colombian flavor. They serve a variety of traditional entrees, offering everything freshly prepared using the finest ingredients. Lunch is served daily between 11 AM and 3 PM and dinner is from 7 to 19:30 PM each night.

Colorful street vendors in the Old City

* El Baron – Located on Carrera 4 at #31-7 on Plaza de San Pedro Claver, this is a very popular establishment open for lunch and dinner. Hours are Noon to 2 AM Tuesday thru Saturday and 5 PM to 1 AM for dinner only on Sunday and Monday. The quality, freshness and preparation of your meal is quite good. The menu shows a mix of both North and South American cuisines served in a gastropub atmosphere.

* La Cocina de Pepina – In Gesmani at Calle 25 at # 9a-06, this is a superb restaurant for lunch or dinner. Lunch is between Noon and 4 PM and dinner from 7 to 9:30 PM Tuesday thru Saturday. On Sunday they only serve lunch from Noon to 4 PM. The cuisine is traditional Colombian and Caribbean. Seafood figures quite prominently in their menu. They take pride in using fresh ingredients. They also claim their salads are safe, but I still prefer to exercise caution.

* Restaurante 1621 – Located in the Old City at Carrera 7 and Calle del Curato and only open for dinner between 7 and 11 PM daily. If your ship is staying late, this is then a possibility. It is an outstanding restaurant featuring the cuisine of northern South America served in a very elegant atmosphere.

SHOPPING: For most of you reading this, Cartagena will be your only Colombian port of call. And many of you may be interested in purchasing local crafts. Colombia is a nation of fine artisans who do outstanding weaving, wood carving and produce beautiful ceramics. And for those who want to spend a lot of money, the major focus is upon emeralds since

Colombia is the world's major producer. There are many jewelry shops, but many cruise lines have a personal shopper on board who will often organize small groups and take them shopping for fine emerald stones.

I am recommending the following places to shop for quality Colombian arts and crafts rather than the massive public markets where you really do not know what you are buying with regard to quality. My choices are alphabetical, but I begin with one fine jewelry store that has a reputation for quality emeralds.

* Lucy Jewelry – Located at Calle Santo Domingo #3-19 near the Plaza Santo Domingo, this magnificent store has an excellent reputation for honesty and quality, two factors that are very important when buying emeralds. If you do purchase a gem, make sure you get a certificate of quality from the store. It is important for insurance or resale purposes. The store is open from 9 AM to 8 PM Monday thru Saturday.

* Chino Market – Located along Avenida Pedro de Heredia, this is a fascinating market area of narrow streets that are somewhat chaotic. The streets are lined with small shops selling just about everything you can think of. It is not a tourist oriented shopping area so do not expect to find souvenirs. This is a genuine lower income shopping bazaar that is simply a taste of real everyday life in Cartagena. It is not advisable to wander alone, a guide is important for overall safety.

Chino Market area just inside the city walls

* Colombia Artesanal – Located at Calle de los Escribos # a-104 in the Old City, this is a shop that specializes in fine quality Colombian arts and crafts by well-recognized artisans. Prices may appear to be high, but you will be looking and quality crafts. Do not be afraid to bargain, as it is expected even in a quality store. This shop is open from 9 AM to 11 Pm daily.

* Las Bovedas – Located in the Old City along Carrera 2 at the north end, this long building was once a collection of jail cells. Today each former cell is a small arts and crafts shop, but not of the high quality as Colombia Artesanal. This is more mass produced tourist oriented craft, which still does offer some degree of quality. You just need to be careful and question anything you are told about some items being handmade. These shops are open daily from 7 AM to 8 PM. Be sure to bargain, as it is definitely expected here.

* NH Galeria – At Carrera 2 #33-36, this is a very high quality gallery featuring contemporary Colombian art items produced by well-recognized artisans. Some of the art for sale is from other South American artists, giving the shop a more international feel. You will find the staff most helpful, and yes you can attempt to bargain on the price. The shop is open from 10 AM to 8 PM Monday thru Saturday and only from 4 to 8 PM on Sunday.

Some ship tours offer a carriage ride through the Old City

FINAL WORDS: For many of you this may be your only day spent on the South American continent unless you have been on a cruise through the southern fjords or have visited one of the major countries on a land based trip. Even if you have been to the continent, you will still find Cartagena to be a fascinating city. Its Old City area is now a UNESCO

World Heritage Site and this alone makes a visit very special. It has a romantic colonial flavor that is quite distinctive. The only other old city area in all of South America that in any way comes close to the flavor of Cartagena is the historic old city in Salvador, Brazil, which is also a UNESCO World Heritage Site.

Enjoy Cartagena and feel safe in doing so. The Colombian government has seen to it that the city is quite safe for visitors, especially in the historic Old City.

This is a city of contrasts. Modern Cartagena with its towering skyscrapers is as modern as any big city can be. Suburban Cartagena has many middle and upper class residential districts that are very pleasant to explore. Overall this is a great port of call.

Some cruise lines will sponsor an indoor/outdoor dance performance at Teatro Heredia

PANAMA AS A NATION

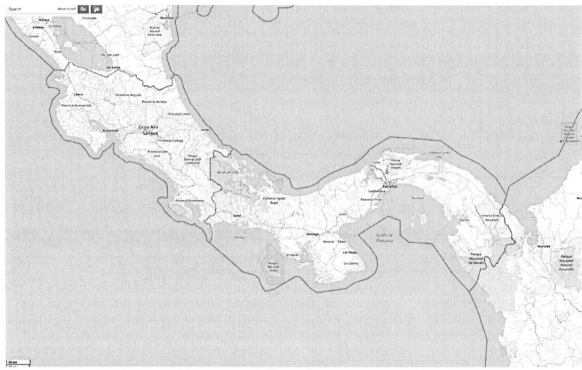

A map of Panama, (© OpenStreetMap contributors)

The Republic of Panama occupies a narrow strip of land that geographers call an isthmus because it connects to larger pieces of land. In this case, Panama is the bridge between North and South America. But to which continent does it belong? As a professional geographer, I could write a whole chapter on that topic but I will not. Suffice it to say that North and South America are separate continents joined at the hip like Siamese Twins. Until the building of the Panama Canal, the traditionally accepted continental border was the political boundary between Panama and Colombia. Now that the canal acts as a water boundary between the two greater landmasses, it is considered to be the boundary. So Panama, like Egypt and Turkey is a nation occupying two continents.

The total area of Panama is only 75,516 square kilometers or 29,157 square miles and the national population is 4,101,000 of which approximately one quarter lives in Panama City, the national capital on the Pacific coast.

THE LANDSCAPE: Panama is a humid tropical country. Its mountain spine runs the full length of the country, but is at its lowest where the canal was built. And that was the reason the location was chosen. To both the north and south of the canal, elevations do rise considerably. The highest elevation is Volcán Barú in the north, which is 3,475 meters or 11,401 feet above sea level. Although part of the Ring of Fire, most of Panama does not have active volcanic or tectonic activity, but the threat still lurks. One reason for building the canal here rather than farther north in Nicaragua, as originally considered, is the far lower degree of volcanic or earthquake activity.

The country is for the most part heavily cloaked in tropical rainforest vegetation, now being protected for the development of ecotourism as well as lessening the dangers of erosion. South of the canal, a region not as rugged as to the north, much of the original growth rainforest was exploited and there are areas today where more of a scrub woodland is found.

The climate is definitely tropical with daytime temperatures generally in the mid to upper 20's Celsius or upper 80's to even low 90's Fahrenheit. The rainy season is generally from December through March, but it can rain just about any time during the year. And humidity is usually quite high, making it muggy and steamy. It was the climate that bred much in the way of insect life, mold and disease organisms. The building of the Panama Canal was plagued in particular by yellow fever, which finally was conquered by a combination of the creation of a preventative vaccine and by draining swamps and spraying for mosquitos. Today visitors to Panama need not worry about serious diseases.

Tropical rainforest seen from on board ship traversing the canal

Many American expatriates have settled in some of the mountain towns in the far western part of Panama close to the border with Costa Rica, especially in the towns of San Andréas and Boquete. This is a beautiful part of the country and at higher altitudes, the climate is quite equitable. It is also in this area that government is attempting to foster ecotourism, as has been successful in neighboring Costa Rica.

A BRIEF PANAMANIAN HISTORY: It is very important for you to know about Panama's history, as just the fact that you will be sailing through the canal is so closely

tied to how the country gained its independence. As a modern nation Panama owes its independence to the United States who in the early 20th century was looking to build a canal in Nicaragua. But the higher elevation, greater earthquake and volcanic danger and potential for political instability were strong negative factors. When the United States finally decided upon the Isthmus of Panama, which was a province of Colombia, the government was not willing to come to terms, asking far too much money for the rights to build a canal.

The early exploration of Panama dates back to 1513, when Spanish explorer Vasco de Balboa crossed the isthmus and laid eyes on the Pacific Ocean. It was a beautiful sunny day with no wind and as he gazed out at the calm blue waters, he named it Oceano Pacifico, the peaceful ocean.

When the Spanish conquered the Inca Empire in Peru and began to exploit the vast gold and silver reserves, the ore was brought to the isthmus on the Pacific side and then hauled overland to be loaded on ships in the Caribbean to sail across to Spain. The Spanish impressed the native people into forced labor hauling the ore or on newly formed plantations under what was called the economienda system, often worked until they dropped.

Dutch, French and British privateers had their eye on Panama and there were raids including the 1671 by Englishman Henry Morgan that totally sacked Panama city, which in a short time had become one of the wealthiest cities in Spanish America. Spain, however, kept an iron grip on the isthmus until revolutionary fever swept through their colonial empire. In 1821, two independence movements occurred, one in Panama City and the other on the peninsula of Azuero where the farmers wanted independence both from Spain and the government in Panama City. Through skillful bribery and political maneuvering a crisis was averted and all of Panama declared independence in unison. Knowing their economic weakness and lack of infrastructure, the government in Panama voluntarily joined with Colombia as a province rather than becoming an independent republic. But later unrest within Panama ultimately led to attempts to break away from Colombia in 1831 and again in 1899.

When Colombia rejected the American bid to build the canal, asking for far too much money and not willing to grant many concessions, rather than pay, the United States supported the local revolutionaries in their bid for independence. After sending a fleet of war ships to the coast, Colombia had to give in since they were no match for the Americans. This was a classic example of Theodore Roosevelt's policy of speaking softly but carrying a big stick.

* THE CANAL ZONE: In the conclusion of a treaty, the United States was granted full sovereign rights to a zone 16 kilometers or ten miles wide and 81 kilometers or 50 miles long over which it would have full jurisdiction and fly its own flag. And it was within this zone that the Panama Canal would be dug.

Over the years of American dominance and despite the strong economic boost it gave to Panama, there was strong resentment to a foreign swath of territory bisecting their nation. Agitation continued to fester, as Panama saw its share of dictatorial and military governments, but most of the leaders did support the American presence. They both feared the American military and also welcomed the constant infusion of American capital.

Former American military headquarters outside of Panama City

The Panama Canal was completed in 1914 and became the great link between oceans, serving both commercial and military traffic through the decades of the 20th century. The United States administered the Canal Zone as a territory, holding total sovereignty over every aspect of its activities, considering it to be American soil. Panama remained independent of the Canal Zone, essentially a constitutional democracy, but not totally without domination of its wealthy elite who essentially corrupted the system

* PANAMANIAN UNREST; From the late 1960's onward there was continual political unrest over the domination of the United States over the Canal Zone and its overall impact upon the independence of Panama as a nation. The country underwent sweeping changes during the 1970's with a change in the constitution in 1972 brought about by the military to clean up corruption. Omar Torrijos became the national leader, proclaimed by the military and ruled until his death in a plane crash in 1981.

By 1983, General Manuel Antonio Noriega came to power, heading both the military and civilian governments. Noriega wore two hats, one as the dictator of the nation and the other as a drug smuggler and money launderer, engaging in a variety of illegal enterprises. And unfortunately the United States turned a blind eye to this criminal undercurrent because Noriega was also working with the Central Intelligence Agency to assist the Nicaraguan Contras in their efforts to overthrow Daniel Ortega's socialist regime.

In June 1987, a series of uprisings by the Cruzada Civilista or Civic Crusade began to undermine the Noriega government, this after a retired military officer had openly denounced Noriega of electoral fraud and other underhanded activities. Hundreds died in street fighting or by the hand of the government. The United States hit the government with numerous economic sanctions, froze all government assets and in essence crippled the economy. The 1989 election saw the opposition win over Noriega, but he annulled the results and continued in power.

The United States, in part to protect its national security interest in the Panama Canal chose to invade the country in December 1989 with the intent of not only toppling the government, but also to capture Manuel Noriega. The basis of the American action was to stop the flow of drugs being funneled into the United States by actions of the Noriega regime. In addition to drugs, Noriega was using Panama as a conduit for illegal migrants from China being smuggled into the United States, a very lucrative operation for Noriega.

The invasion was unprecedented. The United States is a charter member of the Organization of American States, and for it or any other member to invade another's territory was a serious breach of the charter as well as of the United Nations charter. Because Noriega was viewed as a hemispheric pariah, none of the other member states complained.

* THE END OF AMERICAN DOMINATION: After Noriega was captured and taken to the United States for trial and later incarceration, the people of Panama set about to restore the capital city. With American economic assistance and advisory aid, Panama was restored to a level of order with free elections.

President Jimmy Carter negotiated a series of treaties that would ultimately end the Canal Zone and put the canal under Panamanian control. On January 1, 2000, the Panamanian Flag was raised over the Canal where it flies today. Under the terms of the final treaty, the United States would have the sole right to intervene if the canal ever came under foreign or domestic threat.

Today the canal is Panamanian, but many of its key personnel are American because of their knowledge of its operation. But more and more Panamanians are being trained to run the canal fully on their own.

The nation of Panama has seen great economic success. It has one of the lowest unemployment rates in the world, being under three percent. The agricultural base produces a surplus and the country has a healthy balance of trade. However, poverty still exists among the less fortunate mestizo and native communities. The slums of Panama City are a testament to that ongoing problem. Yet overall Panama is considered to be an emerging second world nation with an overall high living standard.

Much of the success of Panama is due to the revenue generated by the canal. And Panama City has become a major financial and market hub for Central America. The United States did invest 5.25 billion dollars in the building of the new, wider and longer locks that now enables greater volumes of shipping and generates larger revenue streams. With the expanded volume of shipping through the canal, new light industries and marketing operations are being encouraged to invest in Panama, and this simply further boosts the country's growth potential.

In the mountains the government is allowing increased exploitation of copper and gold. But some of these deposits are within areas formerly designated as ecological reserves. This action riles many conservation groups at home and abroad and could have a negative impact upon ecotourism. I personally hope that the Panamanian government looks closely at the success of Costa Rica in capitalizing upon its tropical rainforests in developing a very major and sustainable ecotourism trade.

Hundreds of tourists at the Miraflores Visitor Center watch as a major cruise ship passes through the Miraflores Locks

Tourism plays a massive role in the Panamanian economy. Tourism is predicated upon visiting the ecological reserves, viewing the canal and most importantly the buying of real estate for second homes or retirement. Special tax exempt zones have been established to make either temporary or permanent living quite appealing. Over 2.2 million visitors come to Panama on average each year, and this does not count those who view a slice of the country from the deck of a cruise ship. Although ship passengers do not spend money in the country, if it were not for Panama Canal cruises, the overall revenue of the country would diminish by the loss of the heavy transit tolls that cruise ships pay. Generally the average toll is in excess of $100,000 for a single transit.

Panama City has become one of the most spectacular modern cities in Central America. Its population is roughly one quarter of the entire nation. Panama City has also become a major air hub for Central America with flights arriving and departing for the United States, Canada, the Caribbean and all major centers in Latin America as well as Europe.

The dynamic skyline of Panama City as seen by cruise ship passages through the Panama Canal

SAN BLAS ISLANDS

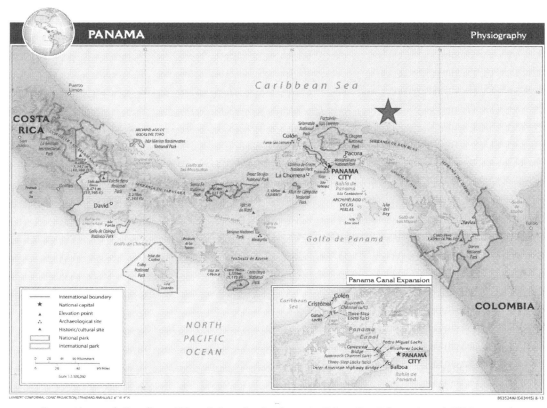

Location of the San Blas Islands designated by the blue star (CIA map)

This brief chapter is for the benefit of those who are traveling on one of the more upmarket cruise lines that will make a special stop at one of the San Blas Islands of Panama to allow guests to visit among the Kuna Indians. This is a very special experience, one that is quite memorable. It is unfortunate that these small islands cannot accommodate thousands of visitors at one time, which makes it impossible for the larger ships to visit. And all ships that do visit must anchor well offshore and tender their guests to shore because there are absolutely no docking facilities for anything the size of even the smallest cruise ship.

THE LANDSCAPE: The San Blas Island Archipelago lies off the northeast Caribbean coast of Panama. The group consists of 335 very tiny, low coral islands of which only 49 are inhabited. They comprise a necklace of sandy islands that are just a mere few meters or feet above the highest storm waves. Fortunately hurricanes rarely track into this part of the Caribbean. Many of the islands are so small as to simply have a handful of palm trees and a bit of undergrowth making them the proverbial desert island that we see in cartoons or movies where someone is shipwrecked. They have no sources of fresh water, as they are too small to have streams or lakes. Inhabitants must depend upon collecting rainwater in order to survive. But fortunately rain is a commodity that falls in abundance.

The San Blas Islands are among several low lying coral islands in the world that are in great danger of disappearing should sea levels continue to rise this century as a result of global warming. But unlike several of the world's other coral island groups, the Kuna Indians are citizens of Panama and would therefore benefit by being absorbed even though their homes would be lost.

Approaching the San Blas Islands

A BRIEF HISTORY: Until the Spanish came to Panama the Kuna were one of the several tribes inhabiting the northern coast of the isthmus. They lived by hunting and fishing and had few tools. They also did not practice any farming. The Spanish saw them as essentially sub human and either killed them of drove them off the mainland to these tiny coral islands where took refuge and survived.

They were a simple people who wore little or no clothing and painted distinctive geometric designs on their bodies. When Catholic missionaries started to spread out across Panama, they were horrified by the Kuna and quickly set about to get them into clothes. So the Kuna began to create their same designs out of scraps of colored cloth and sew them onto their garments. Today what are called "molas" are popular trade items that represent the artistic nature of the Kuna, an outgrowth from body decoration in pre missionary days.

Over the years, especially into the late 19th and early 20th centuries, some Kuna men ventured to the mainland where they took primarily menial jobs, learning skills that could lead to more than a subsistence life. A few men went to work for the Panama Canal Company when it was still under American ownership and today they have a pension that enables them to live somewhat above the average. Most chose to return to their native islands and to live a simple life among their own people.

When visitors come the Kuna display their crafts in hopes of earning a few dollars

VISITING AMONG THE KUNA: There will be no organized tours. You will be free to walk around the island where the tender drops you. And you will simply be allowed to mingle with the locals in a way that is very special.

Kuna women generally remain at home. Women maintain the traditions of the past and engage in the production of craft items, especially molas in the form of dresses and shirts. When a cruise ship visits the Kuna dress in their most colorful garb and offer their wares for sale. It is quite a colorful experience to walk among the narrow paths of a Kuna village and see the colorful people. Thanks to tourism, the Kuna have learned to ask for money if you wish to photograph them, usually one dollar per subject. When you come ashore you need to have at least 25 single dollars if you want to do any photographing. The women also set up tables along the narrow streets and in the town square to offer their colorful creations for sale at very low prices. Remember that these items are all handmade, so the prices asked are very reasonable. I recommend against bargaining since this is such a vital source of income to a people who live at the poverty line.

You will see many young school age children, as many do not have an opportunity to gain an education. On some of the larger islands the children do have a government provided primary school but to go beyond means sending a child to the mainland, which few Kuna ever do.

The inhabited islands are not very beautiful, as the Kuna build their wood and thatched houses close together and there are few trees left standing. A few houses have generators, but otherwise there is no electricity. Outhouses are the only source of waste disposal and they are built at the ends of the piers out over the water, which provides for continuous disposal. Garbage is strewn along the shore and in the water and can at times smell quite ripe. Of course the surrounding waters do become highly contaminated, yet you will see young children swimming.

An elder in her colorful garb

Clearly there are no restaurants, and therefore I have no recommendations for places to dine. And shopping is handled by individual families with the prices being pretty much standardized. Credit cards are for the most part not used, so cash is essential. In Panama the currency is the United States Dollar.

Visiting the Kuna is a chance to come into direct contact with a people who live a third world lifestyle. Today they are finally allowed to settle on the mainland, but for centuries these islands have become their homeland. For so long they were denied the right to live on the mainland. Many of the men did and still do leave to work on the Panamanian mainland and have come to understand modernity, but when they return the come back to a primitive existence.

You will find the people to be quite friendly. And if you are walking alone or in a small group you may sometimes be invited into a private home. Please be courteous and do not show your dismay over the conditions under which these people live. It is hard for us to absorb a lifestyle so alien to our own, but by being gracious you will be rewarded with a rare opportunity to cross that huge gap between us and the Kuna.

Normally the Kuna will not offer you anything to eat or drink, as they somehow know that we would prefer not to sample their food. So it is very rare for you to be confronted with the decision of whether to eat or not to eat.

A mother and daughter dressed to receive visitors and be photographed

FINAL WORDS: As noted before, most cruise ships do not stop in the San Blas Islands. This chapter only applies to such cruise lines as Silversea, Seaborn or Regent. It is not that the larger companies look down upon such a visit. It is just that logistically it would be impossible for thousands of guest from a large ship to be landed on one of these small islands.

COLÓN

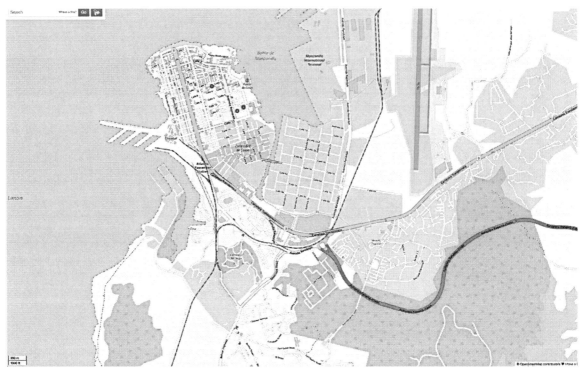

A map of Colón, Panama, (© OpenStreetMap contributors)

Colón is the Caribbean port city just to the east of the entrance into the Panama Canal. It is the eastern gateway to Panama, a major port and is actually the second largest city in the country with a metropolitan population of just over 240,000 residents. Few cruise ships make a port call at Colón, but this chapter is included for the benefit of any reader who may be booked on a cruise which such a stop. Most cruise lines avoid Colón in favor of Cartagena, Colombia, as it is a far larger and definitely more enticing and exciting city for cruise passengers. Colón has seen a lot of deterioration in its infrastructure since the 1980's, especially in its role as a tourist center in good measure because of the increased popularity of Cartagena. Today the unemployment rate in Colón is in the 40 percent range. It has also seen a dramatic rise in drug trafficking leading to a significant street crime problem. The city has massive barrios that of course tend to breed crime. The government in Panama City appears to be ignoring the problem and thus while Panama City is vibrant and booming, Colón has lost most of its charm and the enticement it once had. There are a few nice venues in the city, but they tend to be outweighed by the negatives.

HISTORY OF COLÓN: The city owes its founding to American interests in the building of the Panama Railroad, which ran its first passenger train in 1855. The primary motive for such a railroad was to shorten the distance to the California gold fields since there was no transcontinental railroad across the United States. One could take a ship from an east coast port to Colón and then take the short 76.6 kilometer or 47.6 mile railroad journey to Balboa and take a ship to San Francisco. This cut about two months or more of sailing around the bottom of South America through the Straits of Magellan and then up the west coast of both South and North America.

During the period before the Panama Canal, the railroad carried both passengers and freight between the two coasts of the United States, thus serving essentially American interests. In 1881, the French bought the controlling interest in the railroad because it was to play a major role in their attempt to build a sea level canal across the isthmus. As you already know from an earlier, chapter, the French company went bankrupt, leaving the railroad unmanaged and in a position to deteriorate under the hot tropical sun and high humidity.

In the historic older section of Colón, (Work of Astrid Rios, CC BY SA 3.0, Wikimedia.org)

In 1904, the United States bought the French assets when they abandoned their effort to build a canal, and the railroad restoration began as a prelude to the American building of the canal. Today the railroad handles local freight between the two major cities, but it also carries canal workers, local residents and tourists across the isthmus. They operate a fleet of very nice quality passenger carriages. In 2001, a major restoration and upgrade took place and today's trains are very impressive. Freight is still an important source of revenue for the railroad, but passenger traffic is also significant. Many tourists who are visiting Panama City will often ride the train to Colón and back just to have better views of the canal.

As Colón has seen deterioration because of a loss of its economic significance, it has also been politically ignored since its once wealthy families have relocated to Panama City. The primary population today is a mix of West Indian and Panamanian of the peasant classes, primarily menial workers and their families.

WHAT TO SEE: You may at this point wonder why a cruise ship would even stop here, and that would be a fair question. The sole purpose for those companies who do schedule Colón as a stop is to enable passengers to choose from among several tour options that give you a chance to see some of Panama as a country. When transiting through the canal, you catch glimpses of Panama City's skyline and you see the tropical rainforest along the shores of the Chagres River and Gatun Lake. But there is much more to Panama that is otherwise missed and a visit to Colón gives you that opportunity. The city itself is not at all attractive and too dangerous for you to go off on your own.

* **TOUR OPTIONS FOR COLÓN:** If your ship is going to pay a visit to Colón, I would strongly advise you to book one of the tour options being offered, or have the cruise line arrange a private car and driver/guide. Otherwise it will be a long and rather boring day. Even if a shuttle bus is provided into the center of Colón, there is little to hold your interest for an entire day and personally I do not advise walking around because of the high street crime rate. And I also do not recommend hiring a local taxi to tour around, again for safety reasons.

A view of the nicest part of Colón from the ship's deck, (Work of Balou45, CC BY SA 4.0, Wikimedia.,org)

There is only one interesting sight in Colón if you have a car and driver to take you there because it is difficult to reach and not safe to even attempt going on your own. That venue is Fort San Lorenzo, originally built by Spain in 1595, ordered by King Philip II to protect the new settlements along the Panamanian shore of the Caribbean. The setting high upon a cliff overlooking the mouth of the Chagres River and the sea is quite spectacular and the fort is in a very good state of preservation. It was built to protect against raids by the British, French, Dutch and privateers or pirates.

The tour options that cruise lines offer during a port call in Colón are:

** Countryside drive – You will be taken on either a half-day or full day drive through the beautiful and lush Panamanian countryside. There are various routes, each offering photo stops and/or visits to local plantations. What is offered will depend upon what your cruise line has engaged. For those who do not wish to engage in any major walking or urban activities, this is a relaxing day where you enjoy a drive through Panama. And depending upon the length of the tour, lunch may be included at a nice countryside restaurant.

** Day in Panama City – The national capital and most vibrant city in Central America is only an hour by motor coach from Colón. On an all day tour you will have a chance to see rainforest country while en route to Panama city. And then once there you will visit the historic old districts, the modern beachfront areas and also have lunch in a nice restaurant included. The next chapter discusses Panama City for the benefit of eastbound canal transit itineraries that do spend a day in the capital. The information in that chapter will provide you with all you can see when on a tour out of Colón.

** Gamboa Aerial Tram – This aerial tram ride takes you through a portion of the rainforest at treetop level and has a very great appeal for those with some spirit of adventure. At points along the way your tram will be over 61 meters or 200 feet above most of the canopy, giving you an amazing look at the rainforest. At the end of the ride, you will be deposited on a hilltop where you will have great views over the canal and the countryside. A guide is with you on the tour and points out all of the important features. The tram operates every day of the week except Monday.

** Gatun Lake Cruises – You will be taken by small motorized boats around the shoreline of the lake, stopping at various islands where you will be able to enjoy monkeys and birds up close while going on short walks through the rainforest with a guide. Be aware that for such a cruise you need to wear a hat, sunglasses and also have insect repellant to use when going onshore.

** Panama Canal Operations – You can see the workings of the Panama Canal from a landward perspective, which is totally different than what you will see from onboard ship. If your cruise includes a full day stop in Colón, I highly recommend this tour because you will gain a working knowledge of the canal by witnessing its operations before your ship transits through the next day. Depending upon the tour operator your cruise line chooses, you may tour the new Agua Clara Lock system or the older and more historic Gatun Lock System or quite possibly both.

An aerial view of Fort San Lorenzo, (Work of Garcia, dennis, CC BY SA 4.0, Wikimedia.org)

DINING OUT: If you are booked on a full day excursion, lunch will be included, but you will not have a choice of restaurants. Normally the cruise lines arrange for a group lunch at one of the nicest restaurants in the area you are touring. When going out with a private car and driver, I would recommend that you tell the driver what you have in mind for lunch and leave it to him to choose. I have found that drivers will always take you someplace that is reputable and offers good food. If you invite the driver to join you, that will definitely guarantee a pleasant meal in the area you are visiting.

If you are simply walking around Colón on your own and not doing a tour, I would recommend that you return to the ship for lunch. I prefer not to recommend any in town restaurants, as I believe you would not be satisfied.

SHOPPING: For souvenirs there is Port Colón where most cruise ships will dock. There are souvenir and craft items available and it is open 24-hours per day. And the one item most people want to buy are Panama hats, which by the way, are made in Ecuador. It is not really safe to go walking outside of the terminal.

STRUCTURE OF THE PANAMA CANAL

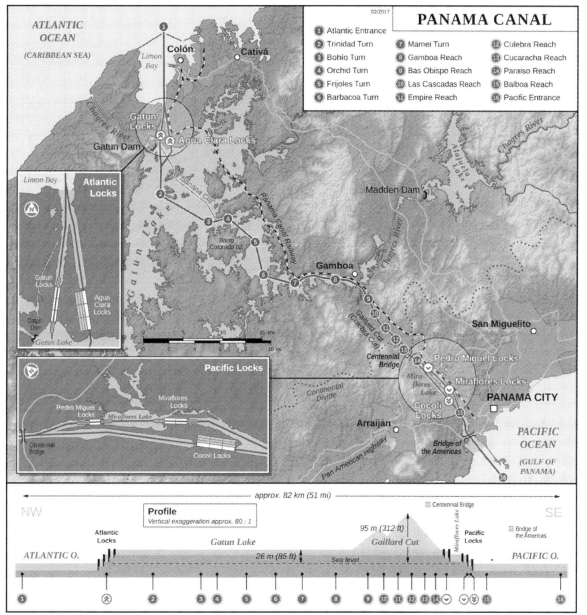

The canal layout, (Work of Thomas Römer, CC BY SA 2.0, Wikimedia.org)

A transit through the Panama Canal is one of those once in a lifetime events for most passengers on a cruise ship. I feel fortunate in having made the journey four times, twice westbound and twice eastbound. Actually I should say southbound and northbound. The actual orientation is from northeast to southwest when viewed on a map oriented with north at the top. The way in which the Isthmus of Panama is arched, the Caribbean shore is actually to the north and the Pacific shore to the south. One quiz question used on many game shows asks the question, "Which side of the Panama Canal is farther west, the

Caribbean or Pacific." The correct is answer is the Caribbean, as the route of the canal when traveling to the Pacific follows a northwest to southeast track.

Most of you will be making the transit through the canal utilizing the old locks that have been in service since 1914. The new and larger locks are only accepting ships too large to utilize the original locks, which rules out the majority of the cruise ships that do the Panama Canal experience. I found that the new locks, despite their size, somehow lacked the majesty and excitement of the original locks. Also I have found that the journey from the Caribbean to the Pacific is more exciting when going through the original locks because of the fact that you enter the triple Gatun Lock system traveling up, which is so much more dynamic than coming back down. On the Pacific side, the Miraflores and Pedro Miguel Locks are separated and therefore you do not get the full scope of being lifted upward when entering the canal. So my advice is to book a westbound cruise to the Pacific.

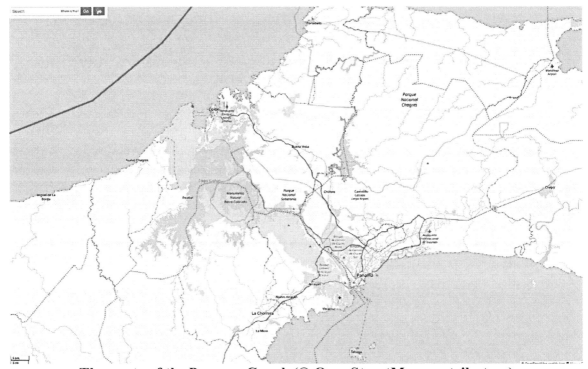

The route of the Panama Canal, (© OpenStreetMap contributors)

BUILDING THE CANAL: France was the first nation to attempt to build a canal across Panama. In 1881, a shareholding company founded by Ferdinand de Lesseps, builder of the Suez Canal, attempted to dig a sea level canal across the isthmus. He was fresh from his success in digging the Suez Canal, which is a sea level waterway connecting the eastern Mediterranean with the Red Sea by crossing the Sinai Peninsula. This eliminated the long journey around the southern tip of Africa. Fortunately for de Lesseps, the western edge of the Sinai where it connects Asia to Africa is very flat and sandy. And there are no major tidal or current differences between the Mediterranean and the Red Sea.

By 1889, the company was bankrupt and de Lesseps was ruined and disgraced. Miscalculation regarding the rather difficult geology, the impact of malaria and yellow fever and the primitive nature of the available digging equipment combined to cost the company the loss of 22,000 human lives and $28,000,000, which in today's value is in the billions of dollars. Allegations of corruption ultimately Charles de Lesseps, the builder's son, in jail.

Assuming that the company had been successful, what they did not recognize was the great tidal variance between the Caribbean and Pacific sides of the isthmus. Tidal surges of up to 6.7 meters or 22 feet on the Pacific Side of the canal would have torn through the sea level canal and made transit so dangerous as to have been impossible. And the erosive power of such a tidal surge would have damaged or destroyed the banks of the canal. Such a surge twice each day would have swept fish and other crustaceans from the Pacific into the Caribbean and altered the natural balance with who knows what sort of devastating effect.

It is a thrill to watch the gates swing open when your ship passes from one lock into the next, here seen in the Gatun Lock system

* ENTER THE AMERICANS: In 1894 a second French company was created to continue work on the trans-isthmus railroad and maintain the equipment in working order to hopefully be able to attract a buyer for the project. In 1904, the United States took over the assets and found that the French equipment and infrastructure had little value because most of it has rusted in the humid tropical climate.

The first two American project directors found it difficult to work within the bounds of the Isthmian Canal Commission and both resigned before making any progress. President Roosevelt then appointed John Frank, the engineer responsible for building the Great Northern Railroad. Frank bypassed all of the bureaucratic structure and ultimately worked directly for the President and Secretary of War. He set about to first make life comfortable, safe and disease free for the thousands of workers, something the French company had never considered. His chief sanitation officer, Colonel William Goras, was given wide latitude in seeing to it that the living sites remained habitable. Dr. Carlos Finlay and Dr. Walter Reed recognized that yellow fever and malaria were transmitted by mosquitos. Spraying was then instituted to greatly lessen the danger.

By 1907, Frank had resigned and the final engineer appointed was George Washington Goethals of the Army Corps of engineers. With his West Point background and strong leadership skills combined with a brilliant engineering background, he saw the project through to its ultimate completion. He wisely kept in place all of the changes instituted by Goras with regard to health and sanitation, thus keeping the work force fit for duty.

Unlike the French effort at a sea level canal, the American plan was to build a dam to hold back the Chagres River to a depth of 36 meters or 85 feet behind the dam. The river flows northeast to the Caribbean Sea and often would rampage during the rainy season. The dam was to create Gatun Lake to regulate the flow of water. This massive manmade lake flooded the lowlands, leaving a chain of islands that today add great beauty to the landscape. In the first century since completion many species have been cut off from one another and deviations are being seen in accordance with Darwin's Galapagos observations.

Locks were built to raise and lower ships through the system. A lock is a large concrete chamber that is flooded with water to equal sea level where a ship is waiting to enter. The ship then sails in and the rear gates close. Then more water is added to raise the ship to the level of the next lock, or water can be released to lower a ship in the case of ships exiting the system. Once a chamber is filled to a higher level or drained down to a lower level the front gates open and the ship sails out at a higher or lower level depending upon whether it is entering or leaving the canal.

* THE OLD LOCK SYSTEM: Three massive pairs of locks were built to raise and lower ships 26 meters or 85 feet in or out of Gatun Lake on the Caribbean side. These locks are 33.5 meters or 110 feet wide and 320 meters or 1,050 feet long. Their height is not equal in every case, but in combination they enable the raising or lowering of ships by the required 26 meters or 85 feet. On the Pacific side of the canal, one lone lock called Pedro Miguel was built followed by the two Miraflores Locks about 1.6 kilometers or one mile farther south because the geologic structure underlying the canal was not capable of supporting three contiguous locks.

The walls of all the locks are massive in thickness starting at 14.9 meters or 49 feet at their base and tapering to 2.9 meters or 9.8 feet at the top. The center wall separating the parallel sets of locks is 17.9 meters or 59 feet thick and rises to accommodate the workstations and two sets of tracks for the diesel-electric locomotives that help steer a ship through the canal. There are also tracks along the outer edges of the locks, thus providing for an equalization of the position of a ship within the locks. Ships do use minimal power, as the locomotives, known as mules, do not actually pull the ships through. Their role is to keep them straight through the use of thick cables that they can loosen or tighten as needed. All action between the locomotives is coordinated by a series of bells that you will hear being rung throughout the time the ship is in the lock.

The locomotives known as mules steering a cruise ship through the single Pedro Miguel Lock

The steel doors at each end of the locks are enormous, varying from 14.2 to 24.9 meters or 47 to 83 feet in height and they are over 2.5 meters or 7 feet thick. Each gate has two leaves that are 19.8 meters or 65 feet wide, closing to form a "V" shape. The gates are operated by hydraulic equipment that is water operated utilizing hydraulic struts installed in 1998.

To fill or empty one lock chamber is quite an undertaking, as it involves 101,070,494 liters or 26,700,000 gallons of water for each use. The water is recycled to avoid the massive waste that would otherwise occur, especially during the drier season. It takes only a few minutes to fill or drain the water in the lock chamber to enable a ship to be raised or lowered.

The low mountain barrier that crosses the isthmus in the middle had to be breached, as this was also the continental divide. Steam shovels were put to work to cut a channel through the mountains, today known as the Culebra Cut. It is 12.5 kilometers or 7.8 miles long. This has had the effect of allowing water from the Atlantic side of the isthmus to now channel through to the Pacific side.

Two smaller reservoirs had to be built to regulate water flow for the locks on the Pacific side of the continental divide and to accommodate the strong tidal range. The geology of the

Pacific side is such that only two pairs of locks and one lock at the western end of the Culebra Cut can accomplish what the triple Gatun Lock complex does on the Caribbean side.

A large cargo container ship starts to scrape the wall in the Gatun Lock system, as it is being lowered to the Caribbean Sea

The maximum size of a ship that can transit the old lock system is referred to as Panamax class. The ship must be capable fitting into the lock with various minimum limits as to clearance. The height of the ship's tallest mast or funnel must be able to fit under the older Bridge of the Americas at Balboa. And the ship cannot draw more than 12.4 meters or 41.2 feet of water. The new Panamax standard for the just opened larger locks enables ships of 25 percent greater length, 51 percent greater width and 26 percent deeper draught to be accommodated. But there will still be a sizable number of ships too large to pass through these locks. American Navy aircraft carriers have always been too wide to pass through the Panama Canal and still are today.

* THE NEW LOCK SYSTEM: In 2016 new larger locks were put into service after many years of construction. They now increase the size of vessels capable of using the Panama Canal, but they somehow lack the drama of the original locks. Until these locks were opened for use two thirds of all the ships afloat today were unable to use the canal. Even with the greater size of the locks, approximately half of the cargo ships and all aircraft carriers still cannot transit the Panama Canal.

The new Panamax Class is based upon the greater size of the new lock system, a transit through which will form a separate chapter later in the book. Now ships of 54.86 meters or

180 feet in width, 426.72 meters or 1,400 feet in length and a maximum draught of 18.29 meters or 60 feet can pass through the canal, still utilizing the now deeper and wider Culebra Cut. The maximum height remains the same, as on the Pacific side of the Canal, the Centennial Bridge limits the height of all ships passing through the system.

There is a chapter coming up that discusses the impact of the new locks upon the overall importance of the Panama Canal. And it also looks at the fine details of how the new system operates.

When the new locks were inaugurated in 2016, the first mega cruise ship to pass through the canal, it having a displacement of 83,000 tons. But some of the extremely large cruise ships in the 100,000 ton category will still be too large to utilize the canal.

The new locks do not have diesel-electric locomotives keeping the ships aligned but rather small tugboats are used. And unlike the drama of the old locks where the doors swing outward, in the new canal system, the locks slide into a large slot on the outer side of the chamber instead of rotating. Although these gates are massive they just somehow do not have the grandeur of the old canal system. The gates are 57 meters wide, 30 meters high and 10 meters thick. They were made in The Netherlands where similar sliding gates are used in the dyke system to protect the lowlands against storm surges.

A sliding gate on the new Panama Canal lock system, (Courtesy of
Power Transmission World)

One great advantage in the new lock system is that for each lock there is a massive holding reservoir of water that enables 60 percent of the water for each lock to be reused thus saving millions of gallons of water that otherwise would be lost, as has been the case with the older lock system. If you transit through the new locks, you will see these reservoirs on the outer side of each of the lock basins.

THE ORDER OF PASSAGE: On the Caribbean side of the canal there is a massive breakwater providing protection for ships that are waiting to enter the locks. For a higher transit fee, ships can prearrange a transit time, but many of the lesser shipping lines do not incur that fee and can wait hours or days for their turn to transit. Ships must have a trained pilot on board provided by the Panama Canal Company. The pilot essentially becomes the temporary master of the ship, but in consultation with the ship's captain on all matters impacting the ship's transit. These highly trained pilots have an intimate knowledge of the canal from long experience that a ship's captain cannot possess.

Cruise ships need to prearrange, as a nighttime passage would not be compatible with the whole concept of a Panama Canal cruise where passengers want to be out on deck and enjoying every moment. Normally cruise ships arrange to arrive at the canal in the early morning and begin their transit shortly after sunrise. The Panama Canal Company also provides on board guides who broadcast a running commentary from the bridge of the ship to enhance the experience. As a destination lecturer and consultant for Silversea Cruises I had the opportunity of doing the live narration from the ship's bridge on four separate occasions, an experience I will long remember.

The three Gatun Locks on the Caribbean side are the most dramatic when seen on the inbound experience of a passage to the Pacific. Both sets of locks can be used for one way traffic inbound or outbound in six hour time blocks when the canal is especially busy, as two way traffic with large vessels is potentially dangerous. At night one set of locks is used for inbound traffic and the other for outbound, as the volume is much lower than during daylight hours. This same pattern holds true for both the old and new sets of Agua Clara Locks on the Caribbean side when traffic is heavy.

The volume of traffic varies from day to day or week to week. Schedules are drawn up for transit through the canal in both the old and new locks. Those ships that have prearranged a transit are given priority over those that simply show up and then ask for passage. And of course maintenance issues or breakdowns have to be factored into the operational schedule. There is never an absolute guarantee that a ship will complete its transit in the average ten hour time frame allowed. And the schedule of staff on board a ship is not considered as a factor by the Panama Canal Company. When a ship is given the green light to transit, it must be ready at whatever time it is authorized to begin. Only cruise ships are given the courtesy of daylight transit and the highest priority since the operators of the canal know that passengers have paid for their cruise with a daylight transit in mind.

There are strict speed restrictions when in transit across the waters of Gatun Lake and even stricter restrictions in the Culebra Cut to avoid creating a wake that could damage the earthen walls.

At the western end of the Culebra Cut stands the Pedro Miguel Lock, the only single lock in the old lock system. The same traffic pattern holds true in that inbound traffic passes through both sides in the morning and outbound traffic passes through in the afternoon. And at night two way traffic is permitted.

Speed through the Miraflores Lake is highly restricted as the distance between the Pedro Miguel and Miraflores Locks is so small. And the same inbound and outbound policies hold true for the two Miraflores Locks.

In the new lock system, at the Pacific end there are three contiguous locks collectively known as the Cocoli Locks. Inbound morning and outbound afternoon traffic patterns are maintained when traffic is especially heavy.

The new Cocoli Locks on the Pacific side, (Work of ArnoldReinhold, CC BY SA 4.0, Wikimedia.org)

* COST TO TRANSIT THE CANAL: Fees for a transit through the Panama Canal are based upon a vessel's size and draught, which is its displacement measured in tons. For cruise ships there is a complex fee schedule that also takes into consideration the number of passenger beds that are occupied at the time of transit. It is quite a complex set of calculations that goes into the fee structure such as the cargo and for container ships there are separate chares for full or empty containers. On average, a small personal yacht or motorboat will be charged rom a few hundred dollars to as much as over $3,000 to transit, and will be grouped with other small vessels occupying the same lock basin on a communal basis. Large cargo

container ships have paid as high as just over $400,000 to transit the old locks and over $1,000,000 for a single transit through the new locks. The lowest transit fee ever charged was 35 cents to swimmer Richard Halliburton in 1928. I doubt if today a swimmer could be accommodated.

Fees to transit the canal must be paid 48 hours prior to transit. Bank transfers must be completed before a ship will be given permission to enter the canal. It is quite lucrative an operation, but you must also consider that the operating costs are also quite major.

Close up of a diesel-electric locomotive steering a huge container ship
Through the Pedro Miguel Lock

FINAL NOTE: Regardless of whether your ship will transit through the old locks now in their second century of operation or through the very modern expanded lock system, you will find the transit to be the highlight of your cruise. In my four transits of the canal I have never met a fellow passenger that was not in awe of the magnitude of the entire operation. But I must note that there is a greater degree of excitement and enthusiasm generated by a passage through the original lock system. Thus my recommendation is for you to book your cruise on a ship still capable of passing through the original locks.

TRAVERSING THE CANAL EAST TO WEST

Entering the Gatun Locks in the morning

The vast majority of cruise ships still transit the Panama Canal utilizing the old lock system, which as I have noted before is far more spectacular and exciting. The next two chapters in this guide will present a virtual tour of a transit through the Panama Canal from the Caribbean to the Pacific and then in reverse from the Pacific to the Caribbean. I will try and convey the events in words and pictures to help you appreciate the adventure.

I then have a chapter that follows and details the flavor of a transit through the new Agua Clara and Cocoli Locks. It was impressive simply based upon the magnitude of these larger locks, but so many of the visual and audio elements of the old canal were missing.

APPROACHING THE GATUN LOCKS:

Normally by dawn your ship will be entering the massive breakwater at the eastern or Caribbean entrance to the Panama Canal. As the sun rises, you will see many cargo ships or tankers dotting the horizon, anchored and awaiting their turn to travel westbound through the canal. Fees are lower for unreserved travel and generally the smaller or less affluent shipping companies simply wait and take their chances that they will be able to transit within a few days. The major shipping lines and all the cruise lines will form a queue in the order they are given to begin the approximately one hour transit through the three contiguous Gatun Locks

Generally cruise ships are placed at or close to the head of the line. The Panama Canal Company recognizes the value of good public relations that will be spread by the thousands of cruise ship passengers when they have a memorable transit.

The nearly completed Atlantic Bridge across the Caribbean opening to the Panama Canal, (Work of Tinashocker, CC BY SA 4.0, Wikimedia.org)

To further good public relations, a guide comes on board with the pilot by motor launch just before entry into the first lock. I am a qualified lecturer on the Panama Canal and worked in tandem with the guide and we did joint narrations each time, which gave the guests two viewpoints.

The majority of passengers will be forward on the upper decks for the best view of the transit through the three Gatun Locks, which takes an hour to 75 minutes. Just prior to reaching the first Gatun Lock, your ship will sail under the new Atlantic Bridge, the world's longest prestressed concrete bridge with a central span of 530 meters or 1,750 feet. It will be fully open to traffic sometime in 2019, but at the writing of this edition it is not yet open. Slowly the ship sails alongside the middle wall, inching its way forward. When it is close enough to where the cables can be attached from the diesel-electric locomotives, henceforth called mules, waiting on either side, men in small boats come out to bring the lines close enough to where ship's crew can reach down with a hook and bring them on board to be attached to one of the winches.

Approaching the Gatun Locks for the start of the transit

Once the ship is fully attached to two mules forward and two aft, the ship slowly sails into the lock and stops. Behind the ship the massive steel doors start to close. And within moments water begins to flood upward from the many openings in the bottom of the compartment. It takes less than ten minutes for the millions of gallons needed to raise the ship to the level where it will be level and equalized with the middle lock.

With the ringing of bells, the mules coordinate their positions while the forward lock doors slowly rotate open. Now ahead of the ship is the middle lock into which the ship slowly sails while being kept in a straight path by the tightening or loosening of the steel cables by the mules. Once in the middle lock, the process is repeated. The rear gates, which are much taller than those in the first lock chamber, clos and soon the water level begins to rise, as millions of gallons flood into the lock. And within a few minutes the forward doors rotate open and the third lock becomes visible.

The final lock has now raised the ship to its maximum height and it sails out into Gatun Lake. Most cruise ships continue on through the lake, which is absolutely beautiful. There are small verdant hilly islands cloaked in tropical vegetation that dot the lake. And some will be passed so close that you will see monkeys in the trees and alligators basking on the shore. Most of the islands are part of a Panamanian national park to preserve their pristine and isolated beauty. If you look back once entering the lake you can see the rear of Gatun Dam, which is the cornerstone of the entire canal system. It holds back the waters of the Chagres River, thus regulating the supply of water for the older lock system on the Caribbean side. Some of the water from the lake also is used to operate the locks on the Pacific side as well

The ship awaits the flooding of the first lock to raise it to the second level

The speed limit while traversing the lake is around 10 knots per hour, which is very slow and it enables you to enjoy the richness of the surroundings. In some ways it is like going on a sightseeing tour of a part of the Panamanian rainforest. If the weather is nice, the richness of the surrounding rainforest is quite striking set against the deep blue of the lake and a sky normally dotted with white cumulous clouds. By late morning, if there will be any rain, you can see thunderheads massing along the continental divide.

The widest part of Gatun Lake is where the Chagres River leaves the highlands and is joined by several tributaries in a broad valley. It is here that the Gatun Dam was built just to the west of the Gatun Locks, holding back the waters that form the lake. But several islands narrow the lake down where it approaches the highlands, the largest being Barro Colorado Island, which narrows the main channel to less than one kilometer or mile in width. It is here where excavation and dredging was necessary, as the course had to proceed through the Continental Divide. This narrower channel enables passengers to get very close up views of the rainforest vegetation and many of its animals, especially the arboreal ones, especially birds and monkeys. On the shores of the lake you will see large local alligators known as caimans. Depending upon the time of day, you may even see the caimans swimming in the lake close to shore. Generally the on board lecturer or Panamanian guide will be pointing out these details over the public address system.

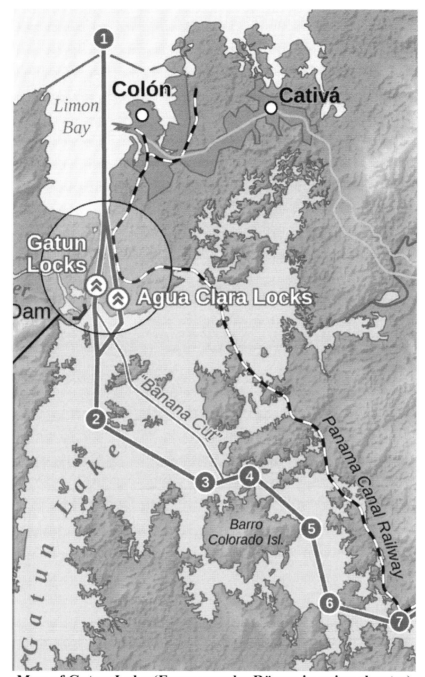

Map of Gatun Lake (From map by Römer in prior chapter)

As the ship actually enters the flooded narrows of the Chagres River, it will pass the only important town along the route, which is Gamboa reached about midway through the journey, an average of four hours after first entering the Gatun Locks. This is the major maintenance center for current canal upkeep. Gamboa originated as the site for the digging and dredging equipment when the Culebra Cut was being opened. Today it is home to the Panama Canal Dredging Division, its location at the point where the Chagres River makes a sharp turn to the south and the actual cutting into the Continental Divide began. It is also here that the main highway and railroad line cross the river along their route between

Panama City and Colón. If you are fortunate enough you may see a passenger train crossing the bridge. If a train and ship happen to be present at the same time, the train will usually stop to give its passengers a chance to watch the ship sailing by.

Crossing the blue waters of Gatun Lake

Gamboa today is only a shadow of what it was during the digging of the Culebra Cut. Today only a handful of families live here, but there are fine examples of the residential architecture, mostly built of wood, that characterize the American adaptation to this hot, tropical climate.

The main highlight in Gamboa is seeing one or two of the massive dredges in their docking facility at Gamboa. The large red and white crane you will see tied up in the docking area is used when it is necessary to change out one of the massive steel gates in the lock system. It is one of the largest such cranes in the world. The dredges are used to keep the upper end of the lake and the Culebra Cut at their new maximum depth of 18.3 meters or 60 feet to enable the deepest draught vessels unhindered passage. Small slides from the walls of the cut and debris washed down river by heavy summer rains cause buildup that needs to be dredged to keep the entire waterway open.

After leaving Gamboa, your ship enters the Culebra Cut, a 12.5 kilometer or 7.8 mile long channel that was dug through the Continental Divide where hills only rise to heights of less than 305 meters or 1,000 feet. This is the prime reason the location was chosen since it is the lowest spot on the dividing ridge that is the spine of Central America. Given the technology available at the start of the 20th century, it was a major feat of engineering to dig this channel.

Fortunately the American geologists recognized that digging to sea level would prove disastrous the project was capable of being completed.

Passing the Titan, the massive crane docked in Gamboa

You will notice both the steep walls that have been terraced and in some areas heavily planted in thick vegetation, both being ways to lessen the degradation of the slopes because of the heavy, tropical rain. And in some locations you will see wire mesh designed to hold back the loose rock that can also be brought down into the water by occasional mild earthquakes as well as the heavy rains.

With the addition of the new and wider locks that parallel the original lock sets, it was necessary to widen and dredge the Culebra Cut, and some of that activity will be ongoing for years to come apart from the normal maintenance. With a wider cut, in some areas the walls are now more fragile since part of the former supporting rock at the base had to be removed.

Toward the Pacific side of the Culebra Cut, the ship will pass under the beautiful Centennial Bridge, a suspension span that was opened in 2004 celebrating the centennial of Panamanian independence. This bridge carries the rerouted Pan American Highway, the main artery connecting the two halves of Panama, now carrying the bulk of the traffic across the canal. And with the canal recognized as the continental boundary, this bridge is the link between North and South America. And it is just past the bridge that you will see where ships passing through the Cocoli Locks on the newer and wider segment of the canal join with or depart from the Culebra Cut. The actual locks are close enough to see, especially if ships are in the chambers at the time, which is most likely.

Dredging is ongoing in the Culebra Cut

The single Pedro Miguel Lock is the next phase of the passage through the original canal, this being the start of the lowering of your ship ultimately to emerge into the Pacific Ocean. There is a log center divider strip, and depending upon traffic flow, your ship will enter either the right or left side. Somehow in my personal opinion, the passing out process seems to be less spectacular than entering the canal. As you look ahead to the lock all you will see is the already filled chamber, which is at the same level as the Culebra Cut. And the massive doors are already open. Thus your ships slowly sails in after first being hooked up to the sets of mules that will guide its passage after the lines have been brought out in a small boat. Although the procedure is the same, there just is not the drama of being raised with the massive doors first opening to admit your ship and then the next set of doors looming ahead. It is simply a matter of visual perception. Of course in the Pedro Miguel Lock there is no second chamber. The doors in front of you are already closed to contain the water into which you sail. They will open once the water level in the chamber has been lowered, and I will admit that part of the procedure is quite dramatic. So be sure to have a good vantage point at the front of the ship.

Once inside the Pedro Miguel Lock, the rear gates will close and the water will be drained out rather rapidly, lowering the ship to the level of the Miraflores Lake, which is 9.4 meters or 31 feet lower than the Culebra Cut waters. Once the front gates open your ship sails into the Miraflores Lake for its short passage of 1.9 kilometers or 1.2 miles to the Miraflores Locks.

Again you will see the long center pier jutting forward. And on the left hand side you will see the small dam placed across the Pedro Miguel River to create Miraflores Lake, filling a basin that is dredged deep enough for ship passage.

Approaching the Pedro Miguel Lock on the outbound leg toward the two Miraflores Locks with the entry doors already open to admit the ship

As your ship is again hooked up to the mules to begin the process of entering the first of the two Miraflores Locks, there will not be the same level of drama as there was when entering the Gatun Locks. But again this is purely a perceptual matter since the process is just working in reverse in that you are entering a lock chamber already filled and ready for your ship. This first chamber of the two Miraflores Locks will lower your ship by half of the 15.4 meters or 54 vertical feet, which the second chamber will complete to bring your ship to sea level.

The Miraflores Lock Visitor's Center is a very popular attraction for tourists visiting Panama City as well as for those on board ship. As your ship descends into the second chamber you will be face to face on the left or port side of the ship with the balconies on the four levels of the visitor's center. Normally on a nice day the balconies are thronged with tourists waving at you and some even shouting across to ask where you are from or where your ships is heading next.

If you are on the port side you are close to the throngs at the visitor's center watching your ship being lowered into the final lock

When the final gate opens to admit your ship to the waters of the Pacific side, quite often ship captains will blow their deep throated ship whistle to the delight of those lining the balconies in the visitor's center. The ship slowly enters the final stretch, the water of the Balboa Reach, a stretch of eight kilometers or five miles before the ship reaches the Pacific Ocean.

When sailing through the Balboa Reach you will have excellent views of the skyline of Panama City, its towering skyscrapers attesting to the wealth of the country. You will also see what look like old early 20th century military barracks and government buildings. These are the remains of Fort Clayton, once the center of command for the United States Army in charge of the security for the former Canal Zone. Today this massive facility is used in part for residential purposes, mixed business and educational services, part of it being known as ciudad de Saber, the city of knowledge. It is a collection of academic institutions brought together by a foundation of the same name to promote higher learning in Panama. It is located just on the edge of Panama City, but today it is all fully integrated into the urban area since there is no longer a Canal Zone. In the days of American occupation of the Canal Zone it was essentially foreign soil as far as the Panamanians were concerned. All of the property, buildings and equipment within the former Canal Zone became a part of Panama with the handover.

This final leg of the passage is still interesting despite being beyond the locks and now into Pacific waters. The ship will pass the local Panama city yacht marina and the large cargo container terminal both serving Panama city. The final major structure is the Bridge of the Americas, which was the original Pan American Highway bridge across the canal that once carried all road traffic across the canal. Today it carries only local traffic because of the new Centennial Bridge.

Entering Balboa Reach, now leaving the actual Panama Canal

The view of the Panama City skyline is definitely important because most ship passengers find it startling to see such a dramatic and highly urbanized skyline. Some equate it to that of Hong Kong, but without the dramatic mountain backdrop. Although it is an impressive skyline and the most dramatic in all of Central America, it in no way really can be compared to that of Hong Kong, as any of you who read this and who have visited China will be able to recognize. But it is still an impressive skyline.

Beyond the bridge is the very long breakwater protecting Balboa Reach from storms or tidal surges. Remember that on the Pacific Ocean side of Panama there are definite tidal ranges that ultimately precluded the building of a sea level canal.

As the ship starts to gain a bit of speed, the pilot boat comes alongside to take the pilot and guide back to shore. Now your ship is free to navigate out to sea, and you are left with the memories and photos of your transit through the Panama Canal.

The Panama City skyline, as your ship sails out into the Pacific Ocean

FINAL WORDS: No matter how creative I attempt to be in my writing of the virtual chapters on a passage through the Panama Canal, it is impossible to truly convey the experience. This is one of the manmade wonders of the world and must be experienced firsthand to be truly appreciated.

TRAVERSING THE CANAL WEST TO EAST

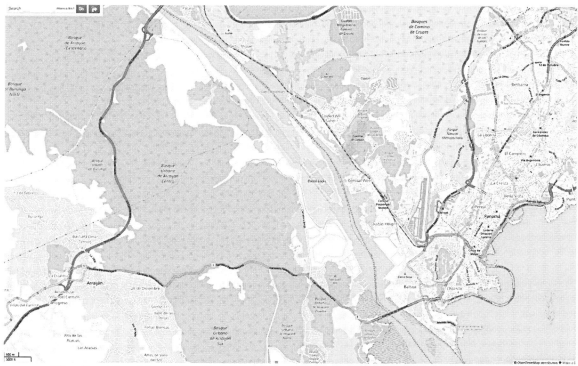

The Pacific side of the Panama Canal, (© OpenStreetMap contributors)

Now we take a virtual journey through the Panama Canal, but this time from the Pacific Ocean eastbound to the Caribbean Sea using the old lock system, which the majority of cruise ships will continue to use. And as I noted before, there is a far greater sense of drama and excitement when making the traditional transit through the locks that are now in their second century of operation. The entire picture changes, as each transit direction carries its own imagery and sense of wonder. After making numerous transits in both directions, I personally favor the east to west crossing of the isthmus simply because there is a greater sense of drama when seeing the three Gatun Locks upon entry rather than upon exit. Although I must admit that seeing them in the afternoon, as the ship is slowly lowered through each of the three locks is also a dynamic sight.

It is early morning just as the first light of day is setting the eastern horizon aglow. The ship is passing the long breakwater on the Pacific side of the Panama Canal. It is several kilometers or miles in length, designed to protect the entry estuary known as Balboa reach free from extreme storms surges or tidal ranges. On the Pacific side of the canal the tidal range can be as high as 6.7 meters or 22 feet whereas on the Caribbean side it is negligible and averages less than one meter or three feet.

In the early morning the twinkling lights of the Panama City skyline's beachfront apartment blocks will be flickering out with the approach of sunrise. Soon the pilot boat will bring both the official pilot who will guide the ship and a Panamanian guest guide who will provide guests with a running commentary while the ship passes through the canal, a journey that will take approximate seven to eight hours. I have had the great pleasure of working right alongside the Panamanian guide to provide a joint commentary from the bridge while the ship is making the crossing both on the eastbound and westbound transits. And I always have found it quite a rewarding experience to share my observations with the passengers.

The ship will pass under the Bridge of the Americas, which was the first bridge across the canal that once carried the Pan American Highway linking the country together. But today a modern suspension bridge just past the third lock is the main national link. Keep in mind that since the opening of the canal, creating a waterway between two oceans, the recognized divide between North and South America is now the canal rather than the point where the isthmus joins the South American landmass.

You will get your best glimpse of the towering skyscrapers of Panama City just past the bridge when the ship passes the cargo container terminal. Panama City has a skyline some observers claim is as dramatic as Hong Kong minus the mountain backdrop. I do find that a bit exaggerated, but the Panama City skyline is still quite impressive.

The Panama City skyline seen from the Balboa Reach at the container terminal

The approach to the two sets of Miraflores Locks is especially impressive for anyone who has not been through a canal system with locks before. As the ship reaches the outermost center strip, men in small boats bring out the lines for the port side diesel-electric locomotives, which are called mules. The ship will have two mules on each side to help guide it through the locks, but the ship's engines will power the actual forward motion. By loosening or tightening the steel cables the mules keep it centered within each lock. Most people who have seen documentaries on the operation of the canal are under the impression that the mules actually pull the ship through. By the use of a series of ringing bells, the mule operators communicate from one side of the lock to the other as to which guides need to be adjusted to keep the ship straight. Hearing the ringing of the bells is a part of the total experience of doing the canal transit through the original sets of locks.

The center wall carries two sets of tracks, one for each direction while the outer walls have a single set. Two way traffic is primarily used at night, but with heavy volume the canal authorities generally prefer one way traffic in both sets of locks during daylight hours, alternating between eastbound or westbound every few hours. Actually even though you are traveling eastbound to the Atlantic side, the actual direction of travel is to the northwest given the orientation of the Isthmus of Panama, as noted earlier. When you emerge into the Caribbean Sea, your ship will actually be slightly farther west in longitude than when it entered from the Pacific Ocean.

Entering Miraflores Lock Two going eastbound

The two Miraflores Locks will raise the ship 16.4 meters or 54 vertical feet above sea level in two stages. The ship will enter the first lock at sea level. The rear gates will rotate shut. Then within ten minutes 26,000,000 gallons of water will flood into the lock chamber from below, raising the ship 8.2 meters or 27 feet in elevation. At this point the forward gates will slowly rotate open and the ship will sail into the second lock, guided carefully by the four mules. And the process will begin again with the rear gates closing, the lock chamber flooding and the forward gates opening after the ship has been raised another 8.2 meters or 27 feet.

But here at the second gate you will be greeted by tourists on the four levels of balconies overlooking the operation. This is the Miraflores Visitor's Center where cheering crowds wait for ships to enter the locks during morning hours or descending through the locks during the afternoon hours. And each cruise ship with its hundreds or thousands of guests are also lining the upper and forward decks. There is a lot of cheering and waiving of hands along with snapping of photographs from both sides.

Crowds at the Miraflores Visitor's Center cheering the ship as it passes

Normally the captain will please those onshore by blowing the ship's loud whistle to salute the crowd when passing the Visitor's Center. And this sends up a roar of approval from those watching the ship pass. I often wonder if for those watching whether there is a bit of envy for those of us fortunate enough to be onboard and making the crossing.

After approximately 45-minutes, the ship will exit the Miraflores Locks and transit the 1.9 kilometers or 1.2 miles of the Miraflores Lake, which was created by building the small dam on Pedro Miguel river, which you will see from the starboard side. This small lake regulates the depth of water so as to enable ships to continue on into the single lock that will raise the ship to the level of the Culebra Cut. The single Pedro Miguel Lock will raise the ship an additional 9.4 meters or 31 feet in elevation. The Culebra Cut through the Continental Divide, the Chagres River and Gatun Lake are all maintained at 25.9 meters or 85 feet above sea level. The reason the Pedro Miguel Lock is separated from the two Miraflores Locks is because the geological structure of the rock layers on the Pacific side was such that three consecutive locks was not feasible. Small fault lines made linking three consecutive locks risky. But in the adjacent new Cocoli Locks were able to overcome that problem given a greater degree of modern technology a century later.

Approaching the single Pedro Miguel Lock traveling eastbound, with a great view of the Centennial Bridge over the canal

As the ship reaches the outermost forward edge of the center strip, once again men in a small boat bring the lines out so that the ship's personnel can lower a hook and pull the lines up to the winch. This procedure also takes place on the opposite side. Depending upon traffic volume, the ship can be assigned to either the right or left lock chamber. It takes approximately 30-minutes to transit the Pedro Miguel Lock.

When the ship leaves the lock it is now 25.9 meters or 85 feet above sea level and ready to enter the Culebra Cut. This channel was dug with steam-powered shovels after sections were first blasted with dynamite during the original construction over 100 years ago. The cut is 12.5 kilometers or 7.8 miles in length and crosses the Continental Divide. Here in the middle of Panama the tall mountains that form the main spine and watershed divide of the country are less than 305 meters or 1,000 feet high in contrast to the border area with Costa Rica where the mountains are ten times taller. It was easier to dig the channel here than anywhere else and that is what initially prompted the French to make their attempt at building a canal. But the layers of rock are not well consolidated and thus the slopes had to grade gently away from the canal. By terracing, using concrete retaining walls and wire mesh they have been deemed stable. On occasion there are slippages or slides that dump debris into the channel and thus dredging is an ongoing process. The Culebra Cut had to be widened to accommodate the larger ships that now pass through the new lock system and this created a need for further stabilization of some of the walls.

Approaching the Centennial Bridge in the Culebra Cut on the eastbound transit

After leaving the Pedro Miguel Lock you will see the point where traffic using the new Cocoli Locks merges into the Culebra Cut just before passing under the Centennial Bridge. The Pan American Highway crosses via this beautiful span that was built to commemorate the first century of Panamanian independence.

The Culebra Cut merges with the Chagres River at a point where the creation of the massive Gatun Lake raises the river water level to the required depth necessary for ships to transit. At the point where the ship leaves the hills by way of having traveled through the Culebra Cut and enters the river channel you will see two bridges on your starboard side. Both the highway and railroad that run parallel to the canal cross the river. And if you are fortunate to be passing at the right time you may see one of the passenger trains that travels between Panama City and Colón. Generally the railroad engineer will stop the train so that passengers onboard can enjoy the view of a passing cruise ship and passengers onboard the ship can photograph one of the sleek trains that make up the fleet. The passenger trains carry both local workers, shoppers and tourists between the cities at the opposite ends of the canal, affording tourists a great series of views of the total canal.

The town that is up ahead on the starboard side of the river is Gamboa. It developed as the staging area for the equipment and personnel that were needed to dig the Culebra Cut. And today it is home to the Panama Canal Dredging Division, which works constantly to keep the channel open. Gamboa is today only a shadow of what it was during the construction period over a century ago. Only a handful of families live here now, but there are many fine examples of the residential architecture, mostly wood, that characterized the American adaptation to this hot, tropical climate.

One of the modern passenger trains stopped at the Chagres River Bridge to watch the passage of a cruise ship

The highlight of passing Gamboa is seeing one or two of the massive dredges in their docking facility at Gamboa. The dredges are used to keep the upper end of the lake, which is actually the wide Chagres River, and also the Culebra Cut at a constant depth to enable the deepest draught vessels unhindered passage. The current maximum depth is 18.3 meters or 60 feet. The large red and white crane that you will see tied up in the docking area is used when it is necessary to change out one of the massive steel gates in the lock system. It is one of the largest such cranes of its kind in the world.

Soon after leaving Gamboa the ship will enter the wide main body of Gatun Lake that will take about an hour to traverse. As the lake widens out, there are numerous large islands, which represent higher ground that became separated from the mainland by the rising waters of the lake building up behind Gatun Dam. The largest of the islands is Barro Colorado Island, which you will pass alongside. Here you will have a chance, with the aid of binoculars, to see the many species of monkeys and birds in the thick rainforest canopy. Today the mammals of these islands are isolated from one another, leading to the start of genetic variation just as Charles Darwin observed on the Galapagos Islands. There are also large alligators, known as caiman, that you will see along the shore or in the immediate offshore waters. Usually your guide will point out the animal life over the ship's public address system. This lake is the cornerstone of the entire Panama Canal in that it both provides for the passage of ships through the center of the isthmus and also regulates the flow of the mighty Chagres River to insure that there is always a steady amount of water to operate the locks. When you consider the hundreds of millions of gallons of water needed each day, you can appreciate the importance of Gatun Lake.

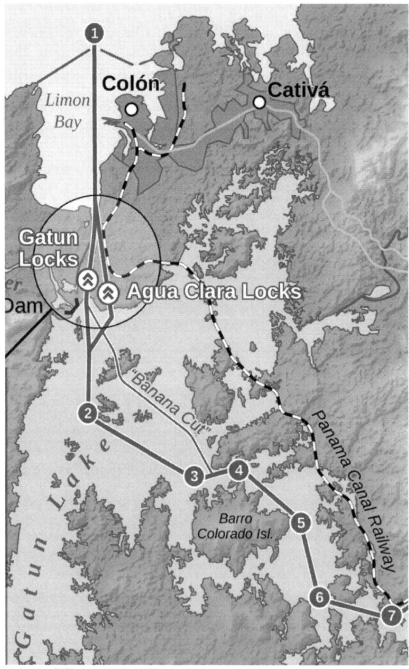

Map of Gatun Lake (From map by Römer in prior chapter)

Sailing into the heart of Gatun Lake

As you sail across the lake you will see many ships sailing toward the Pacific side. These are ships that entered the Gatun or Agua Clara Locks in the early morning and are soon to reach the Pedro Miguel and Miraflores Locks or the new Cocoli Locks, heading to the Pacific Ocean. When I was doing narrations from the bridge I would often point out the country of registry of many of the ships we passed. Always look at the aft end of a ship when it passes and note the home port written across the stern. Two of the most popular ports of registration are Monrovia, Liberia or Panama City. Among German ships you will find Hamburg dominates and you may also see many Chinese or Japanese ships through such names as Shanghai, Osaka or Yokohama. Most cruise ships are registered in Nassau, Bahamas or Hamilton, Bermuda and some European cruise ships carry Valletta, Malta as their home port. Registration is based upon where a shipping company or cruise line gets the best tax advantage and most liberal employee regulations.

Once your ship enters the heart of Gatun Lake you will be on the final leg of your transit across Panama. It will take about an hour to cross the width of the lake. By looking either to port or starboard you will see the greater dimension of this manmade body of water that is quite impressive. You will also notice many small container ships or tankers anchored in the lake. These are vessels belonging to smaller shipping companies that have been transiting the canal without a prior reservation. They will sometimes need to anchor and wait until they are given a slot to pass through the locks on either the Atlantic or Caribbean side. Cruise ships are always given the highest priority and never enter without having booked.

Your final transit will be through the Gatun Locks, the impressive triple lock set that will now take your ship through the descent of 25.9 meters or 85 feet back to sea level for entry into the Caribbean Sea. The Gatun Locks are at their most impressive when entering from the Caribbean Sea, but your transit will be to exit the canal. Once your ship has made the full descent, you can go to one of the aft decks and get pictures of the full height and grandeur of the lock system. Even during the descent, you will find these locks to be impressive, especially if there are ships ahead of you. When your ship is in the upper lock and you look down to ships in the middle or bottom locks you will appreciate the full impact of the enormity of the descent.

A view from the upper lock now equalized to admit the ship into the middle lock where it will be lowered to the next level

Once again the procedure is the same as during the entry into the Miraflores Locks. The ship will sail up to the edge of the middle wall and have the lines brought out by small boat for the ship's crew to pull onboard to attach to the winches. Then the ship will advance slightly to have the outer lines brought on board, either starboard or portside depending upon which lock set has been assigned. Once the mules adjust the cables to keep the ship in mid channel, it will slowly sail into the uppermost lock. Only this time after the rear gates close the water will drain out, lowering the ship approximately 8.5 meters or 28 feet to equalize it with the middle lock. Once the proper level is reached, the forward gates will rotate open and the ship will sail into the middle lock where the process will be repeated, lowering the ship approximately another 8.5 meters or 28 feet.

As you watch your ship being lowered through the locks it is also interesting to keep your eye on any ships ahead of you in the adjacent lock set or in the lock chamber immediately ahead. On some occasions where there is a very large container ship that only has less than a meter or a couple feet of clearance on either side it may send up a large cloud of pulverized cloud of concrete, as it rubs up against and damages the wall of the chamber. With very large container ships that are at the maximum Panamax size it is not uncommon for them to damage the walls of the canal.

A container ship rubbing against the port side wall and damaging the lower lock chamber

As the forward gates of the middle chamber rotate open your ship will sail into the lowermost of the three Gatun Locks. Again the rear gates will close once the ship is in the final chamber and the water level will be lowered to sea level. When the forward gates rotate open, your ship will sail slowly out of the Panama Canal, stopping briefly to have the cables removed. At this point it has completed its transit through the Panama Canal. All that is needed now is for the ship to sail between the marker buoys to the breakwater where the pilot boat will be waiting to take the pilot and guide off the ship. Now your vessel is free to resume its normal speed and sail out into Caribbean waters, ready to continue to its next port of call.

FINAL WORDS: As you look back at the towering Gatun Locks you will be reminded of the day you have spent in transit through the Panama Canal. This is a memorable experience and one that most passengers are unlikely to repeat in the future. In all my years of traveling through the canal, I have never spoken with a passenger who was not impressed by the entire experience. Even a transit through the new, larger locks is impressive, but to a lesser degree since modernity has taken away a bit of the majesty of the old lock system.

A last close look at the mules that guided your ship here to the end of the line

THE NEW LOCK SYSTEM

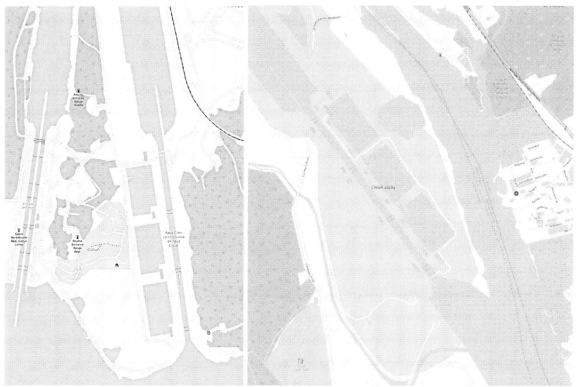

Maps of the new Agua Clara Locks (left) and new Cocoli Locks (right) now permitting much larger ships access to the Panama Canal, (© OpenStreetMap contributors)

THE NEW LOCKS: On June 26, 2016 the Panama Canal Authority opened the new lock system to traffic after several years of work, including numerous delays. It had been hoped that the new locks could be opened to celebrate the 100th anniversary of the original opening of the canal, but delays made this impossible. This new lock system doubles the volume of traffic through the canal by allowing for larger ships to pass that previously could not fit into the older lock chambers.

The project entailed building two new sets of locks along with excavating the channels that would link them into the existing Culebra Cut and Gatun Lake portions of the canal. The Culebra Cut had to be widened and dredged deeper, which in itself was a major task.

The locks on the Atlantic side run immediately parallel to the Gatun Locks and are known as the Agua Clara Locks. This system, like Gatun, consists of three chambers and feed directly into Gatun Lake. On the Pacific side, the new Cocoli Locks also consist of three chambers and they are to the west of the Miraflores and Pedro Miguel Locks, but not as easily visible as the parallel locks on the Atlantic side.

The government of Panama put the construction of these new locks up to a national referendum in 2006 given the massive sum to be invested. The yes vote was 76.8 percent in favor and this gave the green light for the project. The estimated cost in United States dollars was expected to be 5.25 billion, and the final accounting essentially held close to that estimate.

Now the government of Panama is considering even more massive projects expected to cost over 17 billion dollars that will enable the largest ships in the world to pass through the isthmus. If completed, this would make the Panama Canal the most vital link in the entire global transport network in that every ship afloat would be able to travel safely between the waters of the world's two greatest oceans.

With the new Agua Clara and Cocoli Locks now open, projected annual tolls are expected to top over six billion dollars annually. Even deducting the operating costs, it should not take the government long to pay off the second lock sets before the third or fourth projects will take form.

Viewing the new Agua Clara, (Work of ArnoldReinhold, CC BY SA 4.0, Wikimedia.org)

BENEFIT OF THE NEW LOCK SYSTEM: With the new sets of locks now open to traffic, a new Panamax size capability has been created. As a result of the larger ships now capable of utilizing the new locks, ports along the Atlantic Coast of the United States and even ports in the United Kingdom had to invest in new infrastructure and docking facilities to handle ships coming from Asian ports that previously could not be accommodated other than on the western coasts of the United States and Canada.

Another benefit of the new locks has been the transferring of ships right at the old Panamax size to the new locks to eliminate the recurring damage that these tight fits were causing. I have witnessed on numerous occasions the clouds of powdered concrete that were being thrown into the air, as the mules attempted to keep these huge vessels centered in the middle of the old locks, but with little success. I was told by one of the Panama Canal pilots that this had become a regular occurrence that required almost constant repairs to the lock chamber walls. Overall transit time for these large vessels had to be reduced to minimize these incidents. And often one set of locks would be shut to traffic to effect repairs and thus delaying overall transit times. The old lock mechanisms require a large amount of down time for maintenance and now with the new locks in operation, the volume of traffic does not create backlogs as was happening.

The old Panamax size was based upon the capacity of the old locks, which are 33.53 meters or 110 feet wide, 320.04 meters or 1,050 feet in length and have a draught of 12.56 meters or 41.2 feet. The two bridges crossing over the canal, however, have set the maximum height limit of any ships at under 57.9 meters or 190 feet. The size and depth of the old locks essentially preclude two thirds of today's present ships, including the largest of the cruise ships. The new Panamax size is now 54.86 meters or 180 feet in width, 426,72 meters or 1,400 feet in length with a maximum draught of 18.29 meters or 60 feet. Because of the two bridges, the height maximum remains the same. This greatly expands the number of ships that now are using the Panama Canal, shortening the distance between ports in eastern and southeastern Asia with those on the eastern coast of North America and with Western European ports.

There are other important features that make the new Agua Clara and Cocoli Locks far more efficient and also reduce the overall time for ships to transit. The first of these is the amount of water being saved with each use. There is one water storage basin for each lock chamber with a total of 18 such basins. The storage basins and lock chambers fill or empty utilizing gravity rather than mechanical pumps, making them more energy efficient as well as faster. And by reusing three fifths of the water in each lock basin the saving is vital. Panama does have its drier seasons and with climate change there are more frequent periods of lower rainfall, thus the savings is critical. The second feature is the use of sliding gates rather than rotating ones where it takes two gates to open from and close to the middle. Now a single massive gate slides into its own slip to the side of the lock chamber when in the open position.

The one new feature that somehow has taken away the mystique, charm and flavor of the old Panama Canal is the elimination of the diesel-electric locomotives or mules that keep the ships centered in each lock. Now small tugboats accompany each ship and work to keep it centered in the chamber. This also cuts the cost by millions of dollars and improves the transit time since ships do not need to wait for lines to attach them to the mules and then be disengaged after passage. But it was the mules with their intricate bell system of communication that gives a certain level of excitement and mystery to the operation of the older locks. Call me a traditionalist, but I find the new locks to be too sterile and efficient to the point of taking away the thrill of the ship I am on being slowly raised and lowered through the locks. Now it hardly seems like anything is happening even though it is at a much more efficient and faster level.

Looking north over the Agua Clara and their water saving basins, (Work of ArnoldReinhold, CC BY SA 4.0, Wikimedia.org)

The first large cruise ship to pass through the new locks was the Disney Wonder, a relatively large 83,000 ton vessel that passed through in May 2016. Most cruise lines that have mega size ships in the 100,000 ton category will be able to pass through the new locks, but a few of the largest in the 130,000 ton or larger category are too wide or long for passage. Most of these massive ships are used for short cruises in the popular Caribbean market, but those capable of passage through the new Panama Canal locks will be used for the summer Alaska cruise season, thus only passing through the canal twice per year during their repositioning cruise between the Caribbean and Alaska.

Ships used for the South America cruises or that do the once per year around the world cruises will for the most part be capable of passing through the new locks. For those cruises advertised specifically as Panama Canal cruises the older locks will be utilized because the whole charm and mystique surrounding such a passage can only be felt when experiencing the original Panama Canal. As one who has experienced both, I personally would only wish to do another Panama Canal transit if it were through the original locks.

If you are planning a cruise that will include the Panama Canal, check the dimensions of your cruise ship. If it exceeds the old Panamax limit, but the canal is part of the itinerary, you will be transiting through the new locks. Perhaps I am just a traditionalist, but I would prefer to continue to make the crossing through the original locks because of the history, nostalgia and excitement that such a transit generates.

Old and New – ships in transit through the Miraflores Locks (foreground) and the new Cocoli Locks (background), (Work of ArnoldReinhold, CC BY SA 4.0, Wikimedia.org)

TRAVERSING THE NEW LOCKS: The traverse of the new lock system does not have the majesty of the old locks that most cruise ships still fortunately are using. Only the largest cruise ships use the new locks because they exceed the old Panamax dimensions for using the original locks. Rather than have two additional chapters on the traverse, I am summarizing it in this chapter. I am not attempting to lessen the accomplishments in building the new locks. They have a majesty of their own simply because of their larger dimensions and the smooth manner in which they operate. But gone are the diesel electric locomotives known as mules. Gone are the sounds of the bells coordinating the operation of the mules on each side of the ship. Gone is the thrill of watching the massive steel doors on the locks swing open and closed. They have been replaced by a single door that simply glides into a slot to one side of the lock. There is no fanfare so to speak with regard to the whole operation. I found it impressive by scale, but lacking in the excitement generated by the older locks.

Fortunately most cruise ships that make the transit still fit within the old Panamax size definition.

When you enter the new locks from either the Atlantic or Pacific side, the actual process of entering the lock under the ship's power but guided by tugboats rather than the mules gives me a feeling of disconnect in that the ship is not becoming a part of the canal itself. Once inside the locks, they fill or empty quite rapidly, much faster than the older locks and this of course speeds up the process of proceeding to the next lock.

On the westbound journey once passing through the Agua Clara Locks the ship enters Gatun Lake and follows the same route that ships using the Gatun Locks follow. So this part of the transit is exactly the same. Your ship will then pass Gamboa, enter the Culebra Cut and pass under the Centennial Bridge. But here is where the transit through the new locks diverges, as your ship enters the newly constructed passage that bypasses the Pedro Miguel Lock and the Miraflores Locks to descend to the Pacific Ocean through the Cocoli Locks before entering the final channel to the sea. But unlike the older lock system, you do not have a chance to see Panama City up close or any of the former operational buildings of the Canal Zone.

PANAMA CITY

A map of central Panama City, (© OpenStreetMap contributors)

PORT CALL: There are very few cruise ships that make a port call in Panama City. It is simply a matter of logistics that precludes ships from docking. If you are traveling from the Atlantic/Caribbean to the Pacific through the canal, most transits are completed by the middle of the afternoon. For a ship to then dock in Panama City to give its passengers time to explore this fascinating city would require an overnight stay. This adds to the length of the itinerary and the cost of an overnight stay would no doubt add significantly to the cost of the cruise. Traveling from the Pacific to the Atlantic through the canal would also require an overnight stay because guests do not expect to transit the canal at night when they cannot enjoy the spectacle of the operation.

The only practical option for visiting Panama City is based upon a westbound passage from the Atlantic to the Pacific with an overnight stop in Colón. Port fees are far less than those in Panama City and it is easier to maintain control over guest movements since they are reluctant to leave the ship at night given the high crime rate in Colón. Likewise tour operators providing daytime excursions can more easily visit the important venues since they are closer to Colón.

GEOGRAPHIC SETTING: Panama City is set amid forest covered hills and fronts directly on the Pacific Ocean but lacks sandy beaches because of the nature of the underlying rock layers and the onshore currents. There are two small bays along the main coast, but they offered little to no shelter for ships and thus the original harbor was adjacent to the city at Balboa. But today that original anchorage has been dredged out to create Balboa Reach, the Pacific entry into the Panama Canal.

The hills separating the main city from the canal have become a nature preserve known as Parque Natural Metropolitano, filled with many birds, monkeys, tapir and puma. And caimans can be found lazily sunning themselves along the marshy shores.

There are several green hills that have become upscale residential districts because of their view out over the largely flat coastal fringe. But Ancon Hill adjacent to the small peninsula that is home to the original settlement, now known as the historic old quarter, is where you get the best views of the city skyline.

The dramatic Panama City skyline from Ancon Hill

The climate of Panama City is hot, humid and has a distinct rainy season from December through March, but no truly dry season. Despite the heat and humidity, Panama City has attracted thousands of expatriate retirees because it offers affordable luxury living in a modern environment with all the amenities retirees desire. Today the population of the metropolitan area is approximately 1,500,000 making it the second largest city in Central America after Guatemala City. But when it is viewed based upon its modernity and luxury, it outclasses any other city in the region.

A BRIEF HISTORY: Panama City has both a very old, historic component side by side with its swanky apartments, condominiums, banks and hotels. As noted before, some visitors equate it with Hong Kong albeit on a smaller scale. It is the financial center for all of

Central America and a major cultural and travel crossroads. It has become a travel destination for many tens of thousands of visitors, partly because it is adjacent to the Pacific side of the Panama Canal, but also for its luxury resort hotels, fine restaurants and historic charm.

Arriving by motor coach into the heart of Panama City, (Work of flam3boy, CC BY SA 3.0, Wikimedia.org)

Panama City dates to August 15, 1519 when Pedro Arias de Ávila established the first settlement. The date is significant, as once it was established, it became the launching site for Francisco Pizarro's expeditions that would lead to the conquest of the Inca Empire in Peru and the establishment of Lima as a major cultural and administrative hub. Panama City then played a major role as being the port where Peruvian gold was offloaded for the overland journey by mule to the Caribbean shore where it would then go by sea to Spain.

Because of its role as a trade center, Panama City grew wealthy and became a target for pirates and privateers to attack, similar in its fate to Cartagena. In 1671 it was pillaged and burned by Henry Morgan. Today that original site is a major tourist attraction, the ruins never having been restored. The new Panama City, which today is the old historic quarter is thus not the original city.

When the Spanish colonies in both North and South America began their quest for independence, Panama ultimately ended up as a province of Colombia, but did maintain a sense of its own identity and autonomy. During the middle of the 19th century when gold was discovered in California, Panama City and Colón became the two terminal cities for the Panama Railroad that would ferry thousands of gold seekers across the isthmus rather than having to take the long sea voyage around South America. The railroad began operation in 1855, but by this time tens of thousands had already traversed the isthmus by carriage or made the long sea voyage since the gold discovery began in 1848.

The historic cathedral in the old city district, (Work of Danistrada01, CC BY SA 3.0, Wikimedia.org)

The greatest impetus for growth was the American arrival and the building of the Panama Canal. Not only did this bring great prosperity to Panama City, but the American assistance in helping Panama gain its independence from Colombia secured Panama City as the new nation's capital. However just on western the edge of the city was the border of the Canal Zone, territory under American jurisdiction for the remainder of the 20th century.

One great benefit to the heartland of Panama bordering the canal was the development of a healthy infrastructure where the provision of clean water, insect control and the building of adequate housing led to what is today the most modern region in all of Central America. And the provision of employment by the Panama Canal Company has made this one of the most economically stable areas in the entire region. There is still a strong American presence in the workforce because many of the most highly skilled and technologically oriented employees are American. And there is a strong expatriate American population living in Panama City today among retirees.

Economically Panama City has become a major international center for banking, and unfortunately there has also been an underground economy based upon drug trafficking and money laundering. But since the removal of General Manuel Noriega the government has been far more proactive in controlling criminal activities.

TOURING PANAMA CITY:
For those who are booking a cruise through the Panama Canal with a stop in Panama City there is an opportunity to visit the most vibrant city in Central America. If your ship is stopping in Colón, I strongly urge you to take the group tour to Panama City. You will be able to see all the major sights in the presence of a competent guide and without having to attempt to plan your own itinerary. From Colón it may also be possible to have the cruise line arrange for a private car and driver if you prefer the comfort and convenience of more personalized travel.

* TOURING OPTIONS: If your ship is making a port call in Panama City, which generally only occurs on eastbound itineraries, then you will have a greater degree of freedom to explore this vibrant city. The most commonly used option is that of becoming part of a ship sponsored all day tour of the city, which often includes lunch at a nice restaurant. Other options include:

** Private car and driver can be arranged through your cruise line if you prefer the more personalized option of sightseeing without being part of a group. Drivers are very competent and also generally serve as your guide. But you have the freedom of choosing exactly what you want to see and how much time to spend in each location. There are several companies listed on line. My recommendation is for you to check *www.panamayourway.com* for further details, as they are a reliable and safe service.

** Hop on hop off bus service exists in Panama City. Your ship will most likely offer a shuttle into the city where you can join the hop on hop off bus at the Visitor's Center. There is only a single route with 13 stops, but it gives you a good look at the major highlights of the city. For more details visit on line at *www.city-sightseeing.com* where you will find a detailed map and explanation of sights.

** Taxi touring of the city is offered by several different companies, but the one most often named by various travel services is Amber Moon Panama Taxi Service. They do have an outstanding reputation for high quality and safety. Check their web page at *www.ambermooncab.com* for details and booking information.

** Train service between Panama City and Colón is one option to get a rolling view of the entire canal, but I would only recommend this option if you want to just have a pleasant train ride and not spend any time in either city. It does afford a good chance to gain a different perspective of the canal. You could simply ride to Colón and return without going into either city other than going from the ship to the railroad station and back by taxi, which in Panama City is safe. If you wanted to do this in reverse from Colón I would be more hesitant to recommend a local taxi. For information on the train visit *www.panarail.com/en/passenger* for details.

* **MAJOR SIGHTS TO SEE:** Panama City is for the most part rather new with its gleaming high rise towers along the waterfront that give many visitors the impression of being a small Hong Kong, or to me it looks more like a small Dubai. The old historic quarter known locally in Spanish as Casco Viejo does date to the 1600's and is somewhat ramshackle but still quite fascinating. Much of it could stand to have a good facelift, as for example in the old historic district of San Juan, Puerto Rico, which is approximately the same age.

The modern waterfront of Panama City, (Work of Mariordo (Mario Roberto Durán Ortiz, CC BY SA 3.0, Wikimedia.org)

These are what I consider the must see sights in Panama City, most of which will be shown to you on a ship sponsored tour or using the hop on hop off bus. They are listed here in alphabetical order:

** **Amador Causeway** – This three kilometer or nearly two mile long breakwater stretches into the Pacific Ocean and affords dramatic skyline views of Panama City and also of the entrance to Balboa Reach, which is the Pacific gateway to the canal. There are restaurants and shops along part of the causeway.

** **Avenida Balboa** – The main boulevard along the waterfront gives you a chance to enjoy the skyline of the city when walking. It is safe during the day, and locals claim this to be true after dark. Some of the finest shops and restaurants in the city line Avenida Balboa.

** **Biomuseo** – Here on Calzada de Amador you will find a museum dedicated to the natural history and geology of the Isthmus of Panama. It tells the story of how the geological origin of the isthmus altered the biodiversity of this part of the world by cutting off the flow of water between the two great oceans. The exhibits are very well presented and the architecture of the museum itself is quite dramatic. The museum is open Tuesday thru Friday from 10 AM to 4 PM and Saturday and Sunday from 10 AM to 5 PM.

** Casco Viejo – This is the old historic district of the city whose architecture is classic colonial Spanish, but much of it in need of restoration. Despite its somewhat ramshackle appearance, it is still a major tourist attraction since it represents the development of the city following the pillage by pirate Henry Morgan in 1671. The original old city is to this day in ruins, but Casco Viejo does date to post 1671.

A typical street in Casco Viejo, (Work of MuskieAnimal, CC BY DSA 4.0, Wikimedia.org)

** Cinta Costera – This is a very lively street that connects Casco Viejo with the more modern beachfront. It is lined with street vendors and small shops where you can begin to absorb the flavor of Panamanian life. The Fish Market is one place to stop in and check out the local bounty of the sea. The Costera has beautiful plantings, fountains and often is the venue for local street musicians. Many tours of the city will drive along the Costera, and the hop on hop off bus will enable you to stop, stroll and then hop back onto the next bus.

** Miraflores Visitor Center – Located adjacent to the two Miraflores Locks on the Panama Canal, a visit here will allow you to have a different perspective than what you will have when your ship passes through the canal. Such a visit is rare for ship passengers since so few pay a port call to Panama City. When you visit it can be at a time when there is a lull in traffic or when it is especially busy. Essentially it is a gamble, but most motor coach tour operators try to time it when they know the locks will be busy. And if you happen to visit when a cruise ship is passing, you will be able to then contrast your experience that which you will have from onboard your ship when you pass by. The center is open daily from 8 AM to 6 PM.

Many of the old buildings in the poor barrios are worn and present you with a chance to capture a lesser seen side to Panama City

DINING OUT: If you are on an all day tour of Panama City offered by your cruise ship lunch is normally included at a nice restaurant. If you are touring on your own with a private car and driver, using the hop on hop off bus or taxi, then lunch becomes your responsibility. There are many great restaurants in Panama City where you can have lunch. I have chosen to list those I am familiar with that offer you a great atmosphere, good food and service. My listings are shown alphabetically to avoid any prejudice.

* La Vespa – This very popular Italian and Mediterranean style restaurant is locally said to be the top place for lunch in Panama City. It is located in the new city and you would need a car and driver or taxi to reach it, but it serves outstanding seafood, pizza, salads and desserts. Their hours are daily from Noon to 11 PM. It is recommended to pre book your table by calling 507 396 3407.

* La Vespa Vista Mare – At the Trump Ocean Club, this is one of the finest restaurants in the city and will combine a great atmosphere with incredibly good seafood prepared primarily in an Italian or Mediterranean manner. The quality of the food and service make this a true dining experience. It is open daily from Noon to 11 PM and reservations are advised. Call 507 830 4770 to book a table. You will not be disappointed.

* Rene Café – One of the best restaurants for lunch in Casco Viejo, it is located on Calle Pedro J. Sosa. The menu is definitely Latin with an emphasis upon Panamanian and other Central American dishes. The ingredients used are fresh, well prepared and served in a

congenial environment. They do have a prix fixed price lunch daily, and yes they cater to tourists, but they do a great job of satisfying their customers. Lunch is served Monday thru Saturday from 10 AM to 3 PM, dinner is served Monday thru Saturday from 6 to 9:30 PM.

* Santa Rita Casco Viejo – Located at Avenida Eloy Alfaro at the corner of Calle 11, this is a fine restaurant with a Latin American vibe, especially that of Argentina. Their menu does include traditional local dishes, fresh seafood and vegetarian options. It has a fine reputation for freshness combined with flavor. I would say it is one of the best in the city. Their hours are from 7 AM to 11 PM Tuesday thru Saturday, but only open for dinner Monday from 5:30 to 11 PM. You may wish to book a table in advance at 507 303 0991.

* Solomon's Deli – Yes a Kosher style deli in Panama City is one of the most popular spots among local expatriate Americans and Canadians. Located in the modern new city on Calle Ramon H Jurado, this is a great place for mile high sandwiches made with fresh smoked meats imported directly from Montréal. They also make fantastic burgers, great salads and have a wide array of dessert items. It is not what you would expect in Panama, but for North Americans it is comfort food. They are open Tuesday thru Thursday from Noon to 9 PM, Friday and Saturday from Noon to 10 PM and Sunday from 11 AM to 7 PM. You can pre book your table by calling 507 388 3354.

SHOPPING: You will find plenty of small shops and street vendors in Casco Viejo and along Cinta Costera. Panamanian handcrafts are similar to what you will later find in both Costa Rica and Guatemala if you are traveling north, or what you will have already encountered on your way to Panama. Be aware that the Panama Hat, which is so symbolic of the country takes its name from the country, but they are traditional to Ecuador and are imported.

* Multiplaza Pacific – Here you will find the largest and best shopping mall in all of Panama City. It is located in Punta Pacifica on Punta Darien Street. It can be reached with a private car and driver or taxi and some ship tours may include a brief shopping stop. The mall offers the finest high end stores in Panama City along with a mix of regular price shops so that it has something for everyone. But the majority of the merchandise you will find is what is available in North American and European shopping malls. The mall is open Monday thru Saturday from 10 AM to 7 PM and Sunday from 11 AM to 8 PM.

FINAL WORDS: Most of you who read this book will not be on a cruise that stops in Panama City. You will get a good look at the skyline when the ship either exits or enters the Miraflores Locks, but that will be your extent of seeing this rather unique city that blends of old and new lifestyles. Panama City is the most dynamic city in Central America, but it has more of an American flavor than it does a true Latin vibe.

PORTS ON THE PACIFIC COAST

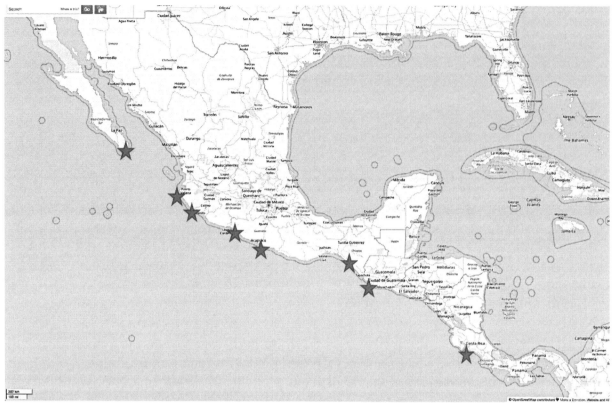

Map showing the Pacific Coast of Central America and México, ((© OpenStreetMap contributors) Stars indicate the ports of call normally visited.

There are far more ports of call on the Pacific Coast, most of them in México that are included in Panama Canal itineraries. The distance is far greater than that between southern Florida and the Panama Canal and there are far fewer cruises that traverse these waters than in the Caribbean Sea. The Mexican Riviera cruises out of Los Angeles or San Diego are either operated on three, seven or ten day itineraries and the farthest destination is Acapulco on the ten day cruises. Three day cruises operate between Los Angeles, Santa Catalina Island, San Diego and Ensenada while seven day cruises will transit as far south as Puerto Vallarta.

On Panama Canal itineraries there would be room for more ports of call, but to include any more than the standard one shown in this book would lengthen the cruise to more than the present-day itineraries that are no more than 16 days in length. This would add to the expense of the cruise and would not really expand the overall experience. Until recently no ports of call were included in El Salvador because that country has undergone so much strife and is still reconstructing itself, but a few ships are visiting Acajutla to see how well the guests like this small port. Nicaragua is attempting to encourage more tourism and San Juan del Sur is managing to attract a handful of cruise ships as of 2019.

The total list of ports of call possible is therefore expanding and as of the writing of this book in the summer of 2019, here is the total list of Pacific Coast ports of call being visited for the upcoming 2019-20 cruise season, shown from Panama north to the United States

Acapulco, México is the largest Central American port visited by cruise ships

PANAMA

* **Panama City**

COSTA RICA

* **Puntarenas**

* **Puerto Caldera (essentially a container port that is part of greater Puntarenas)**

NICARAGUA

* **San Juan del Sur**

EL SALVADOR

* **Acajutla**

GUATEMALA

* Puerto Quetzal

MÉXICO

* Puerto Chiapas

* Huatulco

* Acapulco

* Ixtapa/Zihuatanejo

* Puerto Vallarta

* Cabo San Lucas

VISITING COSTA RICA

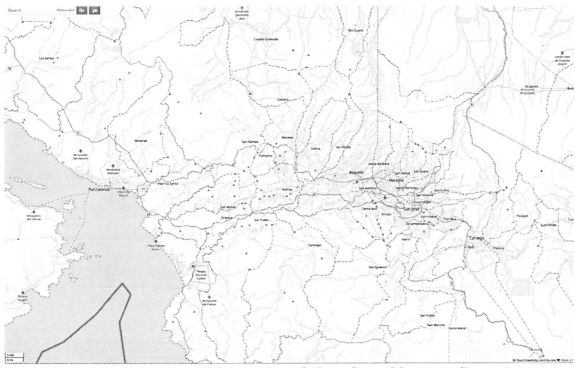

A map of the heart of Costa Rica, (© OpenStreetMap contributors)

I need to admit to a personal bias in that my choice of Central American countries is without question Costa Rica. This small nation has the highest overall standard of living in Central America when viewed relative to the distribution of wealth. It has the highest literacy rate in all of Latin America. It has excellent public health care in place. And it has no standing army. Until recently its crime rate was exceptionally low, but unfortunately the drug cartels that operate in neighboring Nicaragua and Panama have infiltrated the more remote rural areas and Costa Rica has seen an upturn in drug related crime. But street violence is still relatively low and visitors are rarely impacted.

Costa Rica is located just northwest of Panama and south of Nicaragua where the landmass of Central America is rather narrow. The linear distance between the Pacific and Caribbean shores of Costa Rica is only 120 to 201 kilometers or 75 to 125 miles in average width. The total size of the country is 50,901 square kilometers or 19,653 square miles, making it about the size of the Baltic nation of Estonia. The total population of Costa Rica is slightly over 5,100,000.

COSTA RICAN LANDSCAPE: Earlier I pointed out that the Caribbean side of Costa Rica is a low lying tropical rainforest with a hot, humid tropical climate that is responsible for thick rainforest. This is the least inhabited part of the country and has never been seen as desirable even back in Spanish colonial times. Plantations of bananas and cocoa have been the mainstay of those who chose to settle here.

The heart of the country is a rugged series of volcanic and uplifted mountains with intervening valleys at high elevation where the altitude moderates the climate. Here the Spanish found ideal conditions for agriculture and this became the national heartland. The mountain region, however, lies on a series of very active faults and both earthquake and volcanic activity have made this a precarious place in which to develop a nation. But despite these ongoing threats, the people of Costa Rica have built a thriving nation. Despite the potential for disasters, the highlands of Costa Rica are exceptionally beautiful and the people have developed a great love for their land. Costa Ricans have been the world leaders in environmental preservation and have developed ecotourism as one of their major economic priorities. Lush mountain valleys are home to the major cities and towns, plantations of coffee, cocoa and basic food crops along with the raising of cattle and sheep. Much of the land is still pristine and many national parks now preserve the local beauty.

Coffee plantations in the mountainous interior

The central spine of mountains is known as Cordillera Central and it is essentially part of the great mountain rib that runs from Alaska to Chile, known in Canada and the United States as the Rocky Mountains, in México as the Sierra Madre and in South America as the Andes. The highest elevations in Costa Rica are 3,810 meters or 12,500 feet above sea level. There are numerous active volcanoes, Volcan Arenal being the most persistently active and a major tourist attraction. Lava flows and ash fallout from eruptions have for thousands of years enriched the fertility of the highland regions. When combined with a humid tropical climate, the end result is a high degree of fertility. The highlands offer great biodiversity with over 12,000 species of plants and a wide array of wildlife. Reptiles, amphibians, birds and small mammals have made these uplands home and the rivers and sea abound with over 180 species of fish and marine life.

Earthquake hazard is a given fact of life in the mountains and Pacific Coast region, but the people of Costa Rica generally build their structures with this danger in mind.

The mountains extend to the Pacific Coast of the country, giving this side of Costa Rica a spectacular landscape of high mountains, rushing rivers, deep coves and bays the large Gulf of Nicoya. The climate is tropical but with a distinct dry season that does place a degree of stress upon the vegetation and limits the extent of agricultural productivity. But with less settlement, this area has seen a great expansion of national parks and reserves and it is becoming a major center for ecotourism. Also the coastal fringes have become home to thousands of foreign visitors who continue to purchase vacation property.

Costa Rica does maintain a good network of roads in the interior highlands and on the Pacific Coast, tying together all of its major towns and national parks while the Caribbean side of the country still languishes.

Costa Rica's national environmental policies are considered the finest in the Western Hemisphere and among the five best in the world. And economically ecotourism has been a major boost to the national economy.

There is only one highly developed urban complex and that is in the Valley of San José, which is the national capital region. It occupies a high mountain valley surrounded by volcanic peaks, but is connected by multiple roads to the Pacific Coast, which is on average 65 to 80 kilometers or 40 to 50 miles by road to the coast.

A BRIEF COSTA RICAN HISTORY: The typical Latin American history unfolds with the Spanish arriving in search of mineral wealth, killing or exploiting the native population and developing a two class system of wealthy European overlords and an impoverished mestizo peasant class. Costa Rica saw a totally different development than all of its neighbors.

Prior to the arrival of Spanish colonists, the land was inhabited by a few simplistic hunting and gathering tribes scattered across the land. There were no native civilizations of sophistication ripe for plunder. The Spanish who did arrive came seeking land to settle upon as farmers. There were no conquistadors among them. Thus unlike Guatemala or Nicaragua, the majority of Costa Rica's population is pure or very close to pure European Spanish and other nationalities. There is a very small indigenous population base and thus exploitation never occurred as it did in México or the other Central American countries.

Why was Costa Rica spared the cultural devastation that the Spanish wrought upon the native peoples of the other Latin American nations. Costa Rica had no great mineral wealth and thus the Spanish Crown saw it as worthless. The colonists who settled came seeking a simple life were left to their own, as the Spanish authorities were far away in Guatemala.

Rugged yet beautiful Pacific Coast landscape

The settlers were essentially isolated and left to their own. The colonists engaged primarily in subsistence farming and ranching and developed an internal culture based upon mutual dependence, barter and had little of value to interest the authorities. But the settlers did place a great value upon education. When the wave of revolution spread from México southward, the people of Costa Rica did become a member of the Federal Republic of Central America, which lasted from 1823 to 1839. It was considered to be the most impoverished of the component states. They withdrew from this confederation in 1838 to charter their own course of independence and became isolated from their neighbors.

Economically Costa Rica was weak because the only cash crop they had was fine mountain coffee, exported via the Pacific Coast. Colorful oxcarts brought the beans down from the highlands to Puntarenas. Then the coffee beans faced the long route around the bottom of South America to Europe. What the country needed was a railroad to the Caribbean Coast. It took 20 years to complete and by 1890 coffee could more easily be shipped overseas. The project did employ numerous Jamaican, Chinese and Italian immigrants and their descendants still make up much of the population of Puerto Limón, which Costa Ricans still see as a backwater. The banana production on the Caribbean was begun by American venture capital and employed many of the former railroad workers, and this is in part why Costa Ricans in the interior look down upon the Puerto Limón region as if it were an infestation upon the nation.

During the early 20th century, Costa Rica's government was influenced heavily by United Fruit Company and it was run by a dictator, but only briefly. General Granados was overthrown in 1919 and democratic rule was restored. But in 1948 a disputed presidential election led to a 44-day civil war that resulted in over 2,000 deaths. It was the worst event in the country's history.

The Spanish colonial architectural heritage is well exhibited on the streets of the capital city of San José

Once the new government took office, it dismissed the military and to this day Costa Rica maintains law and order with a civil police force. The constitution that was adopted in 1953 has given the nation total stability. There has been no political violence ever since. Elections are peaceful and there is a respect for law and order. But now the drug problem is one that has the government and people both worried, as some violence has spilled over Costa Rica's borders.

CRUISE SHIP VISITS: The majority of Panama Canal cruises include at least one stop in Costa Rica, visiting the port of Puntarenas on the Gulf of Nicoya. The actual port and town offer little to nothing of interest for passengers, but the port of call is based upon offering a variety of tours to sites of great environmental beauty. And at least one tour is generally offered to the capital city of San José, which is one hour away by motor coach or automobile for those who prefer to have a more cultural experience. San José is a very comfortable city to visit, home to outstanding examples of colonial Spanish architecture, but it is not as rich in historic or cultural monuments as Cartagena, which had a more dynamic history.

The next chapter is devoted to Puntarenas and the potential sightseeing activities available from that port of call, since the town itself is not a real tourist destination. It is the deep anchorage and berthing facilities that make it the primary stop for cruise ships when they visit the Pacific Coast of Costa Rica. Today, however, the mega cruise ships have exceeded the capability of Puntarenas, so many itineraries show the stop as Puerto Caldera. This is simply a container port with major facilities to handle large ships, but it is technically a part of greater Puntarenas.

Docking on the long pier in Puntarenas

PUNTARENAS

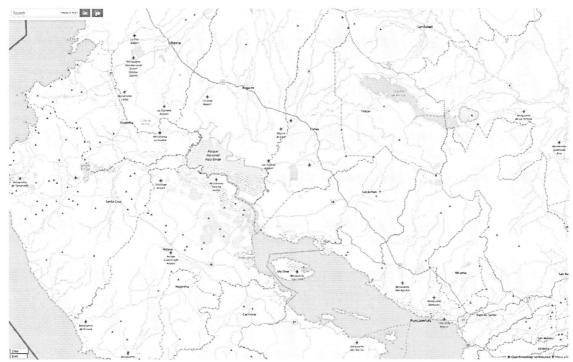

A map of the region north of Puntarenas, (© OpenStreetMap contributors)

The majority of cruise ships show Puntarenas on the Gulf of Nicoya along the Pacific Coast as the stop for Costa Rica. It has its long pier for passenger vessels of small to medium size. The large mega cruise ships that are now being used by the mass market cruise lines dock in Puerto Caldera, which as noted in the prior chapter is essentially a large container port about 16 kilometers or 10 miles south of the main town of Puntarenas, but is still a part of the metropolitan area, which has about 44,000 residents.

THE LANDSCAPE: The coastal plain along the Gulf of Nicoya's eastern shore is very narrow. It is covered in a scrubby woodland that is part of the west coast wet and dry tropical rainforest. During the drier winter months many of the trees actually lose their leaves, giving the land a somewhat bleak appearance, but when the very heavy monsoonal rains come in summer, the land becomes quite green and reflects its true tropical nature.

The western edge of the major cordillera that runs through the heart of Costa Rica is less than 30 kilometers or 18 miles from the shore. The land rises rapidly into the highlands and the temperature and vegetation change quite drastically. It takes an hour to drive from Punta Arenas on the new divided highway to San José and you see and feel the difference with each passing kilometer or mile.

Puntarenas is built on a very long sandbar and is only a few blocks wide. It has a definite ramshackle appearance, as the nicer residential areas are found just to the east and west of the major express highway to San José. There are several small beachfront communities where expatriates are buying property well to the south of Puerto Caldera.

THE TOWN: Puntarenas only dates back to 1840 so it has no colonial history. It developed as a deep water port for San José and other interior communities for the purpose of being able to both ship and receive goods. Coffee exporting became the major commercial crop that necessitated the port. And once the Panama Canal was open, its role as a port increased with the ability to now ship coffee to the east coast of the United States and Canada and to Europe. There are no historic monuments or major attractions in Puntarenas and the main town on this narrow spit of land is not at all representative of life in Costa Rica.

SIGHTSEEING OPTIONS: Do not plan to waste a day by staying in Puntarenas because there is nothing to see or do and you will be both bored and disappointed. It is imperative that you take a tour since the purpose of this port call is to enable you to experience Costa Rica's natural or cultural landscapes.

* SIGHTSEEING OPTIONS: Unlike major ports of call, you do not have many options in Puntarenas, as this is a very small town. Here are my recommendations:

** The majority of guests will explore via a motor coach tour to one of the national parks, reserves or action oriented sites. There is also a cultural tour offered by most cruise lines into San José, which is the capital and major city of Costa Rica.

** For those who wish to have the privacy and convenience of a private tour, your cruise line can organize a private car with a driver/guide, but given that this service must be provided out of San José it can be rather costly. If this is your choice, make certain to book it preferably before boarding the ship.

** If you wish to arrange a private car and driver on your own, I suggest that you check out Gray Line of Costa Rica at www.graylinecostarica.com for details as to what private arrangements they can offer.

** There is one company that offers reliable private shuttle service for small groups to do sightseeing out of Puntarenas. Tropical Tour Shuttles is considered a reliable and safe company. Check their web page at www.tropicaltourshuttles.com for full details and prices.

** There are no hop on hop off busses in Puntarenas, as it is too small and has nothing worthy of seeing.

I do not recommend attempting to negotiate with any of the local taxi operators that may be waiting outside the pier or dock in Puntarenas or Puerto Caldera. Their reliability and the safety of their vehicle is always in question.

* MAJOR SIGHTSEEING VENUES: Each of the venues noted in this section represents a place that has been chosen by one or more cruise lines for an all-day or half day excursion

from Puntarenas. Most are based upon the ecotourism concept. I have listed them alphabetically to avoid any personal bias.

** Monteverde Cloud Forest – One of the most spectacular of national parks in Costa Rica, this high altitude tropical rainforest is located at such an elevation that when most inflowing air is intercepted by the surrounding mountains, the forest is shrouded in clouds.

The Monteverde Cloud Forest living up to its name

A visit to Monteverde is a full day, taking about 2.5 hours travel time each way. The last portion of the road is still unsealed. But you do get to travel through beautiful, rugged countryside that is very sparsely inhabited. The changes in altitude reveal the different layers of vegetation in Costa Rica. Monteverde is at over 1,525 meters or 5,000 feet above sea level in the Cordillera de Tilarán where it intercepts streams of warm Pacific air laden with moisture. The condensation produces thick fog giving the landscape a haunting and very ethereal look.

The park is home to over 2,500 species of plants including large numbers of orchids, 400 species of birds 120 reptilian species and over 100 different types of mammals. There are also numerous insects, but none that are pesky or harmful to humans.

Most cruise visitors are treated to a traditional Costa Rican lunch of roasted meats, chicken, rice, beans, bananas and salad topped off with fresh Costa Rican coffee. Remember that in Costa Rica the level of sanitation is quite high so you can eat with confidence that you will not experience any intestinal upset.

** Volcan Poás – An exciting tour is a visit to the simmering caldera that is Poás, located about a two hour drive by motor coach from Puntarenas. Poás is actually quite close to the capital city of San José and your coach will skirt the suburban edge of the capital en route.

Poás is a massive caldera, which is an expansive crater containing several vents, representing past explosive eruptions of unimaginable fury. Today the volcano is relatively calm; most of its activity is in the form of steam eruptions with occasional outbursts of lava over the lip of one of its smaller interior craters. But the potential for a violent eruption to occur is present even though the probability is relatively unlikely. Volcanoes must always be treated with great respect for their fury is uncontrollable.

On the outer rim of Volcan Poás, (work of Leonora (Ellie) Enking, CC BY SA 2.0, Wikimedia.org)

The massive bulk of Poás rises to a height of 2,708 meters or 8,885 feet. Its northern crater is filled with a lake of highly toxic sulfuric acid at high temperature. The southern crater lake contains fresh water. Because of the toxic gasses and the condensation from rising moist air, it may be impossible to see the crater from its rim, so a visit is always a gamble.

On a Poás tour lunch is usually had at one of the fine local restaurants set amid the coffee plantations near the base of the massive mountain. The combination of mountain air, good food and freshly brewed Costa Rican coffee are a hard combination to beat. And then the return drive is often through the arts and crafts city of Sarchi where the famous Costa Rican miniature and highly decorated ox carts are created.

** San José – A visit to Costa Rica's national capital and largest city is the perfect tour for those who want to enjoy a cultural experience. It takes just over one hour on the country's new expressway from Puntarenas, climbing rapidly through the western coastal mountains into the high valley where San José sits beneath slumbering volcanoes.

In the heart of bustling San Jose

On the way into the city, your coach will pass alongside Escazu, a community that has attracted numerous expatriate Americans and Canadians who are taking advantage of a high quality of life at a lower cost. Escazu exhibits many high rise condos and smart shops set amid bowers of trees.

San José is quite unlike any of the other capital sin Central America. It is the most prosperous, yet not in an extravagant way, as it represents the greater equity between wealth and poverty than what is seen in neighboring countries. There are fewer grand palatial mansions in San José and likewise far fewer poverty stricken barrios. Even the presidential palace is just simply a nice residence. This is a city where the vast middle class dominates.

Around the city center you will find rows of colonial houses with their heavy doors and iron bars on the windows, dating back to the era of Spanish colonization. In the outer suburbs the homes are individual and do not have the layers of security you see in Panama or Guatemala.

San José is frequently shaken by earthquakes and often showered in ash fallout from its neighboring two active volcanoes. There are signs in almost every public venue that point out what to do during an earthquake. The people are simply accepting of the risks with which they live. You also see signs that simply say, "Pura Vida," the Costa Rican expression that means "the good life."

The grand colonial Post Office in San José

In the event you are visiting San José on your own with a private car and driver, these are the major sights you should attempt to include in your visit, shown alphabetically:

*** Catedral Metropolitan – The baroque cathedral is not as grand as in larger Latin American cities, but it is still a traditional Catholic house of worship and faces onto one of the major city plazas.

*** Correo de Costa Rica – This 19th century post and telegraph building is one of the finest examples of grand public architecture in Central America. The building is open for business weekdays from 8 AM to 6 PM.

*** Mercado Central – This is the grand food market in the city center. It is exceptionally clean, yet filled with a lot of local color and charm, and it shows you what is available to eat in the country. Located at Avenida Central and Avenida Uno, it is open daily from 6:30 AM to 5:45 PM except Sunday.

*** Museo de Arte Costaricense – This museum features a good collection of graphic and three dimensional works of art representative of all aspects of the nation both through time and today. It is located at Parque Metropolitano and open from 9 AM to 4 PM Tuesday thru Sunday.

*** Museo Nacional de Costa Rica – You will find an excellent collection of items and exhibits from the natural to the cultural aspects of Costa Rica. This museum helps you fully understand the true nature of the nation.

*** Simón Bolivar Zoo – If getting out into the countryside on one of the all day tours is not what interests you, visiting this zoo might be just the right venue for you to see the rich Costa Rican animal and bird life, but in a comfortable city setting. It is open daily from 9 AM to 4:30 PM.

*** Teatro Nacional de Costa Rica – This elegant, but small opera house is the pride of the city, dating to 1897 during the height of the coffee plantation era. Located at Avenida Dos and Calle Cinco, you can visit during daylight hours. The museum is found on Avenida 17 between Avenida Central and Avenida Segunda. It is open Tuesday thru Saturday from 8:30 AM to 4:30 PM and on Sunday from 9 AM to 4:30 PM.

Teatro Nacional de Costa Rica

** LESSER SIGHTSEEING VENUES: There are numerous less significant, but equally enjoyable ecotourism venues closer to Puntarenas. Each cruise line offers what it finds most welcomed by its guests, mainly through trial and error. It is not possible for me to list them all, but I am giving you the most distinctive of the various options, ones I personally have had experience with and am comfortable recommending.

*** **Aerial Tram and Zip Line Adventure** – This is a more active tour for those who are quite physically fit and have no fear of height. You will zip through the forest canopy after first riding through part of the forest on an aerial tram. This is an all day tour and most cruise lines do include lunch.

*** **Miravalles Hot Springs Resort** – For anyone looking to relax and enjoy the warm therapeutic waters that result from the volcanic activity under the Costa Rican mountains, this is a perfect way to spend a few relaxing hours. The drive into the highlands to the resort is quite an added bonus. Depending upon how your cruise lines organizes this tour, it may or may not include lunch.

*** **Natuwa Sanctuary** – Here you have a chance to visit a wildlife sanctuary where the emphasis is upon preserving the rich bird life of Costa Rica, especially the Scarlet and Great Green Macaw. If you are a bird lover, this tour is right for you. It is a half day tour and quite easy for most guests.

*** **Sky Walk** – For those who want to have a chance to enjoy the forest from a higher perspective, this sky walk adventure offered by several cruise lines is a half day adventure where you walk on aerial bridges high in the forest canopy. It is not far from Puntarenas and is a relatively easy tour, but only recommended if heights do not bother you.

*** **Tárcoles River Mangrove Cruise** – Here you have a chance to cruise through the lowland estuary of the river and enjoy the guided tour of this habitat and its unique plant and animal assemblages. This is normally a half day tour.

DINING OUT: Costa Rican cuisine is based upon the availability of local ingredients and usually includes grilled beef, chicken or port generally served with beans and rice, corn on the cob, fried plantains and one or more vegetables. The most popular dessert is one called tres leches in Spanish, meaning three milks. It consists of a rich cake served with heavy cream or whipped cream and is quite delicious.

On all of the full day tours your cruise line will offer lunch is generally provided and most likely at a well-respected restaurant. If you are out for the day with a private car and driver, then you are on your own for lunch. I am recommending restaurants that I have visited and find worthy of inclusion in my book. These are my personal recommendations shown alphabetically.

* **Freddo Fresas** – Located on Carretera Principal a Volcan Poás, this is a perfect spot if you are visiting the famous volcanic caldera. It is generally on tour itineraries, so call ahead to reserve a table at +506 2482 2400. The cuisine is typical of rural Costa Rica, and they have incredibly good desserts and local coffee prepared in a very unique manner.

* **La Esquina de Buenos Aires** – Located in downtown San José on Calle 11, this is a great restaurant known for its fantastic soups and grilled meats served in the traditional style of Argentina. They also offer a fine array of pasta and great salads. Lunch is served Monday thru Thursday from 11:30 AM to 3 PM with dinner between 6 and 10:30 PM. Friday these serve straight through to 11 PM. Saturday they open at Noon and serve until 11 PM and Sunday from Noon to 10 PM. Reservations are not required.

* Restaurante la Terrasse – This is an outstanding fine dining establishment in a very old house on Avenida Nuevo in San José. I would consider this quite gourmet oriented and dining here is a memorable experience. It is only open for dinner, but if your cruise ship is staying in port into the late evening, it is possible to enjoy a fine dinner. Reservations are a must and your guide can call them at +506 8939 8470 to book a table. They are open from 7 to 10:30 PM Tuesday thru Sunday.

The making of Costa Rican coffee at Freddo Fresas

* Restaurante Nuestra Tierra – In San Jose at Avenida 2 and Calle 15, this is a true local establishment that is not fancy or formal. This restaurant is down home Costa Rican, but one I trust because the food is fresh and nicely served. You will experience what most middle class Costa Ricans would eat at lunch, mainly grilled meat and rice with beans plus vegetables. And yes they do serve tres leches for dessert. Reservations are not required and they are open daily from 6 AM to Midnight.

* Taller Gastronómico el Punto – Located in Escazu, this is one of the most artful and innovative dining establishments where lunch is a work of art. Most guest are in awe at the novel and elegant cuisine that is served. Hours for lunch or dinner are Tuesday thru Friday from Noon to 10 PM. Monday they only serve dinner from 7 to 10 PM and Saturday they

serve both lunch and dinner from 1 to 10 PM. Have your driver book a table by calling them at +506 2215 0387.

Restaurante Nuestra Tierra in San José

SHOPPING: There are nice arts and crafts to be purchased in Costa Rica and of course many shops that sell typical souvenirs. Puntarenas is very limited and I have found only one store that sells some craft items and souvenirs. It is called Lime Coral Jaco and located on Calle Jaco Sol.

* San Jose- There are two good venues for traditional arts and crafts in the capital city. These are:

** Galeria Namu – Located on Avenida 7 in the city center, They feature both traditional and indigenous works of art. Hours are from, 8 AM to 6:30 PM Monday thru Saturday and from 1 to 5 PM Sunday.

** Holalola Souvenirs – Located on Los Yoses Boulevard, this shop is known for its fine quality traditional arts and crafts. They are open from 10 AM to 6 PM Monday thru Saturday.

** Mercado Publico – Arts and crafts stalls will be found in the vast public market, which is a venue on my list of important sights in the city.

* Sarchi – On your various tours the motor coach may stop for souvenir or arts and crafts shopping, but it cannot be guaranteed. If you are out on your own with a car and driver and in the highlands north of San José, I highly recommend the town of Sarchi. It is known for its many small artisan shops and the most typical item that people buy is the miniaturized replica of the famous highly decorated ox carts. There is a guild in Sarchi that is the best venue for quality painted ox carts. The two producers of these hand crafted art objects are *Fabrica de carretas joaquin Chaverri* and *Fabrica de carretas Eloy Alfaro*. Both offer a good selection at somewhat affordable prices. Remember these are handmade and painted.

A life size handmade ox cart in Sarchi, too big to take home

FINAL WORDS: A visit to Puntarenas gives you several choices in tours to different parts of Costa Rica, varying from the national capital city to a massive volcanic caldera to a mountain cloud forest. This port call is one of the most diverse you will find on the entire cruise. Puntarenas just happens to be central to so many distinct venues, each with its own specific local environment. The only problem with such a one-day visit is trying to choose where to go. I have recommended several venues because over the years I have been able to sample them all. Thus where you choose to spend the day will depend upon your specific taste. But in the end no matter which venue you choose, you will come away with a positive image of this small Central American country.

VISITING NICARAGUA

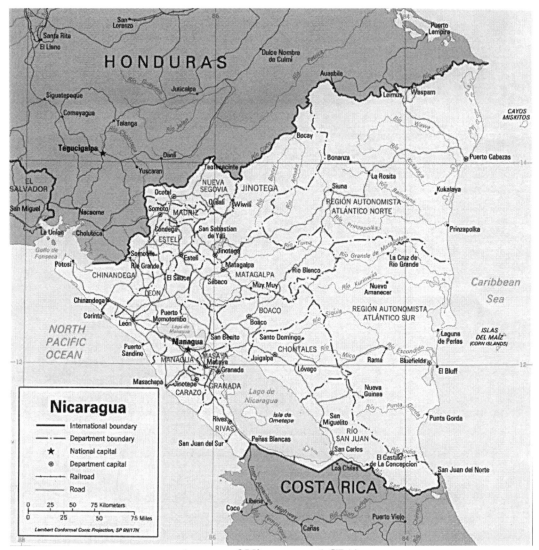

A map of Nicaragua (CIA)

Very few Panama Canal cruise itineraries will include a stop in Nicaragua for a variety of reasons. Costa Rica is so popular and so devoted to ecotourism that it has built a global reputation for its beautiful rainforests, mountains and volcanoes. The majority of people looking at a Panama Canal transit also consider the ports of call, especially on the long Pacific Coast, and the majority are very enthused about a visit to Costa Rica. Nicaragua is not well known to people who regularly cruise, as it is a country that has received so much negative press because of its years of dictatorship followed by Communist government and more revolutionary upheaval. And it is a shame because the country does offer some incredibly beautiful landscapes, especially along its Pacific Coast and in the mountainous highlands.

THE PHYSICAL LANDSCAPE: Nicaragua is a moderately large country for Central America. It extends over 120,375 square kilometers or 50,338 square miles, but almost two thirds of that land area is relatively flat tropical rainforest extending from the mountain rib in the west to the Caribbean Coast. This is the least settled part of the country because it has low productivity given the hot, tropical nature of the lowlands. And it has very shallow and swampy shores. It was also very much a zone of malaria and yellow fever, even having received the nickname as "The Mosquito Coast."

The majestic beauty of Lake Nicaragua, (Work of Adrian Sampson, CC BY SA 2.0, Wikimedia.org)

The mountainous rib of high volcanic peaks with fertile high altitude intervening valleys became the homeland for most indigenous tribes and later for the Spanish colonists. It is comfortable because of altitude moderating the tropical heat. And the land is very productive. But like Costa Rica, it is subject to the risk of earthquakes and volcanic eruptions. It is a fragile landscape and one that is frankly dangerous and subject to potential catastrophic events. The mountainous rib sits atop the plate boundary between two of the planet's tectonic plates.

In the central highlands there are two massive lakes, that sit between volcanoes, many of which are active. Lake Nicaragua is the larger and Lake Managua is home to the national capital and largest city of the same name. These are beautiful freshwater lakes along whose shores you find many farming and fishing communities. Lake Nicaragua is so close to the Pacific Ocean and the coastal lowlands, a distance of 24 kilometers or 15 miles, that when the United States was looking to build a canal, their geologists initially considered this to be a perfect location even though it is much wider than Panama. The lake and the outflowing San Juan River would have been utilized, but far more locks would have been necessary since Lake Nicaragua is far higher in altitude than the center of the Isthmus of Panama. What was the ultimate deterrent was the potential for both catastrophic tectonic or volcanic events. Some even considered it in the late 20th century as a viable choice for the larger locks that ultimately were built as part of the Panama Canal expansion.

A reminder of the volatility of Nicaragua, (Work of Jorge Mejia Peralta, CC BY SA 2.0, Wikimedia.org)

A BRIEF NICARAGUAN HISTORY:
The history of Nicaragua is as volatile as its geography. A brief review will make your visit to San Juan del Sur far more meaningful and you will appreciate why so few cruise ships visit the country.

The indigenous people came from several cultural traditions, but they were primarily simple farmers or hunter gatherer types. There were a few tribal groups linguistically related to the Maya

In 1502, Columbus did explore the Mosquito Coast and was not impressed with the landscape. He also did not come into contact with any tribes. The first Spaniard to make any inroad was González Dávila who did invade the southwest corner of what is now Nicaragua. He did come into contact with local tribes, obtained some gold but was ultimately forced to retreat. Actual settlement did not occur until 1524 when Granada and León were established, today seen as historic sites for their colonial architecture. The original León, today known as

León Viejo, is a set of runs because of volcanic destruction in 1610. Granada and the second León are within easy driving from San Juan del Sur and your cruise line may offer an all day tour to either city, but Granada is the best known for its colonial flavor.

In 1655, the British who were active in the Caribbean seized the Mosquito Coast and held it as a protectorate until 1860 when they finally gave it to Nicaragua. But it remained a semi-autonomous region until 1894. To this day it is a cultural backwater and sparsely populated.

The Spanish were brutal in their conquests of the indigenous people in the highlands and their use of many as slave labor. The conquistadors also took wives or concubines and this introduced much disease into the local population, ultimately further decimating most. But the mixed blood "mestizo" people ultimately came to comprise the bulk of the Nicaraguan population, so totally different a story from that of Costa Rica.

Nicaragua gained independence in 1821 but became part of the Mexican Empire for two years and then part of the Federal Republic of Central America until 1828 when it became totally independent and on its own. Leon and Granada held differing political views and leadership of the country balanced on the verge of all out civil war until 1852 when Managua became the national capital.

With California gold seekers crossing the country via the San Juan River and Lake Nicaragua, an American soldier of fortune named William Walker declared himself president in 1856 because the country was divided between political rivals. Surrounding countries united and drove him from power, and finally the country saw stability with the Conservative Party holding on to power.

From 1912 until 1933, Nicaragua was occupied by American forces. The initial justification came when President Díaz asked for aid in putting down a rebellion by the fired army general who had led the military. American Marines occupied the country and it was during this period that the United States was granted a corridor to build a canal, but by this time the Panama Canal project was nearing completion.

During the last six years of American military presence, a guerrilla campaign undermined the country and kept it in turmoil. So when the Americans pulled out in 1933, they left behind a civil guard that was well trained and supported. The conflict between the two main political forces ultimately led the director of the guard, Anastasio Somoza García to seize control by first having the two party leaders assassinated.

The Somoza Dynasty ruled with an iron hand until 1979 even though the elder Somoza was shot in 1956 by a Liberal loyalist, and because it was friendly to the United States, he was given plenty of financial and military support. In the face of the Cuban Communist takeover and Cuba's political influence in the hemisphere, there was fear that they may use Nicaragua's political divisions as a means of infiltrating the country without Somoza in power.

Alas in 1979, the Somoza family was deposed by the Sandinista political movement. The 1972 Managua Earthquake and the siphoning off of much of the aid money by the family ultimately led to the Somoza downfall. The story leading up to this downfall is quite complicated and too detailed to be relevant in this book, but makes for interesting historic reading for those who might wish to follow through. Suffice it to say that in 1979, this all came crashing down.

The new government at first was given support by the United States with millions poured into the country. But when the Americans learned that the Sandinista Government was supporting the rebels in El Salvador, the Reagan Government shifted its support to a group of Nicaraguan opposition groups that were called "Contras." With CIA help, the Contras were trying to undermine the Sandinista Government. Operating from bases in neighboring Honduras, the Contras fomented unrest against the Sandinista Government, and the United States became convinced that Ortega was a Communist and further bolstered this opposition. Arms were shipped via Iran in what became known as the Iran-Contra scandal in which Marine Colonel Oliver North assumed blame to keep President Reagan from taking any political backlash for secretly continuing the program funneled through Iran after Congress had suspended aid, accusing Daniel Ortega, a supposed Communist, of fraudulently winning the election.

In 1990, a coalition led by Violeta Chamorro, defeated the Sandinista Party because there was such a groundswell of support. It was difficult for her to unite the country and to bring in aid and investment because of the Sandinista ties with Cuba and Communism. In the next election in 1996, the Liberal Party won, again defeating the Sandinista Party. So by now you would think that this socialistic party with its taint from the past would be finished. Again to shorten the story, Daniel Ortega and the Sandinista Party returned to power in 2006 as a minority government, but gained public support and in 2011 won a landslide majority. With National Assembly enabling a third term, Ortega was reelected in 2016 even though there have been complaints of fraud. The Sandinista Party and Daniel Ortega have achieved a measure of respectability and Nicaragua has managed to maintain a degree of stability. But opposition has been mounting across the country with many complaints about mismanagement. There have even been violent clashes with police and the Inter-American Commission on Human Rights has been looking into many abuses.

As of 2019, there is political unrest which no doubt will only be resolved in the next election scheduled for 2021. Hopefully the grievances will either be addressed or there is the possibility of a full scale revolution, which would totally destabilize the country and have a spill over impact upon neighboring El Salvador and Honduras.

From a tourist perspective, Nicaragua is relatively safe for visitors. There are the usual petty street crimes, but overall visitors will find the country very comfortable at the same level they find in Costa Rica. Drug violence is also relatively minimal and is nothing for visitors to be concerned about especially in San Juan del Sur where some cruise ships visit.

SAN JUAN DEL SUR: Located on the Pacific Coast close to the border of Costa Rica, San Juan del Sur is a pleasant small resort community that only dates back to 1851. It is 140 kilometers or 87 miles southeast from Managua and occupies a narrow coastal fringe backed up by an equally narrow range of low mountains separating it from Lake Nicaragua. It developed as a fishing community but has become the major tourist destination for American and Canadian visitors looking for sun and surf in a safe environment. Its crescent shaped bay presents a beautiful locale for water sports, and it was this bay that provided for a rest stop for travelers going to the California gold fields in the 1850's. Had the transoceanic canal been built in Nicaragua, this would have been the Pacific base of operations. Today the population is around 16,000 residents, including some expatriates.

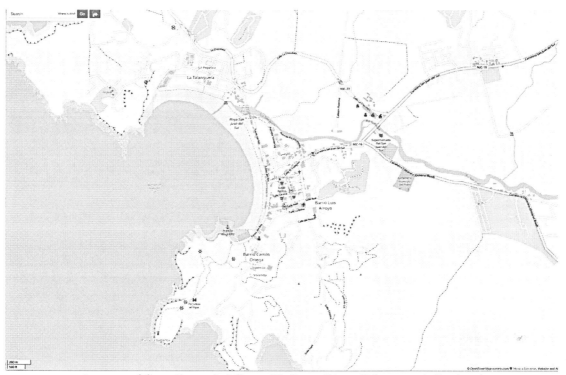

A map of San Juan del Sur, (© OpenStreetMap contributors)

SAN JUAN DEL SUR: The biggest deficit for tourism is the lack of a strongly developed infrastructure, as found in Costa Rica. Nicaragua is developing its national parks and is proud of its growing ecotourism. But there are still far fewer major hotels and resorts. For cruise ship visitors, it is not as easy to find private tours in San Juan del Sur, but the cruise ships that do stop have arranged for a sufficient number of tours to keep their guests happy during a port call.

Here are my recommendations regarding touring while in San Juan del Sur:

* Ship sponsored tours are your best bet for having either a full or half day excursion. San Juan del Sur, Private touring is rather limited with regard to availability. Tours will either be of the small town and its immediate surroundings or if your cruise line has developed a program with local operators you may have the opportunity to visit Managua, the national capital about a two hour drive by motor coach. Managua is a rather sprawling city that unfortunately still has many poor barrios. Its central core was decimated by a massive

earthquake in 1972 just two days before Christmas. The old core has never fully recovered up to the present day. There may also be a tour to Granada, which is a beautiful 16ᵗʰ century Spanish colonial city on the shore of Lake Nicaragua. I would highly recommend the tour to Granada. It is a small city steeped in colonial history and with a rich architecture and offers views along the shores of Lake Nicaragua.

The beautiful bay at San Juan del Sur

* Tours by private car or van may possibly be arranged by your cruise line depending upon their experience. But you may also wish to check out Iskra Travel and Tours, as they are a reputable tour agency. Their web page is *www.iskratravel.com.*

* Taxis will be available and you may wish to negotiate with a driver for a tour of either the local area or an all day tour to Granada. Be sure and agree on a rate prior to departing and do not pay until service is rendered. You can also check on line in advance with Taxi Express Travel at *www.shuttlesairportnicaragua.worldpress.com* for information and rates or Neptune Transport Services at *www.neptunetransportservices.com* for their information and rates.

* LOCAL SIGHTS IN SAN JUAN DEL SUR: This is still a very small town with few specific sights of special interest. The major sights to be seen are shown below alphabetically:

** La Flor Beach Nature Reserve – This small reserve on the edge of town is a small beach where sea turtles come on shore to nest. If you are there at hatching time, you will be able to see baby turtles run nature's gauntlet to get to the sea. If it is the right time of year, a tour will be organized by your cruise line or private operators.

On the beach in San Juan del Sur, (Work of Adam Jones, CC BY SA 2.0, Wikimedia.org)

** **Latin American Spanish School** – Located at Avenida Real on the north side of the central park, this is an important non-profit school where students of all ages can learn Spanish in an immersion program that is quite superior to anything you can buy for private study. Visitors are always welcome to come and watch and learn. Visitors can come between 8 AM and 1 PM on weekdays.

** **Marsella Valley Nature Center** – Located in the mountains north of town, this is a place where you can play disc golf and lounge on the beach. It is not really a nature reserve, but simply a sheltered and shady place to enjoy the fresh air and play disc golf of enjoy the sand and sea. If you are touring privately, call prior to see if you can visit. Their local number is +505 8805 6951.

** **Mirador del Cristo de la Misrecordia** – This is a high vantage point at the western edge of the bay where you will have a fantastic view over San Juan del Sur and the surrounding countryside. The hilltop is also crowned with a large statue of Christ, which looks over the bay and town. It is always open to the public, but it is a rather steep walk to the top.

* **TOURS TO GRANADA OR MANAGUA:** If your cruise line offers tours either to Managua or Granada, the itinerary will be predetermined and lunch will be included. If you decide to visit either city on your own with a private car and driver/guide, you need to trust in their advice as to what to see since both cities offer quite a diverse number of sights.

DINING OUT: San Juan del Sur is rather small, but it does have a few nice restaurants where you can try the local cuisine, and also enjoy the fresh seafood. If you go on a tour to Managua or Granada you will be provided with lunch as part of the overall package, so you will not have any choice of restaurants. If you happen to have a car and driver/guide and leave San Juan del Sur, ask your driver to take you to a good quality restaurant, as they are very familiar with the countryside and what it offers.

In San Juan del Sur I have found that the restaurants are not consistent with regard to quality and service, good one time and not so good the next time I visit. Thus for the three I am recommending, if you look at reviews you will see that the majority are good, but that about five percent of the ratings are low. This is a consistent theme in San Juan del Sur. My recommendations for lunch in San Juan del Sur are shown here alphabetically:

* **Beach House Nicaragua** – On Calle del Paseo del Rey facing the beach in the center of town, this rather rambling house with a big verandah serves the freshest of seafood dishes that are well prepared in local traditional recipes. You will dine with a cool breeze coming off the bay and overall have a relaxed lunch. They are open daily from 8 AM to 11 PM.

* **Café Mediterrano** – Located in the heart of town opposite the municipal market, this restaurant offers an Italian vibe, serving fresh seafood, homemade pastas and breads. The menu also offers both vegetarian and vegan dishes. And they serve nice desserts. Their hours are Tuesday thru Sunday from 8 AM to 9 PM.

* **Dale Pues** – Located in the main road leading into the town center, but there is no address I can give other than it is on Avenida el Tropezón just north of the junction with Avenida el Albinal. This is a somewhat international café with American sandwiches, burgers, fish tacos and British style pub dishes. It is casual and the service is quite good. They are open daily from 7:30 AM to 10 PM.

SHOPPING: There is not a lot of shopping with regard to local crafts, but most people visit the central market in the heart of town. Usually, however, it is mostly food oriented for locals to buy their essentials. But there are a few souvenir and craft items.

As for real shopping, I have found two interesting places, which are:

* **Art Warehouse** – In the heart of town on Calle Mercado, this is an absolutely enjoyable place to visit. It is a combination of artist's studios, art gallery and café that actually serves some delicious light meals. There are also art classes being offered. You can find a nice piece of local art at a reasonable price. They are open Monday from 9 AM to 8:30 PM and Tuesday thru Saturday from 9 AM to 5 PM. You will find it a delightful place to stop or linger.

* Tienda de Artesanias Quetzalcoalt – Located in town but you will need to ask specific directions since no actual address is provided. This shop is administered by a group of artists and crafts people representing the local art community. All works of art are genuine and you will find a wide array of sizes and prices on graphics and handcrafted objects. Unfortunately they do not show any hours of operation so you will just have to hope they are open when you visit, which on a day a ship is in port is most likely.

FINAL WORDS: Unfortunately for most of my readers this port of call will not be on your itinerary. But for those who will visit, you should consider it a rare opportunity to spend a day in a country so little known in the cruise market, a country that has seen so much strife in the past but one trying to develop its tourist infrastructure.

A dramatic view of Lake Nicaragua from the mountains just behind San Juan del Sur, (Work of Wolkenkratzer, CC BY SA 4.0, Wikimedia.org)

VISITING EL SALVADOR

A map of El Salvador, (CIA)

El Salvador is the smallest mainland country in North America, occupying only 21,041 square kilometers or 8,124 square miles. It is located on the Pacific Coast of Central America, bordered on the north and east by Honduras and on the west by Guatemala. This is a country that has seen much political turbulence and violence in the 20th century and therefore has not been a place where tourists consider visiting.

On the cruise itineraries of those lines making the transit through the Panama Canal or offering more extensive cruises along the Pacific Coast south from the United States at present only seven ships will stop in Acajutla in 2019, representing Azamara, Crystal, Fred Olsen, Phoenix Reisen and Regent Seven Seas. At the time of this writing, the 2020 cruise schedule has not been released.

Thus for the vast majority of readers of this cruise guide, you will not be visiting El Salvador, just as has been the case for Nicaragua. But in the next few years it is quite possible that the number of port calls from the lines noted above and others may increase, thus expanding the potential horizons for exploring more of the vast coastline between the border of the United States and the Panama Canal.

THE PHYSICAL LANDSCAPE: El Salvador despite its small size geographically is still quite a dramatic country. It has a very narrow coastal lowland that quickly gives way to the interior highlands composed of parallel ranges of mountains with small intervening valleys where the majority of the people live. The mountains are part of the same structure seen in Costa Rica and Nicaragua, that of being highly volcanic with over 20 volcanoes in such a small geographic area. The highest peak in this small country is 2,730 meters or 8,957 feet high and dominates the landscape. They are all potentially active, but two have erupted in recent years. Being that the country straddles a major plate boundary not only creates a condition for volcanism, but also tectonic activity, giving El Salvador a high frequency of earthquakes with many being relatively intense.

Unlike Costa Rica and Nicaragua, there is no lowland plain leading to the Caribbean Sea because the border between El Salvador and Honduras is still within the mountain zone given that El Salvador is such a small country and only extends inland just over 100 kilometers or 62 miles.

The interior of El Salvador, (Work of Metztli, CC BY SA 3.0, Wikimedia.org)

The climate of El Salvador is tropical, but with the exception of the narrow coastal plain, altitude moderates the country's geographic position, giving most of the land a temperate climate and making it quite hospitable to settlement. Temperatures are generally in the upper 20's Celsius or 80's Fahrenheit, but with a fair amount of humidity. This is a country where drought is rare and rainfall is plentiful. Combined with the volcanic soil, El Salvador has a good geographic potential for farming at the subsistence and plantation level. But it has been the history of violence that has kept the country from prosperity.

A BRIEF HISTORY: The only way to appreciate why this apparently beautiful country is not experiencing a tourist boom, as is the case in Costa Rica, is by taking a quick review of its history. Wherever you go in El Salvador it is impossible to escape the brutality and destruction that has been wrought by its turbulent 20th century history.

Prior to the arrival of the Spanish, El Salvador was home to numerous indigenous groups, including being on the fringes of the Maya civilization. Many of its people were quite sophisticated and prospered in the traditional manner, farming corn, beans, squash and other vegetables native to North America such as the tomato, avocado and chili. And one plant was destined to have a great global impact, that being cacao, better known in its commercial form as chocolate. Native cotton also was utilized in the production of fine quality garments and rugs.

The year 1524 saw the first of the Spanish conquistadors enter what is now El Salvador and by 1525, the largest tribe known as the Cuzcatlec had been conquered, the capital city of San Salvador being established in the heart of their land. As was the case through much of Central America, the native people faced the impact of new diseases along with brutal conquest, those who survived becoming a slave labor class, many having mixed blood because of the ill treatment of their women. Most of the present day population of El Salvador is classed as mixed race or Mestizo and the vast majority live impoverished lives.

San Salvador, the capital city, is overshadowed by volcanic peaks, (Work of Xtremesv, CC BY SA 3.0, Wikimedia.org)

During the long period of Spanish colonization, El Salvador was first under the Viceroyalty of New Spain out of Ciudad de México until 1609 when it became part of the captaincy General of Guatemala. There was very little real contact between the small settlements of El Salvador and the population centers of Antigua and Ciudad de Guatemala. The territory was essentially run by local Spanish authorities as a separate entity.

Revolution began to brew with the first signs of it in El Salvador in 1811 and independence came in 1821. Like Nicaragua, El Salvador became a part of the First Mexican Empire, but in 1823 joined the Federal Republic of Central America, remaining a part of this loose confederation until 1841 when it was dissolved. It was then that it briefly became totally independent, then joined the Greater Republic of Central America with Honduras and Nicaragua. This lasted four years from 1895 to 1898 and the it dissolved.

The more modern history of El Salvador during the last decades of the 19th century and all through the 20th century is one of ongoing political unrest, violence, coup after coup and dictatorial rule. It culminated in the most long lasting and brutal civil war in all of Central America, lasting from 1979 to 1992 and killing tens of thousands as well as displacing more than half the national population. The Chapultepec Peace Accords signed in Ciudad de México created a democratic government in which all sides were given representation, ending the violence and suffering. During the conflict nobody was spared, including the peasant majority, wealthy socioeconomic leaders and members of the clergy. At least the country is at peace and hopefully will stay that way.

The economy is still one in which agriculture is the main form of activity supported by minimal fishing and manufacturing. The government is attempting to encourage more international banking and also tourism. In 2001, the country gave up its own currency once known as the Colon, and now uses the American Dollar as its currency, the same as is done in Panama.

ACAJUTLA:
The main port for the country is Acajutla, located on the northern edge of the coast. It is primarily a cargo port, but the handful of cruise ships now visiting El Salvador dock here. By road it is only 82 kilometers or 51 miles from San Salvador, which is the capital and largest city. Acajutla is small and only has 30,000 residents, the vast majority being relatively poor and working at menial jobs in the port or they are unemployed.

The main cargo being exported is still coffee and sugar cane along with a few minor manufactured goods such as textiles, clothing and furniture.

Acajutla is an old town, dating to the earlies Spanish intrusion into what is now El Salvador in 1524. The town grew in significance as a coffee exporting port in the 1840's, and it has remained the prime port to the present day.

During the civil war, lasting from 1980 to 1992, Acajutla was targeted by rebel groups because of its small oil refinery and its port facilities, since it was vital to the government's military needs. Since the civil war ended, the government has continued to develop the port for handling containerized cargo. It is still refining the oil imported to the country, primarily from Venezuela.

Avenida San Rafael in Acajutla, (Work of Roberto Alas, CC BY SA 3.0, Wikimedia.org)

SIGHTSEEING IN ACAJUTLA: The port town of Acajutla offers nothing for the tourist. You must participate in one of the ship sponsored tours in order to see anything. Staying in port and attempting to walk around Acajutla is definitely not recommended because of both safety issues and the fact that it offers nothing of interest.

* THE CRIME FACTOR: Despite the end of the civil war and the return of a degree of stability, the country is considered to be one of the more dangerous nations in the world. Street crime, much of it violent, still is a major problem. And with regard to tourists, pickpockets are rampant, and sometimes they are bold enough to approach with knives or guns. It is best to not even attempt to do any private sightseeing on your one day port call. Even if you do not enjoy group tours sponsored by your cruise line, this is the safest means of travel in El Salvador.

* GETTING AROUND: As noted above, your safest means of sightseeing is to be part of a ship sponsored motor coach tour even if you normally prefer to do private touring with a car and driver or simply explore on your own. I do not encourage either activity in El Salvador at this time. A private car puts you at risk, especially on the highway between Acajutla and the local provincial capital of Sonsonate or San Salvador. Please play it safe and take the bus tour. Likewise, do not even consider using a local taxi.

However, if you are insistent upon having the freedom of a private car and driver, your ship's tour office may be able to assist. In any event, the driver will need to come from the capital, as Acajutla does not offer such services. There is only one company I would even consider in the future, as to date they have been reliable. It is called El Salvador Custom Tours. Check their web pages at *www.elsalvadorcutomtours.com* for details and rates.

* SIGHTS TO SEE: There are no recommended sights to see in Acajutla. The destinations of interest will be one of the following:

** San Salvador – The national capital city of San Salvador is only a one hour trip from Acajutla. It is not a very exciting city since it is still recovering from the long civil war. However, with a population of 300,000 and a long history dating back to 1525, it does offer some historic buildings of the Spanish colonial era, and surprisingly some modern developments post-civil war.

The main plaza in San Salvador, (Work of Erickssonr, CC BY SA 3.0, Wikimedia.org)

San Salvador offers many interesting sights, but if you are on a motor coach tour you will see only what the tour operator has planned for you. If by chance you have taken the private car and driver/guide option, the sights I recommend are listed below:

*** Catedral Metropolitana – A beautiful example of baroque architecture and this is a must see sight.

*** **Iglesia el Rosario** – This is a relatively modern and futuristic church, built to symbolize the eye of Jesus, and it offers dramatic interior and exterior views. It is a most unusual style for a Catholic church.

*** **Jardin Botanico la Laguna** – This is the beautiful botanical garden on the edge of the city featuring the local flora. It is peaceful and worthy of a visit. It is open daily but no specific hours are given.

*** **Joya de Ceren Archaeological Park** – This park is just to the east of the city and is the remains of a pre-Colombian Maya village. If you have not seen any of the major Mayan ruins in Yucatan, this is definitely a worthwhile stop. It is open daily from 8 AM to 4 PM.

*** **Museo de Art de El Salvador** – A good collection of historic and contemporary art representing the county will be seen in this fine museum open daily.

*** **Museo Nacional de Antropologia** – The museum collection is outstanding and does include many Maya treasures.

*** **Parque Nacional el Boqueron** – This volcanic crater surrounded by thick rainforest vegetation is spectacular and it also offers great views of San Salvador. It is open daily from 7 AM to 9 PM and should be a must see sight.

** **Sonsonate** – A visit to Sonsonate takes only a few hours, as this regional capital is just 18 kilometers or 12 miles. This town of 72,000 residents offers a bit more of a glimpse into the lives of the people of El Salvador. It has a relatively distinct town core with a beautiful cathedral and plaza. There are no specific venues to visit in Sonsonate.

** **Volcanic Landscape Tour** – There are several possible combinations of volcanic peaks that can be put together into either a half day or full day tour in El Salvador depending upon the arrangements your cruise line has made with a local tour operator. If you are interested in seeing the natural landscape and if such a tour is available, it would be quite worthwhile as opposed to spending the day in the national capital.

DINING OUT: The opportunity to dine out is limited to whatever restaurant the cruise line provides on its full day tours. If you are going to have a private car and driver/guide, you would most likely dine in San Salvador, the only city that offers any significant choices. However, I have found that restaurants in the capital are inconsistent. When it comes to recommending one for lunch, I am only able to recommend two establishments with any degree of confidence. There are none in Sonsonate or Acajutla that I am comfortable recommending.

My dining choices in San Salvador are:

Il Bongustario – This is an Italian and Mediterranean restaurant with very good food and service. It is located at Hippodrome Boulevard # 605 in the heart of the city. You will find that seafood, vegetarian and vegan dishes are all part of the menu along with excellent pasta dishes. The surroundings are quite pleasing and very relaxing. They are open Monday thru Friday from noon to 2:30 PM and Saturday from 7 AM to 11PM. Reservations are accepted by calling 503 2528 4200 to book a table.

* Los Balcones – This is a popular restaurant noted for its consistent quality and good service. It is located at kilometer 40.5 on the Autopista Aeropuerto Internactional just outside of the capital. Seafood and traditional Salvadoran dishes combine to provide diners with a good taste of the country. The restaurant also serves vegetarian and vegan dishes as well. The service at lunch is buffet style and you have quite a bit of variety from which to choose. They are open from 5 AM to 10 PM daily.

The cathedral in Sonsonate, (Work of JosueArguera, CC BY SA 3.0, Wikimedia.org)

FINAL WORDS: The majority of those who read this book will not visit El Salvador. But for those who do have that rare opportunity, I trust you will appreciate that this small country is still in recovery mode after its brutal civil war. With many problems to overcome, especially grinding poverty, drug smuggling and infrastructure that needs to be built, whatever you see should be accepted at face value. You are being given an opportunity to be at the forefront of what hopefully will be a tourism revolution in the future.

VISITING GUATEMALA

A map of Guatemala, (CIA)

Over the past few years Guatemala has made newspapers and television in North America and Europe with regard to the high rate of violence perpetrated against the peasant population by both the military and drug cartels, giving the impression that it is not safe for visitors. This impression would hold true for any tourist wanting to explore the backwater areas of the country. But as a cruise ship passenger, you most likely will take part in an organized motor coach and/or walking tour or you will have a private car and driver for your visit. I have been to Guatemala numerous times by ship and although I prefer going out on my own, I refrained and instead took ship tours, still coming away with a good understanding of the country on each visit. Even when on a group tour, you will have some free time in Antigua, Lake Atitlán or Tikal, these being the three main destinations for group tours. And in these major destinations you will be totally safe.

THE LANDSCAPE: Guatemala is a much larger country than Costa Rica, having 108,888 square kilometers or 42,042 square miles. Its population is over 15,800,000. By comparison it is about the size of the European nation of Austria or Hungary with its population being slightly below that of the Netherlands.

Along the edge of the Guatemalan Central Highlands

Guatemala is located south of Mexico and shares also shares borders with Belize, Honduras and El Salvador. It has a small window of coastline on the Caribbean, but its major coast is along the Pacific.

Cruise ships stop in Puerto Quetzal, a commercial port located on the Pacific Coast Plain, giving easy access to the historic colonial city of Antigua or the capital of Guatemala City. There is a local airport that provides charter flights to the far north of the country for one day visits to the ancient Maya ruins of Tikal. Other one-day trips are made by motor coach from Puerto Quetzal to the active volcanoes you see on the horizon, to Antigua or Lake

Atitlán. And some upmarket cruise lines will also offer a tour by air to Copan, another ancient Maya ruin, but this one being across the border in Honduras.

The physical environment of Guatemala consists of a narrow Pacific coastal plain, a major highland region that consists of high volcanic mountains with very fertile intervening valleys similar to that of Costa Rica, but only much more expansive. To the north, and occupying about 40 percent of the landmass is the relatively flat limestone plain of the Yucatan, which extends on into México to form a large peninsula that juts into the Gulf of México.

Guatemala is geologically a volatile land that is wracked by frequent earthquakes and volcanic eruptions. In 2018, a major volcanic eruption of Volcan Fuego nearly severed the road between Puerto Quetzal and Antigua. The core of the country straddles a major plate boundary between the North American and Caribbean Plates, gigantic blocks of the earth's crust. A third plate, called Cocos, lies off the south coast in the Pacific Ocean. It is subducting below the Caribbean Plate, creating the country's many active volcanoes. The highest mountain in all of Central America is Volcan Tajumulco at over 4,220 meters or 13,845 feet above sea level. There are also several deep lakes, each filling a volcanic caldera, set amid the volcanic field, the most famous being Lake Atitlán. The scenic beauty of the lake and its surrounding volcanoes belies the potential for a catastrophic event in the near future. Past cataclysmic events have destroyed Antigua and Guatemala City, and the danger looms on the horizon for the future.

Northern Guatemala is flat, covered in a stunted forest or woodland and lacks flowing rivers because it is underlain by limestone that acts as a giant sponge. Yet it was here that the once mighty Maya civilization once flourished. Northern Guatemala is also within the path of potential hurricanes and has seen its share of such disasters.

A BRIEF HISTORY: It is vital to appreciate the history of Guatemala to enable you to fully grasp the significance of the various sights you may see depending upon what tour you choose. This is a nation steeped in Pre-Colombian history followed by a long Spanish colonial heritage.

Guatemala was once home to the Maya civilization, which grew out of long occupancy dating back to over 14,000 years. No matter where you will visit other than if you choose to climb one of the volcanic peaks (offered by some cruise lines) you will be exposed to some aspect of the country's history. Civilization is believed to have begun around 5,500 years ago, but it was the Maya who reached the greatest heights of architectural and scientific development around 2,000 years ago. Maya influence spread throughout the highlands and the Yucatan Peninsula. Many traditions are so much a part of today's Guatemalan villagers that many of their cultural practices continue.

The Spanish began to explore south from central México and by the early 1520's, Guatemala became an important province of New Spain. Between 1520 and 1541, the capital had to move twice because prior settlements were devastated by native attacks, earthquakes or floods. Finally Antigua became the capital, but it too was heavily devastated in 1773 and 1774 by earthquakes, finally forcing a third move to what is today Guatemala City.

Acatenango Volcano near Antigua with a mild eruption of steam

Antigua had been the capital long enough to have developed magnificent colonial architecture, and despite rebuilding after the last major earthquake, it still has managed to retain its historic importance. Today Antigua is a UNESCO World Heritage Site.

Guatemala led the independence movement in 1821 that united the former provinces into the Central American Federation, but it dissolved by 1840 after civil war had erupted in most of the member provinces. Internally Guatemala then went through decades of dictatorship and revolution.

In 1871, under the leadership of Justo Rufino Barrios, the country began to modernize, develop a road infrastructure and manufacturing. Like Costa Rica, first coffee and then bananas became important commercial crops. And later United Fruit Company was very instrumental in maintaining Manuel Estrada Cabrera as dictator for 22 years until 1920.

From July through October 1944 the country was in turmoil by the ousting of one dictator, replaced by a general and then by a military junta. Finally the first freely elected president, Juan Bermejo, managed to stay in office for his full term, reforming the government and improving the lives of workers. Jacobo Guzmán then succeeded him in 1951, and he brought about significant land reforms. However, the next government was overthrown by a coup d'état promulgated by the American CIA, fearing that the new President Árbenz was a socialist. This was at a time when the United States was frantic in its fears over Communism. In 1954, General Armas, with CIA aid, invaded from Honduras, but it did not take long for him to be assassinated in 1957. The next president still had American support, and he was instrumental in providing an airstrip for the ill-fated Bay of Pigs invasion of Cuba in 1961 and the training of 5,000 anti-Castro forces on Guatemalan soil.

If you are starting to question how Guatemala has survived to the present day, the story deepens before it improves. The government of Ydígoras-Fuentes did not last long. The next coup was led by the Defense Minister in 1963 after the failed Bay of Pigs fiasco. This coup also had American backing, and it led to a terror campaign former President Ydígoras-Fuentes.

The baroque cathedral in Antigua

In 1966, free elections were held and the new president was left leaning so rightist groups formed paramilitary units that received open assistance and training from the United States Army. Chaos again reigned. The 1970 presidential election was contested and several guerrilla groups began to develop footholds in many rural areas. In 1974, the election was once again disputed. This led to much tension and instability. The final blow came in 1975 when Mother Nature intervened with a massive earthquake that killed over 25,000 people and severely damaged the infrastructure. Many of the deaths in and around the capital were from substandard housing that simply crumbled. The government did little to aid the people, which only created more unrest, and this was further enhanced by a fraudulent election in 1978. In 1982, after a brutal attack by guerrilla forces on the Spanish Embassy, met by equally strong government response, the government was overthrown.

You still see village poverty en route to Antigua

The military take over the country in 1982, but conditions for the people do not improve. The government uses torture, murder and village burning to root out guerrilla groups, essentially terrorizing the whole nation. The guerrilla groups merge into a single force and conditions for ordinary people become so bad that thousands of peasants flee into southern México for safety, even obtaining Mexican assistance in their plight.

Finally in 1986, a successful coup brought about a new constitution and free elections, but the civil war between the guerrilla groups and the government did not end until 1996. Both sides were assigned equal blame for the violence and abuse during this long period of strife.

The brutality began as an offensive against the intellectual class, but in the end it turned into ethnic persecution against the Maya who make up a good share of the rural population. As many as 250,000 peasants are believed to have died while a further 1,000,000 were displaced and many hundreds of villages were destroyed. Many Guatemalans blame the United States from the early 1950's until the early 1980's for fanning flames of brutality in its attempt to keep Communism at bay. President Clinton finally acknowledged this fact during his administration.

This brief, but rather difficult to read section shows you how tragic life in Guatemala has been since the 1950's. Only now is the country starting to develop some semblance of an infrastructure and democratic elections. But drug violence has started to take a toll on the rural population in particular, as Guatemala has a favored environment for raising marijuana and coca. Yet some degree of manufacturing in Guatemala City and Puerto Quetzal are helping take advantage of a keen labor force and the use of local raw materials.

After reading this historic sketch, many of you may be saying that if your itinerary includes a stop in Guatemala you will stay on board. I hope that would not be the case because as a tourist traveling in a group or on your own with a private car and driver, you will be quite safe. Even if you use your free time in Antigua or at Lake Atitlán to walk around on your own, you will be well received by the locals and not be in any danger. The drug lords and their thugs do not target foreign tourists, especially in the major venues such as Antigua, the national parks or in Guatemala City. So please enjoy your brief visit to Guatemala.

PUERTO QUETZAL AND INLAND: You will be presented with many options for your port of call in Puerto Quetzal. Please take advantage of the chance to explore a beautiful country steeped in a rich history. If you stay on the ship or just wander around the cruise terminal and marketplace, you will have wasted a day that could be well spent.

* TOURING OPTIONS: As in Costa Rica you do have similar options not only in the various tour venues, but in your means of travel. Given the long history of violence and the present problems with localized drug violence, I recommend that you either go on a ship sponsored tour or have the ship's travel desk arrange a private car and driver/guide.

I do not recommend that you hire a local taxi in Puerto Quetzal even if one is available. This is a remote port that is far from any significant city or town. And there is a degree of personal risk in going out for the day not knowing the credentials of the driver or condition of the vehicle.

Attempting to rent a car or van and drive on your own is very risky. The lack of roadside services and the man potential hazards should negate this option. And not knowing the country and its people could put you at risk of becoming a victim of crime.

* TOUR DESTINATIONS: There is absolutely nothing to see in Puerto Quetzal or in the immediate vicinity. The tours offered by your ship or that you can arrange through the cruise line will mostly involve one to two or more hours of driving to reach the venues of importance. To visit the Maya ruins of Tikal or Copan will involve a group charter flight from Puerto Quetzal. Tikal is in the far north of Guatemala with the flight on a chartered prop aircraft taking close to two hours. Copan is in neighboring Honduras and the flight will also take approximately 90 minutes.

** VISITING ANTIGUA: A visit to Antigua is the major cultural highlight of a port call in Puerto Quetzal. The drive takes a bit over an hour, and the route takes the motor coach between two of the country's most notoriously active volcanic peaks – Fuego and Agua. Fuego is the more active, most recently creating havoc in 2018. A third peak known as Acatenango lies to the south and you will see it before seeing the other two. And Acatenango often puts out puffs of steam or ash almost on an hourly basis. There is always the chance for a significant eruption of any of these peaks, which could suddenly alter your plans. But more than likely it will be a calm day with magnificent scenery to hold your interest.

Volcan Fuego towers above Antigua, as does Volcan Agua

The city of Antigua sits in a round bowl flanked by these massive volcanic peaks. As the capital of Guatemala from 1541 to 1774, it developed magnificent churches, public architecture and palatial homes. Even though the great 1773 earthquake destroyed much, many buildings did survive while others were later restored. The city has always remained steeped in its historic charm. Today with its UNESCO World Heritage Site status it is thriving as a major tourist destination. A significant number of expatriate American, Canadian and British retirees have chosen to buy property in Antigua because of its great appeal to those who love Spanish colonial architecture.

A full day tour to Antigua is a great way to learn about the richness of Guatemala's history and engage in a visual experience that is very memorable. Lunch is generally provided at one of the two resort hotels, occupying former monasteries or government buildings.

Antigua is laid out in a grid with a central plaza being the focal hub. The main cathedral and the civic administrative palace occupy two sides of the plaza. The richness of the historic architecture permeates all of the streets of Antigua with many small churches and plazas dotting the city. Inner Antigua contains the traditional adobe walled compounds where the residences face interior courtyards and have few windows facing outward to the street. Most of the streets are cobbled and this will make you feel like you have entered a time warp. There is a definite sense of "magic" to the aura of Antigua and it is a city where photographers cannot resist clicking away. Street life is very colorful and genuine, not put on for show to give the tourists their thrill. This is a genuine working city, but one where life is played out amid historic structures.

El Arco is a clock tower with centuries of history behind it

If you wish to photograph local people in a more close up manner, something that is hard to resist because of the overall color of the city, it is fine to do so but please first ask the individual if you can take their picture. If you do not know any Spanish just point to your camera and to the person you wish to photograph and smile. Most often the gesture will be rewarded. It is expected that you will give them a tip, and the accepted rate is 25 Quetzales, which would be equal to three American Dollars. And they will accept dollars or Euro.

Most tours to Antigua generally involve driving around the city to point out the major highlights followed by a group walking tour where your guide will visit the central plaza, El Arco, the old clock tower, the main cathedral and the government palace or city hall.

One of the important sites is the great cathedral that was devastated by the earthquake in 1773 that resulted ultimately in Guatemala City being chosen to replace Antigua as the colonial capital. In essence that was a premature move since Guatemala City is just as prone to earthquake danger as is Antigua. But had Antigua remained the capital, it would have ultimately become the major city and much of its colonial heritage would have been lost.

You may also visit one of the gem and mineral shops or weavers to watch demonstrations of local crafts. And the Casa Santo Domingo Hotel grounds also include an early set of monastic buildings that are today set aside as a museum.

Depending upon the cruise line, you will have a nice lunch in Antigua, most often at the Casa Santo Domingo Hotel or another comparable venue. For the benefit of those of you who are visiting Antigua with a car and driver or whose tour does not include lunch, I will have recommendations later in this chapter.

The governmental palace decorated with purple banners for Easter

*** MUST SEE VENUES IN ANTIGUA: Casa Santo Domingo Museum – The Casa Santo Domingo Hotel is incorporated with a set of history museums that chronicle the role of the Catholic church and the importance of silver mining in the growth of Antigua. There are several individual museum sectors, silver, glass, pottery, Mayan archaeology and colonial history. The museums are open to the public all day, but no specific hours are shown.

**** Cerro de la Cruz – This high vantage point topped by a crucifix offers fantastic views out over Antigua with the two great volcanoes of Agua and Fuego forming a dramatic backdrop. If time permits, a view near sunset is most dramatic.

**** ChocoMuseo – In town at 4a Calle Oriente, this small museum presents the history of cacao and the making of chocolate, the gift from Central America to the world. The museum is quite fascinating. It is open daily from 10 AM to 6:30 PM remaining open until 7:30 PM on Friday and Saturday.

**** Iglesia de la Merced – This magnificent yellow church was first built in 1548 but nearly destroyed in the great earthquake of 1773, but rebuilt and strengthened. It is almost as important to the people as the main cathedral. It is a classic example of Spanish colonial baroque design and said to possibly be the largest church in Central America.

Iglesia de la Merced, (Work of Raymond Osterlag, CC BY SA 2.5, Wikimedia.org)

**** Iglesia de San Francisco el Grande – On Calle Oriente, this is one of the largest of the old churches of Antigua, but it was left in ruins after the great earthquake of 1773. Today it stands as a stark reminder of the forces of nature underlying the central highland region of Guatemala. Visits to the interior are not permitted, as it is too fragile.

*** DINING OUT IN ANTIGUA: If you are in Antigua on your own or if your tour does not include lunch, I am providing several choices for traditional Guatemalan cuisine, but in restaurants that meet the highest in standards for quality and cleanliness. My choices are shown alphabetically:

**** Casa Escobar Restaurante – Located at #6 Avenida Norte 2, this is essentially a steakhouse, but one with a distinctive Guatemalan atmosphere, serving in local tradition. The cuisine, atmosphere and service are all outstanding. They are open daily from 7 AM to 10 PM and reservations are accepted by calling +502 3248 1675

163

Many tour lunches will be at Casa Santo Domingo Hotel in their outdoor courtyard

**** El Refectorio – At 3a Calle Oriente #28, this is a delightful restaurant serving traditional Guatemalan cuisine that is beautifully prepared. The atmosphere is especially elegant with a distinct Old World charm. They are open daily from 7 AM to 10 PM and reservations are not needed.

**** La Casa de los Sopas – This is a very traditional Guatemalan restaurant serving many local dishes, including a variety of delightful soups. They specialize in caldos or soup type stews and use only the freshest ingredients. They are open daily from Noon to 10 PM and reservations are not needed.

**** Quilitro – This is considered to be one of the finest restaurants in Guatemala, known for its traditional cuisine served in a beautiful environment with impeccable service. The menu is a fine example of what Guatemala can offer, and it does include vegetarian entrees. Hours are Sunday from Noon to 3 PM, Tuesday and Wednesday from 4:30 to 9 PM, Thursday and Friday from 1:30 to 9 PM, Saturday from 1 to 9 PM. Reservations are advised by calling to book at +502 7832 3461.

*** SHOPPING IN ANTIGUA: Antigua is a good shopping destination if you are looking for silver jewelry, Guatemalan jade and hand woven items. The quality can be quite excellent if you compare goods, but your time will be limited if on a group tour. Some tours do include a visit to the jade museum and workshop, which is quite interesting and popular among those who wish to make a significant purchase.

My recommendations are as follows, shown alphabetically:

**** Colibe – This fine arts and crafts shop is found at Avenida 4a Calle Oriente #38 and open daily from 9 AM to 6 PM. They offer a wide assortment of traditional woven wares and other quality Guatemalan craft items.

**** Nim Po't Centro de Textiles Tradiciones – Located at Avenida 5a Norte #29, this is a major warehouse type shop that features outstanding woven wares and other Guatemalan crafts. The woven wares of Guatemala are especially colorful and use a mix of commercial and vegetable dyes with the styles dating to Maya times. They are open from 9 AM to 9 PM with extended closing at 10 PM on Friday and Saturday.

The diversity and color of Guatemalan handcrafts

**** Oriental Jade Factory and Museum – This is often a designated tour stop. It is located in the town center at Avenida 4a Oriente #24. The jade demonstration and lecture are worth watching even if you do not make a purchase. They are open daily from 9 AM to 6:30 PM.

** VISITING GUATEMALA CITY: It is rare for a cruise line to offer a motor coach tour to Guatemala City even though the capital is only 30 minutes beyond Antigua. When you compare the beauty and historic charm of Antigua with the bustle, congestion and air pollution of Guatemala City, it is not a very pleasant or exciting option. For anyone with a private car and driver I would not suggest you visit Guatemala City unless you have some specific personal reason for wanting to tour the city. The traffic congestion in this major city of over 2,100,000 makes sightseeing rather difficult in the short time that would be available after factoring in the travel time there and back. As a major urban center, most of the historic architecture has either been destroyed or is overshadowed by the growing city where much of the landscape is covered in rather unattractive barrios. Therefore I am not offering any recommendations as to sightseeing, dining or shopping.

Guatemala City from the hills showing a haze of air pollution

** VISITING LAGO DE ATITLÁN: The smaller upmarket cruise lines often will offer a full day motor coach tour to Lago de Atitlán, one of the most beautiful sights in Guatemala. This is a long and somewhat tiring tour, but if you enjoy spectacular landscapes combined with culture and history, it is worth considering this tour, if it is offered. The drive is 142 kilometers or 88 miles each way not counting travel distances around the lake. The approximate drive time is just over two hours each way.

Lago de Atitlán is a large and very deep lake with a dark blue color that fills an ancient volcanic caldera. It is rimmed by several towering volcanic peaks and offers an exceptionally dramatic image. The lake is surrounded by numerous traditional villages where the local inhabitants are for the most part of Mayan descent. Without question, the lake and its villages produce the most photogenic landscape in all of Guatemala.

Most full day motor coach journeys to the lake are combined with a motorized launch trip to the most beautiful village of Panajachel, which enables you to savor both the natural and cultural flavors of the countryside.

Not every cruise line will offer this trip because given the distance and infrastructure involved in creating the tour itinerary, it is quite a costly outing. The five-star cruise lines such as Silversea, Seabourn and Regent generally do offer this tour.

Majestic Lago de Atitlán, (Work of Francisco Anzola, CC BY SA 2.0, Wikimedia.org)

If you do happen to be on one of the five-star ships and decide upon this tour, keep in mind that it involves a rather tedious drive on relatively narrow roads through mountainous countryside. But you will be rewarded with incredible scenery and a chance to explore the living Mayan culture of the country. I am not offering any dining or shopping venues because such tours are totally planned and you will not have the flexibility to make your own discoveries. As for going by private car and driver I would recommend against it. The organized tour is a superior option because the tour operator will have coordinated the motor launch, afternoon lunch and guide services well in advance.

** VISITING TIKAL NATIONAL PARK: Tikal is one of the three greatest archaeological sites in the Western Hemisphere. It is an ancient Maya city from the classical period when the culture was at its very peak. It is located in the far north of Guatemala over 600 kilometers or 370 miles by road. The journey would be impossible by motor coach, and would take over 11 hours. Thus the only way to have a full day excursion is to travel by chartered aircraft, normally a turbo prop. Even that flight takes about 90 minutes and you must add to that approximately an additional 30 minutes at each end by motor coach, which adds up to a total travel time of 3.5 hours. A tour to Tikal is essentially a full day event, and it always includes lunch as part of the excursion. It is impossible to take this journey on your own with a car and driver given the distance and the travel time factor. Even if you are not in favor of group tours, there is no alternative.

Tikal became the center of administration for one of the largest and most powerful of the ancient Maya states. Its grand buildings still rise to impressive heights. The largest temple stands over 46 meters or 150 vertical feet in height, the top reached by a very steep staircase. There are numerous temple pyramids and imposing buildings presently reclaimed and restored, giving this site an incredible appearance. Guatemala has designated Tikal as a national park and it has received UNESCO World Heritage Site status.

A view over part of Tikal, (Work of KimonBerlin, CC BY SA 2.0, Wikimedia.org)

Tikal's period of greatness lasted for around two centuries, and it is believed to have been conquered by the ancient city of Teotihuacan in the central valley of Mexico during the 5th century. The new rulers were ultimately absorbed culturally and the city continued to be a major center of power until sometime in the 9th century.

*** COMFORT ON YOUR VISIT: If you are planning on a visit to Tikal from the ship you need to be aware of the travel time of tropical heat and humidity, as it is located in the Yucatan Peninsula at low elevation, thus being especially uncomfortable for anyone not accustomed to the combination of heat and humidity. You will be walking several kilometers or miles, climbing many stairs and exerting a lot of energy, so if you are not in very good physical shape, this is not a tour for you. Also make note that the flight in a turbo prop aircraft over the high mountains of central Guatemala can be quite bumpy to downright turbulent depending upon weather conditions on the day of your visit.

You will be in the company of a guide during your visit, and that is essential because simply wandering about the ruins is rather meaningless. Knowing what it is you are looking at makes the entire experience meaningful.

Lunch will be provided. Do not expect a gourmet meal, but the lunch will be well presented and you do not need to worry about the sanitary conditions around its preparation. Just to play safe, do not eat any raw vegetables, salad or fruits that you have not peeled yourself. It is quite easy to contract dysentery in this hot and humid region.

There is a gift shop within the national park. You will be given some time to purchase souvenirs and some native crafts locally produced. Actual artifacts of Pre Colombian origin cannot be legally sold. Thus beware of vendors who try to entice you to buy what they claim are genuine artifacts.

** VOLCANO CLIMB: For those with plenty of energy and who are in great condition most cruise lines will offer a climb of Volcan Pacaya near Antigua. This can be quite an arduous, yet exciting experience. Most cruise lines will have organized this to our to include climbing the volcano. Whether the tour is actually offered on your specific itinerary is dependent upon the level of volcanic activity of the mountain, as all guides are cognizant of the need to keep their guests safe.

Most tours to climb Pacaya do not include a lunch stop and many guests have the ship's dining facilities pack them a small box lunch. Likewise there are no shopping venues near the mountain, but on occasion the tour will take you via Antigua where a brief stop may be permitted.

** SHORT LOCAL TOURS: It is not possible to point out every possibility with regard to short localized tours, as each cruise line has its specific local personnel who arrange for short three to four hour excursions close to Puerto Quetzal. I have listed below those that I have been made aware of during the past five years by the various cruise personnel with whom I interact.

*** Auto Safari Chapin: This safari park gives animal lovers an opportunity to see much of the native wildlife of Guatemala as well as African game animals in a more natural setting than an urban zoo. The park is located just northeast of Puerto Quetzal about a 30 minute drive by motor coach. This is a drive through zoo where you can observe the animals in their habitat from close range. The park is open Tuesday thru Sunday from 9:30 AM to 5 PM and can be visited on your own if you have arranged for a car and driver.

*** Coffee Plantation Visit: There are several local coffee plantations in the lower foothills of the highland region that are within an hour or less driving time from Puerto Quetzal. With the many volcanoes along the length of the central highland region the soil is rich in nutrients. which when combined with the higher altitude is excellent for the raising of fine quality coffee. Such a visit is often combined with a coffee tasting and a chance to buy some coffee from the plantation you are visiting.

Volcan Pacaya, (Work of Librex, CC BY SA 2.0, Wikimedia.org)

** Visiting a Macadamia nut farm: The Macadamia nut is originally from the Hawaiian Islands and is one of their most popular tropical nut exports. However, in the foothills of Guatemala the conditions are comparable and the nuts are now being raised. A visit to such a plantation is interesting and at least a chance for those not wanting to do anything too strenuous a chance to get out into the local countryside.

FINAL WORDS: In conclusion I wish to remind my readers that you plan to attend one of the excursions your cruise line is offering. There is absolutely nothing for visitors to do in Puerto Quetzal, as this is an industrial port. Yes there is a small visitor's center and local artisans will be displaying their wares for sale, but you will have a long day ahead of you if you do nothing but stay around the ship.

MÉXICO AS A NATION

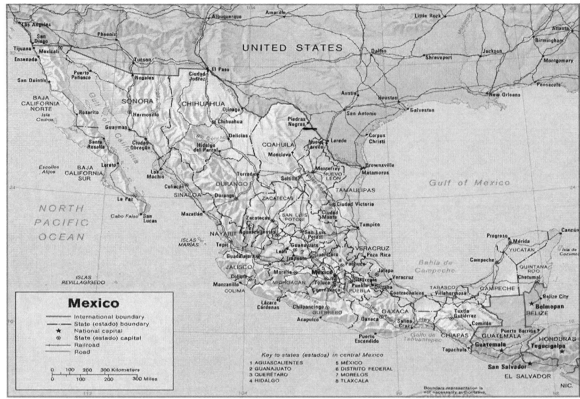

A map of México (CIA)

México is the largest Latin American nation in North America in both land area and population. It is also the largest Spanish speaking nation in the world, and a major political leader within the Latin American sphere of influence. The physical size of México is exaggerated by its elongated shape that gives one the feeling of the country being so much larger in scope than its square kilometer or mile size indicates. México extends over 1,972,560 square kilometers or 761,606 square miles. To travel by air from Tijuana in the far northwest corner to Cancún on the Caribbean coast of the Yucatan Peninsula by road is 4,377 kilometers or 2,720 miles.

México's estimated population is approximately around 130,000,000. No true accurate figures can be more specific, as there are so many millions of peasants in small villages and on farms or ranches that do not get properly counted. The capital city properly known as Ciudad de México (Mexico City) is believed to be in excess of 20,000,000, making it the largest city in the Western Hemisphere.

Your cruise will make several stops in México during its Pacific coast transit between Los Angeles and the Panama Canal. The majority of cruise ships will stop in Acapulco, Puerto Vallarta and Cabo San Lucas at the very least. Depending upon the length of your cruise and the line you are traveling on, other common stops are Puerto Chiapas, Zihuatanejo/Ixtapa, Manzanillo, Mazatlan and Ensenada. Some of the high end cruise lines may offer overnight or two night excursions by air to Ciudad de México or Guadalajara, leaving from one port and returning to the next one either north or south depending upon your ultimate destination. Because México will play such an important role in your overall cruise, it is important to have some geographic and historic background on this dynamic, yet troubled country where a rich and vibrant history and culture is today being submerged by the ongoing news stories about drug violence and massive immigration northward into the United States.

México is a Catholic country where the church figures prominently in daily life

TRAVELING IN MÉXICO: Among Americans and Canadians, México is a country that is familiar to millions because of its popularity as a tourist destination. The majority of the North American visitors, however, tend to patronize the beach resorts that have developed an infrastructure catering to their tastes. Visitors from the eastern state or provinces favor visiting the beaches of Cancún or Cosumel. For those living in the western states or provinces it is the Pacific resorts that are most often patronized, such as Cabo San Lucas, Mazatlan and Puerto Vallarta. Up until the 1980's, Acapulco was the most favored beach resort, but it has become a big city and has lost its luster. Fewer North Americans visit the cities in the interior and that is a shame because the rich tapestry of Mexican history unfolded in the great cities of the Central Plateau. And that is where you find the true Mexican heritage.

The news media has in recent years put quite a scare into North American visitors through their ongoing coverage of the drug cartels and the violence they have wrought upon the country. There is no denying that such violence exists, and that the Mexican authorities have been hard pressed to gain the upper hand. Thousands of innocent people have been

terrorized and/or killed in the last ten years in many regions of the country bordering the United States. But if you look closely at the statistics, it has been rare for visitors to be caught up in these incidents. When traveling in México on your own, or even if you venture away from the ship on your own, here are the important tips that can make a difference between a safe visit and ending up becoming a victim:
* Never enter the poor barrios or market areas without being accompanied by a guide.
* Never walk down dark or narrow streets on your own.
* Do not dress in an ostentatious manner or wear jewelry or watches when out on your own.
* Keep your camera or handbag close to your body.
* Do not count out large sums of money in public.
* Only use reputable taxis that have been called for in advance by a hotel or restaurant.
* Do not walk alone at night.

Having a working knowledge of Spanish is very helpful, especially in creating an atmosphere of confidence when you are off on your own. During the course of the cruise while in México you are best off taking ship sponsored tours or using cars and drivers arranged through the cruise line or known agents.

THE PHYSICAL LANDSCAPE: A brief description of the physical components of the Mexican landscape is necessary to help set each port of call within its proper context relative to rest of the nation. México is large and diverse, especially in its north to south extent. The north has deserts, high snow-capped mountains and rugged canyons. The Central Plateau is capped by large volcanic peaks and has mild grasslands and woodlands and the south is lush and tropical.

The rich landscapes of Guerrero in the Sierra Madre Occidental

* CENTRAL PLATEAU: This is the heartland of México, and it straddles the Tropic of Cancer, having a mild climate despite its location. Altitudes of most towns and cities are between 1,830 and 2,440 meters or 6,000 and 8,000 feet with the highest volcanic peak as high as 4,920 meters or 16,140 feet.

Pico de Orizaba, highest in México, (Work of Veto Zereptram, CC BY SA 3.0, Wikimedia.org)

* SIERRA MADRE OCCIDENTAL AND ORIENTAL: These two great mountain ranges mark the western and eastern edges of the Central Plateau. They are rugged and difficult to traverse, serving as magnificent landscape backdrops to thousands of villages and farms. On the western flanks of the Sierra Madre Occidental is the Barranca del Cobre, one of the world's greatest canyon complexes. Peaks can rise to over 3,050 meters or over 10,000 feet.

* TRANSVERSE VOLCANIC RANGE: This range runs east to west across the middle of México at the southern margin of the Central Plateau. It contains the highest mountains in the country, including Pico de Orizaba towering over 5,636 meters or 18,491 feet. Many of these snow covered giants are still active and from time to time do threaten the country's major cities.

 BAJA CALIFORNIA RANGES: A series of mountain ranges run the length of the Baja California Peninsula, approximately 1,600 kilometers or 1,000 miles, with a maximum height of 3,096 meters or 10,157 feet. Despite their high elevations they are essentially dry and almost barren except for pockets of pine forest at their highest elevations. This is because the Baja California Peninsula is primarily a desert region as a result of its latitude and the cold ocean current washing its shores.

The arid landscapes of Baja California extend right to the seashore, as seen here outside of Cabo San Lucas

* SIERRA MADRE SUR: This collection of ranges extends from the Transverse Volcanic Range all the way into Central America, and it is in the high intervening valleys and plateaus that the majority of the people live because of the cooler and milder conditions in these southern tropical latitudes.

* YUCATAN PENINSULA: As noted in the chapter on Guatemala, the great Yucatan Peninsula is a vast, flat limestone region with very little flowing water because the rock is so highly absorbent. The scrub tropical woodland covering the peninsula presents an almost endless sea of green. It was here that the great Maya civilization took root.

México is also quite vulnerable to natural disasters. Almost all of the country with the exception of its border region with the United States from Arizona to Texas is subject to the danger of earthquakes. This is a highly volatile land in which catastrophic events occur on a regular, but somewhat infrequent basis. The last major devastating earthquake occurred in 1984 when over 15,000 people died in a major event in Ciudad México.

Volcanic eruptions are another natural hazard, but they have tended to have less of an impact upon the population because the volcanos of México are not in locations where the pose an immediate threat to most cities, towns and farms. However, in 1943, Parícutin Volcano erupted out of a cornfield northwest of Ciudad de México and destroyed much of the immediate countryside. This was a major geological event because it was the first recorded volcanic event where humans witnessed and recorded the birth of a volcano.

Because of its size, elevational differences and the extent of the land from the mid latitudes into the tropics, the climates and life zones of México are so varied, giving the country an infinite variety of landscapes. From its northern deserts to its tropical rainforests and high semi-alpine valleys and plateaus, this is a country with a potential for great wealth in its resources. México has diverse agricultural zones, a rich and varied supply of minerals and fossil fuels and an abundance of natural timber. The country should be the most prosperous in Latin America. But like many of the other Latin American countries, rigid class systems, a great imbalance in the distribution of wealth and governmental corruption have combined to keep the majority of the populace in what can only be called peasant status while a handful of elite, well educated people control the power and wealth of the nation. And now add to this the role of the drug cartels and you can begin to see the many problems confronting a country that otherwise should be providing for all of its people.

A BRIEF MEXICAN HISTORY: The exciting and complex history of México could fill a volume many times the size of this travel book. Yet as a visitor who will be stepping off the ship in several Mexican ports of call, it is absolutely vital to have some understanding as to how this vast and potentially important nation came to be where it is today. It would therefore be a disservice to my readers if I were to ignore the history of México because so many of the excursions offered to you in each port are directly tied to sites that are of historic significance.

The Pre Colombian period of Mexican history alone could fill a volume. This land was the birthplace of several great civilizations that built one upon the other and their technological and artistic accomplishments diffused outward to influence native tribes thousands of kilometers or miles away. It is believed that the central valleys in the highlands are the birthplace of farming for North America. The domestication of maize, beans, squash, tomatoes, avocado and cacao were essential to the indigenous diet. And think of the impact these foods have had upon the world since having been taken back to Europe by the Spanish. In addition, native cotton, tobacco, wild turkey and many species of fish figured prominently into the food cultures of the continent.

Civilization has a long history in the Mexican highlands. There were several great nations that arose, flourished and then led into the next era generally through conquest. Names such as Olmec, Toltec and Aztec are familiar to anyone who has traveled in the central parts of the country, as ruins of these great nations are everywhere. And in the Yucatan Peninsula the Maya were the great society that contributed to the overall advancement in science and technology in the greater whole of México and Guatemala.

European history in México begins with Hernán Cortés landing on the Gulf Coast and marching his troops inland to ultimately capture the great Azteccapital of Tenochtitlan in 1519. Soon after conquest a new capital arose on the very foundations of Aztec pyramids and temples – Ciudad de México, today known worldwide as Mexico City. Today the capital is the largest city in population in the Western Hemisphere and among the ten largest cities in the world. It was from here that Spanish rule spread throughout the highlands, forcing native people into second class status and servitude while Spanish overlords became an elite ruling class. By 1600, Spanish rule extended as far north as what is now the United States when settlement was made along the upper Rio Grande at Santa Fe. Great mineral wealth in the form of gold, silver and copper flowed into Spanish hands and helped fuel the building of many magnificent cathedrals and government palaces still gracing Mexican landscapes to the present day.

Architectural reminders of the Spanish colonial heritage in Guadalajara

By 1921, the ordinary people reached the breaking point with Spanish rule and declared their independence, recognized by Spain as the Treaty of Córdoba. But México became mired in dictatorship after having established a constitution.

For three decades until the early 1850's, General Antonio López de Santa Ana ruled with an iron hand. He invited Americans to help settle the frontiers of Texas, but after reversing policies toward them, he precipitated rebellion in which Texas became an independent republic in 1836. But border conflicts with Santa Ana drove the Texans to join the American Union, ultimately precipitating the Mexican American War of 1846 over the recognition of the Rio Grande as the border between the two nations. The end of the war in 1848 under the Treaty of Guadalupe Hidalgo ceded more than half of the northern land area of México to the United States, including the riches of California.

When Santa Ana was defeated in 1854, the country had a succession of leaders, but they all were unable to govern successfully. Debt incurred by Santa Ana led México to borrowing heavily from France, which in 1862 prompted an armed invasion of the country to exact reparations on the unpaid amount. It was also in part the result of conservative forces wanting to establish a monarchy in which they would still hold great power, as in the Spanish colonial era.

The first popularly elected president, Benito Juárez fled to the far north where his supporters waged guerrilla warfare until they were able to overthrow the French and the upper elite class in 1867, capturing the pretender Emperor Maximilian and executing him. Benito Juárez was restored to power, and to this day he is celebrated as the father of the modern nation.

After Juárez died, nobody could match his hold upon the spirit of the people. The country was once more plunged into dictatorship under Porfirio Diaz whose rule despite being despotic did bring about economic stability and foreign investment. Despite economic gains, the majority of the people did not benefit. Ultimately the hand of Diaz became so heavy that people rebelled. The Mexican Revolution that begin in 1911 occurred after yet another fraudulent election. This revolution was quite brutal. Among the various revolutionary leaders Pancho Villa became the most infamous in the eyes of Americans because of his daring raid for munitions, which he lead across the border into Columbus, New Mexico. The American General Pershing chased Villa deep into the northern interior, but to no avail. In México he is seen as a great folk hero. Another revolutionary leader immortalized in a Hollywood movie was Emiliano Zapata. But lesser known to North Americans are the names of Alvaro Obregón and Francisco Madero, both later serving a term as president of the nation.

By 1928, many of the large estancias were broken up and given to groups of peasant farmers under what became known as the Ejido System. And by 1029, one political movement, Partido Revolucionario Institucional (PRI) emerged as the dominant political party controlling the government until the election of 2000.

During World War II, México supplied the United States with many valuable minerals and also with farm laborers under a guest worker program. This helped stabilize the Mexican economy, but still the nagging problem of rural poverty continued, especially with rapid increases in population resulting from better overall healthcare.

By the late 20th century, a combination of over population, ongoing governmental corruption and a growing trend toward drug violence encouraged more illegal immigration to the United States. This problem was exacerbated by the guest worker program having been drastically scaled back relative to the needs of the Mexican population. Both drug violence and illegal immigration reached record highs by the year 2000.

The rule of PRI ended in 2000 with the election of Vicente Fox of the opposition party known by its initials of PAN, Partido Acción Nacional. But 12 years of their rule did not bring great improvements, especially in the war against drugs. In 2012, PRI came back into power with its charismatic leader Enrique Peña Nieto, a handsome young man who pledged to bring about sweeping changes. But by the 2018 election, he fell far short of what had been promised. Now México is placing its hopes in Andrés Manuel López Obrador, a populist who pledges sweeping change. He won 53 percent of the popular vote with his rather leftist political movement known as MORENA, or Moviemiento Regeneración Nacional. Some analysts say this will bring the country into a state of political chaos, but only time will tell. The other major parties have certainly not accomplished anything this century to date.

The country has great potential if only governmental corruption and crime can be reined in. Tourism, which accounts for a large portion of the national income, has been drastically set back. And the immigration issue has done nothing but inflame the sentiments of the current American leadership. Hopefully this new Mexican populist movement will bring about the sweeping changes it proposes. Only time will tell.

PUERTO CHIAPAS

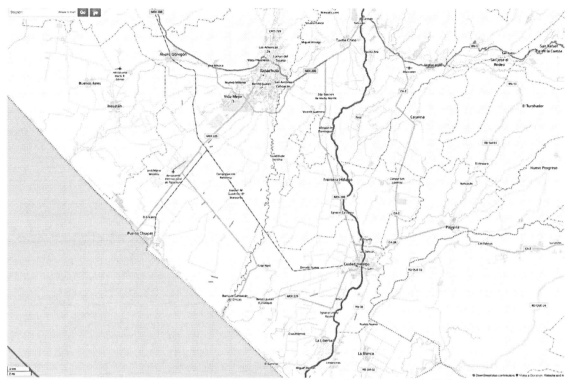

A map of the southern part of the Mexican state of Chiapas,
(© OpenStreetMap contributors)

Puerto Chiapas is a relatively new stop and in 2019 only 13 cruise itineraries included this port of call. Only Holland America, Norwegian, Princess, Seabourn, Silversea and Windstar offered this port on their schedule, with Holland America dominating with eight visits followed by Princess with two stops. Given many of the obstacles to touring around the state of Chiapas, I doubt if the popularity of this port will increase in the next few years.

Chiapas is the most southerly state of México, bordering on Guatemala. It has been a state beset by social and political upheaval throughout the late 20th century and so far into this century because of agitation from its predominantly native and mestizo population that has for over a century felt left out of Mexican political affairs and neglected when it comes to infrastructure development. Their grievances are real, as this state has been looked down upon by Mexican authorities as more of a nuisance than an integral part of the nation.

Puerto Chiapas is part of a program to correct the neglect and focus upon attracting tourism as one means of improving the economy. But it will take more than just the creation of a port to begin attracting cruise lines to consider stopping. One important consideration is the location being so far removed from the major Pacific ports of México that are popular tourist destinations. Puerto Chiapas is over 1,100 kilometers or 685 miles south of Acapulco and only ships that are sailing to or from the Panama Canal will be venturing that far south and making it a turnaround destination. Adding a stop in Puerto Chiapas adds one full day to a

Panama Canal transit itinerary, and for many cruise lines this means the elimination of one other stop to keep the itinerary at 16 days or less without raising the cost of the cruise.

The new port facility at Puerto Chiapas, (Work of APIMADERO, CC BY SA 3.0, Wikimedia.org)

THE LANDSCAPE: Chiapas is a beautiful state dominated over by high, volcanic mountains that are part of the Sierra Madre Sur that continue on into Guatemala. The southerly latitude gives these mountains a thick tropical rainforest cover, providing for lush landscapes with rushing rivers, waterfalls and magnificent vistas. The upland valleys between the high mountain ranges are the favored regions for settlement and it is here that the major towns and cities of Chiapas are found. And it is in this region of semi isolated valleys that there is a strong spirit of rebellion because of the level of poverty among the primarily indigenous and mestizo population.

The coastal region was also once covered in thick rainforest vegetation, but much of it has been destroyed to expand plantation agriculture and agriculture. Bananas are the important cash crop presently grown with a ready market along the Pacific Coast of both the United States and Canada. But the development of a tourist base with large resort hotels is doubtful given that the Yucatan Peninsula to the north is already the most heavily patronized beach property by tourists from the eastern United States and Canada. For residents in the American and Canadian west, there are so many Mexican resorts thousands of kilometers or miles closer in places like Cabo San Lucas, Mazatlan and Puerto Vallarta.

The far north of Chiapas extends into the southern margins of the Yucatan Peninsula and it is here that there are remnant sites of Maya origin plus the local residents are mainly of Maya descent. The most famous ruins are found at Palenque, comparable in many ways to those of Tikal in Guatemala. Most visitors to Palenque are flown in from northern resorts such as Cancun and Cosumel on the Caribbean coast.

Silversea's Silver Spirit docked in Puerto Chiapas, (Work of APIMADERO, CC BY SA 3.0, Wikimedia.org)

A BRIEF HISTORIC SKETCH: Of all 31 states and the Federal District of México Chiapas has the highest percentage of indigenous and mestizo residents, thus making it a region that always fell under the political heels of the government since Spanish colonial days. The national capital is located so far to the north in the Central Valley of México that in the minds of the leaders, Chiapas is a world apart. It has always been perceived of as a backward and less worthy of inclusion. Through the centuries, the people of Chiapas have resisted government officials and military personnel, rising up in arms on numerous occasions. Subjugation and rebellion are two recurring themes that describe Chiapas.

The mid 20th century was the most critical for Chiapas, as large numbers of refugees from political violence in Nicaragua, El Salvador and Guatemala flooded across the border. The Bishop of the diocese of Chiapas attempted to organize the various native tribal groups, and he received support from leftist groups. Ultimately all of this unrest culminated in 1994 when the Zapatistas, a militant grass roots revolutionary group, captured several villages within Chiapas and raided a local military camp for arms and munitions. Up until now despite armed conflicts, the government in Mexico City had been attempting to pacify the region by pouring in economic aid and establishing programs to better the lives of the locals. However, there came to be a standoff that survives to the present. The Zapatista movement is still alive and the government cannot seem to find a common ground with what the group wants. There seems to be no satisfying the vast majority in Chiapas. But at present the status quo is holding and tourism is starting to develop, which may give the locals more incentive to maintain the peace. This is the only one of the 31 states in México that is not committed to a unified nation. Yet the very notion of independence would only make Chiapas one more Central American country torn by drug violence, poverty and neglect. Independence would only present more fuel to the stream of immigrants flowing north toward the United States.

WHAT TO SEE AND DO OUT OF PUERTO CHIAPAS: Just as was the case in Puerto Quetzal, Guatemala, there is absolutely nothing to see or do in Puerto Chiapas. Your cruise line will offer several tours and it is imperative that you select one so that you will see something. Otherwise you can count upon a very boring day onboard with little to keep you occupied for more than an hour.

When your ship arrives at the dock, most cruise lines have pre booked musicians and dancers to perform in colorful costumes as a form of welcome, as this is your first Mexican port of call. There is a rather nice cruise terminal building and a helpful staff to answer questions and also assist you if you choose to go off on your own. And there is a bar and also a nice swimming pool at the cruise terminal.

* LOCAL SHUTTLE: Without any prearranged car and driver you can take a locally provided shuttle bus into the rather historic small city of Tapachula, which is less than half an hour away. But to simply wander around Tapachula on your own without a working knowledge of Spanish or any understanding of where you are is not all that rewarding and can be somewhat risky.

* LOCAL TAXI: As with the local shuttle, there are taxis available and you can negotiate an all day tour of the immediate region. There is a taxi desk outside the cruise terminal and generally the person on duty can assist you in your finding a driver with whom you might have a good day. But you are taking a chance as to the quality of the vehicle, the integrity of the driver and his ability to meet your needs. I have had good luck on one occasion and not been satisfied on the next visit, and keep in mind that I am fluent in Spanish. As for your safety, the cruise terminal personnel do only permit reputable drivers to offer services, so overall safety is not a major concern.

* PREARRANGED PRIVATE EXCURSIONS: Depending upon the relationship your cruise line has with any private tour operators in Chiapas, you may be able to prearrange a car and driver to take you on an excursion identical or similar to the motor coach tours being offered by your ship, or totally tailor something to your specific taste. These excursions are relatively costly, but I find them worthwhile. There is one reputable company that does offer private car and driver services across the country. And they claim to now include Puerto Chiapas. To see what you can arrange, visit them at *www.cruisingexcursions.com* and you may be satisfied.

* SIGHTS TO SEE FROM PUERTO CHIAPAS: The new cruise port is located just north of the border with Guatemala and is connected by a good highway to the city of Tapachula in the interior. The port was started in 1975 primarily for the shipping of bananas, coffee and to service the local fishing fleet. The cruise port opened in 2005 and it is slowly attracting more ships each year, but it is in no way a busy port facility. In a way this is good for you as a visitor because it makes the locals much more eager to please.

** PALENQUE: Not all cruise lines have the capability of offering a tour to Palenque because of the logistics involved. Palenque is in the far north of Chiapas and for a one day port call it requires coordinating a motor coach to Tapachula Airport, the flight to Palenque and then a motor coach to take guests to the Maya ruins that are among the finest in the country. Palenque is comparable to Tikal in Guatemala, as one of the finest examples of the architectural wonders created during the height of the Maya civilization. A tour to Palenque will be an all-day event and will include lunch.

A portion of Palenque, (Work of BIOLOGO JORGE AYALA, CC BY SA 4.0, Wikimedia.org)

** TAPACHULA: The city of Tapachula is relatively interesting. It has approximately 300,000 residents and serves as a regional market center, governmental hub and as the official port of entry for land traffic from Guatemala. There has been an increase in local crime because of the migrant crisis and drug traffic, but as a visitor you should not be bothered if you venture there on your own using the local shuttle. The setting for Tapachula is quite beautiful, as the city sits at the base of Volcan Tacaná, which looms over the urban environment. And the surrounding countryside is essentially a lush rainforest.

The local Palace of Culture in a very beautiful colonial building, (Work of Alejandro Beristain, CC BY SA 4.0, Wikimedia.org)

Among the few specific sites to visit in Tapachula you will find:

*** Planetary Cobach – In Tapachula you will find this small planetarium where they put on a show for visitors, treating you to a glimpse of Maya culture and also their knowledge of the stars. It is located on Avenida Paseo de los Cerritos but no specific hours are given.

*** Soconusco Archaeological Museum – Located in downtown Tapachula, this museum represents ancient artifacts representing the indigenous cultures of the region surrounding Tapachula dating back over the past 1,000 years. It is a tasteful museum that is quite amazing with regard to its archaeological finds. It is open Tuesday thru Sunday from 9 AM to 6 PM and there is a nominal entry fee.

*** Izapa Ruins – Just 11 kilometers or seven miles outside the city to the northwest is this small set of Maya ruins. The small set of ruins dates to approximately 1500 BCE, early in the expansion of the Maya to this southern region from the Yucatan Peninsula. The site is open daily from 9 AM to 5 PM and there is no entry fee.

Volcan Tacaná outside of Tapachula, (Work of eduardo robles, CC BY SA 2.0, Wikimedia.org)

*** DINING IN TAPACHULA: If you are touring on your own and wish to dine in the city, I have two recommendations as to nice restaurants with local cuisine served in a nice atmosphere. And both restaurants meet high standards of cleanliness. My choices are:

**** La Jefa – Located on Avenida Norte 1a Oriente, this is a highly respected Mexican restaurant serving dishes typical of Chiapas. The cuisine, service and atmosphere are all excellent and surprising for this more remote location. They serve from Noon to 8 PM Monday thru Saturday.

**** Tapachtlan – In the city center at Avenida 3a Avenida Sur # 19, this is a fashionable restaurant with a lovely atmosphere, serving both indoors and out on their patio. The menu is traditional and representative of Chiapas. Hours of service are Monday thru Saturday from 7 AM to 11 PM.

*** SHOPPING IN TAPACHULA: The downtown area offers a variety of shops that sell local handcrafted weavings, carvings and pottery items. Bargaining is expected, but be respectful in so doing and you can come away with some nice bargains. I have no specific recommendations, but I suggest you ask a representative in the cruise terminal if you are looking for quality local crafts. And you might check the wares of any locals who are displaying inside or on the grounds of the cruise terminal.

** TOURS IN THE LOCAL REGION: Your cruise line is sure to offer a sampling of shorter tours in the local area that range from four to six hours. Here is my most current listing of the types of tours you can expect to find.

*** Coffee Plantation – In the Sierra Madre Sur you will find a great number of coffee plantations because of the good volcanic soil and the humid tropical climate. Depending upon which plantation your cruise line has contracted with, the drive to the plantation chosen can take anywhere from one to two hours, but it gives you a chance to appreciate the local geography. Seeing how coffee is grown, harvested, dried and roasted gives you a whole new appreciation for the beverage so many of us cannot do without.

*** Mangrove Tour – The coast around Puerto Chiapas is heavily dominated by mangrove swamps that serve as home to numerous types of sea birds. Usually a mangrove tour is short, lasting three to four hours and gives you an opportunity to explore this important biome that will figure in saving many cities with rising seas as a threat.

*** Tuxtla Chico – This town in the Sierra Madre Sur is home to the processing of cacao, which is grown on plantations in the region. It is within an hour drive from the ship and in the shadow of Volcan Tacaná, presenting a superb setting. You will be able to see how cacao is turned into Mexican chocolate and also have the opportunity to both taste and buy some to bring home. Mexican chocolate is generally laced with cinnamon and is of outstanding quality.

FINAL WORDS: Puerto Chiapas has a long way to go before its regional infrastructure can handle a greater variety of offerings. What presently offered is diverse enough to appeal to most tastes. Keep in mind you are visiting a part of México that has been beset by many problems and one that has not been greatly favored by the central government. Yet surprisingly there are some historic gems such as Palenque and to a lesser degree Tapachula.

HUATULCO

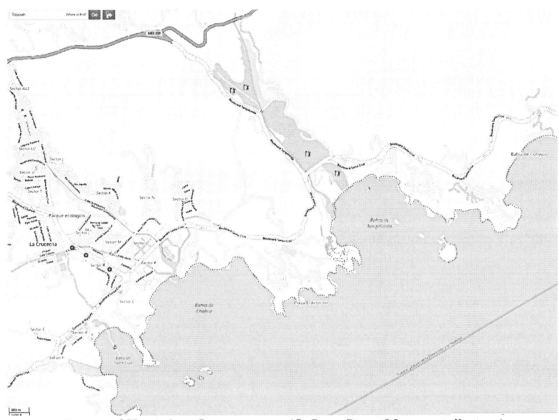

A map of Huatulco, Oaxaca area, (© OpenStreetMap contributors)

The coastal region of Bahias de Huatulco is located on the coast of the Mexican state of Oaxaca, approximately 496 kilometers or 308 miles from Acapulco. The state of Oaxaca is considered by many visitors to be the most historic and romantic state in México, famous for its strong indigenous cultures that are deeply rooted in the great civilizations of the past. And Oaxaca is also famed for its gastronomy, said to be the root of what we commonly call Mexican cuisine, strongly based upon native ingredients. And the state is also very well known in the art community for its fine quality woven ware, lacquered wood and pottery.

Tourism to Oaxaca is normally accomplished by flying into the state capital city of Oaxaca or by taking a motor coach tour and once arriving, then enjoying the local sights and gastronomy. The coast of the state is quite long, and three consecutive small bays that center upon the small town of La Crucecita have been gaining popularity as a hidden gem with regard to its beaches and scenery combined with the charm of its towns and villages.

Cruise ships are just discovering Huatulco, and for 2019, 41 port calls have been scheduled. The cruise lines currently stopping in Huatulco are Celebrity, Holland America, P & O, Phoenix Reisen, Princess, Royal Caribbean, Seabourn and Windstar. The number of port calls and the stature of the cruise lines visiting tells you that this is a port of call to take note of for the future. The majority of port calls are part of what are known as extended Mexican

Riviera cruises of up to two weeks in length, but a few port calls are part of a Panama Canal transit.

PHYSICAL LANDSCAPE: The coastline of Oaxaca is quite rugged and it is indented with numerous small bays, but does not offer up any major harbors. Parralel to the coast is the massive Sierra Madre del Sur, the block of mountains that extends south from the Sierra Transversal that run from coast to coast in the vicinity of Ciudad de México .

The interior of the state of Oaxaca is made up of mountain ranges and intervening valleys and it is where the state capital city of Oaxaca is located. By road it is 235 kilometers or 146 miles from Huatulco to the capital, a distance that does allow for full day motor coach excursions from the coast for cruise passengers.

The climate if Oaxaca is tropical, but tempered in most locations by elevation. Along the coast the summer heat is also ameliorated by cooling breezes from the ocean. Summer in Oaxaca is the rainy season, sometimes even exacerbated by hurricanes. Winter is the height of the tourist and cruise ship season.

Playa Santa Cruz, (Work of danielllerande, CC BY SA 3.0, Wikimedia.org)

There are three major bays that comprise the Huatulco area, the largest being Tangolunda, which is the middle bay. This is the upmarket resort bay where luxury hotel properties are to be found. To the west is the bay of Santa Cruz, which has docking facilities to accommodate one full size cruise ship. Adjacent to the east and separated by a narrow headland is the bay known as Chahué, which is more residential. The beach community of Santa Cruz merges with the larger interior town of La Crucecita.

Bahia Santa Cruz, (Work of Philippe Boulet, CC BY SA 3.0, Wikimedia.org)

The entire Huatulco region actually contains six more small bays along with over 35 beaches and stretches for over 25 kilometers or 16 miles, especially to the east of Tangolunda. Many of these beaches, which are essentially deserted, have excellent surf and are becoming frequented by surfing enthusiasts. Eventually this entire area will be developed with hotels, condominiums and homes, as more people discover the beauty of the region and its proximity to the city of Oaxaca. Fortunately the government has already set aside over 12,000 hectares or 29,650 acres as Parque Nacional Huatulco. It contains tropical lowland, beaches, headlands and most importantly some of the best examples of coral reefs in the hemisphere. This protected region will remain free of hotels or any form of development, which is a major step toward preservation.

A BRIEF LOCAL HISTORY: The rich fabric of history that is part of Oaxaca does not extend to any great degree to the Huatulco region. The great Mesoamerican civilizations were based upon farming and mining in the interior plateaus and valleys. They had little interest in the seacoast since they never developed any boatbuilding sophistication. It is, however, believed that the Toltec civilization did originate in the mountainous region between Huatulco and the city of Oaxaca.

The bays of Huatulco did see some traffic while Hernán Cortés was in control of colonial development in México in the first half of the 16th century. The importance of the bays as anchorage during storms or to take on fresh food and water cannot be overlooked in the days of the Spanish galleons sailing between Acapulco and Peru, and there were privateer attacks by the famous British captains Sir Francis Drake and Thomas Cavendish. But since there was so little actual settlement in the bays of Huatulco, there is little in the way of any architectural heritage left behind, as was the case in the interior of Oaxaca. This cannot be said for the interior, as the city of Oaxaca was a very important colonial center and then after independence it played a pivotal role in the late 19th century history of the country. México's most famous and beloved President Benito Juarez came from Oaxaca as did the late 19th and early 20th century dictator Porfirio Díaz

Up until the late 20th century, Huatulco was essentially a rural backwater, known for its coffee plantations and little else. Tourism began by federal intervention in the region when Fondo Nacional de Turismo managed to obtain and then develop the infrastructure for 21,000 hectares or 51,892 acres for recreational tourism. This was the start of the resort area of Tangolunda. The main population centers are Santa Cruz and La Crucecita while Tangolunda is primarily devoted to resort hotel development.

The name Huatulco comes from the inland community of Santa María Huatulco, which is the only community in the area showing any true Spanish colonial heritage. The name has carried over to the entire beach area with the collective name of Bahias de Huatulco. Most of the tourists who come are wealthy Mexicans for the major cities. Foreign tourism is still in its infancy.

SIGHTSEEING IN HUATULCO: This is one of the safest and cleanest regions in all of México, so visitors can relax and enjoy sightseeing or simply relaxing on the beautiful beaches. Violent crimes are rare and even pickpockets or robberies here are not a commonplace occurrence. And this area is somewhat isolated and not in the mainstream of either drug trafficking or smuggling.

* SIGHTSEEING OPTIONS: Most cruise passengers seem content to walk around Santa Cruz or simply spend the day on the small beach. Some cruise lines will offer a shuttle into La Crucecita, which is the main shopping area. Some cruise lines may offer shuttle service to one of the resort hotels along the beach in Tangolunda. For extensive touring, the offerings will vary with each cruise line. Many offer a half day motor coach tour of the three bays and their associated communities, and depending upon the cruise line, this may also include a visit to Santa María Huatulco. For those cruise lines with more energetic programs there will be a full day motor coach tour to Ciudad Oaxaca to explore this historic colonial capital city.

* Private cars with a driver/guide are available through most cruise lines now that this area has well developed tourist infrastructure, but the cost may be relatively high. If you wish to explore this option on your own, check with Tours by Locals at _www.toursbylocals.com_ and key in Huatulco for information.

* Taxi touring in Huatulco is a less expensive option. The taxis allowed in the port area are all reputable. You can negotiate a tour for a few hours or all day, making sure you set an exact price before leaving. And do not pay more than a deposit upfront. You can also check on line with Taxi y Tours en Huatulco at *www.taxi-y-tours-en-ualtuco-negocio.site* for their services and rates.

Bahia Tangolunda, (Work of kognos, CC BY SA 4.0, Wikimedia.org)

* IMPORTANT SIGHTS TO SEE: Here are my recommendations for the must see venues in Huatulco shown here alphabetically:

** Church of the Virgin of Guadalupe – Located on the main square in La Crucecita, this baroque church is a good example of the religious architecture from Spanish colonial times in an area that was at the time a cultural backwater.

** City Tour – The most popular half day activity that enables you to see the three major bays is the city tour by motor coach, or private car, showing you the old and new settlement. Tangolunda exhibits beautiful hotels and new residences for part-time visitors. La Crucecita does date back to the early Spanish period and has a few historic buildings.

** Hagia Sofia – Located just outside of Santa Cruz where your ship docks, this small reserve has been created to protect the bird life and butterflies that still can be enjoyed in their natural habitat. The reserve is open weekdays from 9 AM to 2 PM and Saturday from 11 AM to 5 PM.

** Parque Eco-arqueologico de Bocana Copalita – Located to the east of Tangoluna Bay, this small reserve to set aside for preservation an early pyramid that dates back over 2,000 years before the development of the great Mesoamerican civilizations.

Santa Cruz harbor, (Work of Marrovi, CC BY SA 3.0, Wikimedia.org)

** Parque Nacional Huatulco – This combination of beautiful coves with white sand beaches and thickly forested hillsides has been set aside west of La Crucecita to protect the natural landscape from future development. The most beautiful beach is Playa San Augustin, which is totally natural and very special.

** Santa María Huatulco – Located just a short distance inland from La Crucecita, this old community is the most historic dating back to Spanish colonial times. Yet there are no major venues within the village.

* A VISIT TO CIUDAD OAXACA – A few cruise lines offer a full day excursion to Ciudad Oaxaca, the capital of the state of Oaxaca. This is one of the most sought after capital cities in México and is a major tourist destination. Oaxaca dates to 1532 and became the major Spanish settlement in the southern highlands of the country. With a metropolitan population of 600,000 it offers both a rich array of historic sites as well as all the amenities of a major urban center. Oaxaca is noted for its pre-Colombian and Spanish architecture, its many small museums and galleries, its artists workshops and above all else for its gastronomy. It is considered to be the most gastronomic of Mexican cities, home to so many important

Mexican dishes, most noted being moles, which are the rich variety of spicy sauces so treasured in the country.

On the magnificent historic streets of Ciudad Oaxaca, (Work of Alejandro Linares Garcia, CC BY SA 4.0, Wikimedia.org)

If you are able to participate in an all-day excursion, I would most strongly urge you to visit Ciudad Oaxaca, given the great historic, artistic and gastronomic place this city holds within México. And all cruise sponsored visits do include lunch where you can sample the gastronomy for which this city is famed.

There are so many major sights to be seen during the few hours you will have, and since most who sign up for this tour will be traveling in a group by motor coach, the sights you see will have already been predetermined. But for those who have a private car and driver/guide, I offer this list of the most important venues that you should visit:

** Andador de Macedonia Alcala – This grand pedestrian street is in the heart of the city. It exhibits the grand Spanish colonial architecture. And it is home to numerous galleries and artists studios.

** Mercado de Benito Juarez – In the center of Oaxaca, this famous city market will show you all of the potential ingredients that go into the making of the famous local cuisine. Among the delicacies you will see are various dried insects, which still make up a part of the indigenous diet. On a more appetizing note, you will find a wide array of chili, spices and chocolates. The market is open daily during daylight hours.

** Monte Alban – A visit to Monte Alban located on the top of a mesa overlooking Oaxaca should be the number one site on your list. Monte Alban is the remains of the once great Mesoamerican city of the Zapotec, a powerful civilization comparable to the Aztec.

Museo de las Culturas de Oaxaca – This is the most important museum in Oaxaca with a treasure-trove of artifacts from the great civilizations of central México. It is open Tuesday thru Sunday from 10 AM to 6:15 PM.

** Templo de Santo Domingo de Guzman – One of the most lavish of old Spanish churches in México, this is considered to be one of the most visited sites in Oaxaca. Visitors are welcome during daylight hours daily.

In the heart of Ciudad Oaxaca, (Work of Alejandro Linares Garcia, CC BY SA 4.0, Wikimedia.org)

There are so many other lesser sights in Oaxaca that can be added to your time in the city, but I prefer to leave that up to your driver/guide if you are touring independently. And if you are on a motor coach tour, the venues will be predetermined. One day in Ciudad Oaxaca is simply not enough time.

DINING OUT: If you are on an all day tour, your lunch will be included and you will not have any choice in the restaurant. But normally the cruise lines offering an inclusive lunch will choose a restaurant that represents the gastronomy of the region. If you are out with a car and driver/guide you may wish to follow my recommendations of carefully selected restaurants in both Huatulco and Ciudad Oaxaca. My choices have been made with great care for authenticity and are shown alphabetically, combining both locales:

* Café Juanita – Located in the Poligono area of Santa Cruz at Boulevard Benito Juarez in the Marina Chahue, this is a very popular local restaurant just a short taxi drive from the dock. The menu is very diverse, combining local Oaxacan flavors with an international mix giving it a fusion approach. Seafood figures prominently at lunch, but in the morning they serve both Mexican and North American breakfast dishes that are well prepared. They are open Wednesday thru Sunday from 8:30 AM to 10 PM and Tuesday from 8:30 AM to 4 PM.

* Casa Taviche – This very popular traditional restaurant is located at Avenida Miguel Hidalgo # 1111 in the city center. It is noted for its fresh ingredients, traditional recipes and outstanding service. Mole and seafood are among the specialties. They are also vegetarian and vegan friendly. They are open Monday thru Saturday from 1 to 10 PM.

** El Quinque – Located at Callejoh Hidalgo # 218 just outside of the city center, this is a great find when it comes to traditional Oaxacan dishes served in a friendly and caring manner. Their diverse menu does include beef and chicken along with seafood and a variety of non-meat oriented dishes. They are open daily from 8 AM to 11:30 PM.

** El Sabor de Oaxaca – Located in La Crucecita at Avenida Guamuchil # 206, it is a short distance from the cruise ship dock, walking distance for anyone who is capable. The name translates to mean the flavor of Oaxaca, and that is what you get. Fresh ingredients and traditional recipes will give you a good introduction to the gastronomy of Oaxaca. They are open daily from 7:30 AM to 11 PM.

* Restaurante Catedral – In Ciudad Oaxaca at Calle Manuel Garcia Vigil # 105, this is one of the finest places for a traditional Mexican lunch where the gastronomic flavors of Oaxaca will give you a taste treat to remember. Seafood plays an important role in the diet of Oaxaca, but for vegetarians and vegans there are menu selections. The quality of the cuisine and the manner of presentation are all superb. Their hours are from 8 AM to 11 PM Wednesday thru Monday. If you wish to book a table to be sure, call 951 516 3285.

* Terra-Cotta – In La Crucecita at Calle Gardenia # 902, it is not far from the cruise dock and anyone who is fit can walk the distance. Taxis are always available and safe. The menu is diverse combining Oaxacan flavors with an international array of dishes, always using the freshest ingredients. They are open daily from 8 AM to 11:30 PM.

SHOPPING: The state of Oaxaca is a shopper's paradise for handcrafted items made with great flair. Woodcarvings, lacquered wood, pottery, woven wares and jewelry are all in the mix. If you are on a group tour to Ciudad Oaxaca you may only have a brief window of time for shopping at whatever venue has been chosen. If you are on your own either in Huatulco or Oaxaca you will be able to venture into one of the shops I list in this section. I have chosen based upon a lengthy experience with Mexican crafts, having once carried them in a gallery I owned in Scottsdale, Arizona. My few good recommendations are shown below in alphabetical order:

* Chocolate Mayordomo – In Ciudad Oaxaca on Mina Street, this is a chocolate lover's dream. Mexican chocolate, especially that from Oaxaca, is a definite must gift item or for

yourself. Often it is laced with cinnamon and is outstanding. They do not show their hours, but are normally open during normal business hours each day of the week.

* La Casa de las Artesanias de Oaxaca – Located in Ciudad Oaxaca at Calle de Mariano Matamoros # 105, this is a good one stop shop for traditional arts and crafts from Oaxaca. They offer a variety of art and craft items in a range of prices where you are sure to find something to take home. Their hours are from 9 AM to 10 PM daily.

* Museo de Artesanias Oaxaquenas – Located in La Crucecita at Calle Flamboyan # 216, which is a short drive by taxi, but too far to walk, this is an outstanding shop where you will find both antique and current object d'art from Oaxaca. Their collection is superb, and normally bargaining is not recommended unless your purchase is quite large. They are open Monday thru Friday from 10 AM to 9 PM.

* Museum of Oaxacan Handcrafts – Located in La Crucecita at Calle Flamboyan # 216, this shop features a wide array of traditional crafts, all carefully selected by the owners for their high level of quality. Bargaining is not customary, but you can always ask. They are always open when a ship is in port, but do not show any current hours.

ACAPULCO

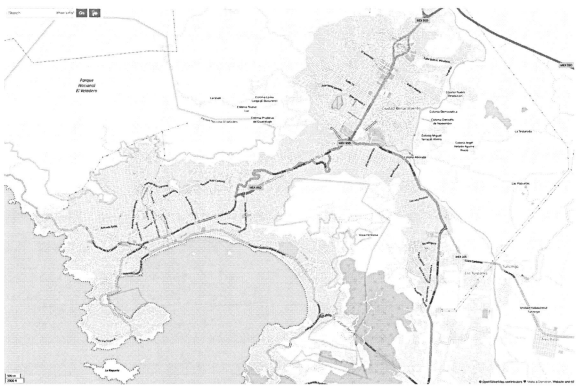

A map of greater Acapulco, (© OpenStreetMap contributors)

Acapulco is the largest coastal city in México with a metropolitan population of 1,100,000. At one time during the first half of the 20th century this was the grand beach resort of the entire nation, a city of great glamour and wealth. But during the last half of the 20th century with the rise of newer, less crowded coastal resorts on both the Pacific and Caribbean shores, Acapulco has seen a significant decline in its position as the crown jewel of the Mexican shores. The massive influx of poor peasants from surrounding rural areas, the infiltration of the drug cartels and the congestion of its narrow coastal fringe combined to make Acapulco far less desirable than Cancun, Ixtapa, Puerto Vallarta and Cabo San Lucas. Today it caters as much to weekend visitors from the national capital and other major interior cities as it does to foreign visitors. Many Mexican scholars refer to Acapulco these days as a "faded grand damme." I have found that cruise passengers have shared mixed reviews over the past few years, many being very disappointed in Acapulco while others have mildly accepted it for what it is. But overall there is a general lack of great enthusiasm, and some cruise lines are even bypassing it, leaving it off itineraries where stops are made along the Mexican west coast.

THE NATURAL SETTING: The main heart of Acapulco wraps around crescent shaped Acapulco Bay, backed up by steep mountains that encompass the entire city, coming down to the ocean both east and west of the city and showing steep seaside cliffs. The newest parts of the city to be developing lie beyond the mountains to the north of the bay and to the east along a flat coastal plain where there is room for growth, but in a far less enticing setting than around the bay.

The poor neighborhoods cling to the upper hillsides behind the bay while wealthier and middle class neighborhoods occupy the lower hillside spurs closest to the bay or the ocean. The wealthiest districts of Acapulco are found on the eastern side of the bay where they have a commanding view of the beachfront skyscrapers of the city heartland. And there is also an older wealthy district between the city center and the ocean on a peninsula along the western side of Acapulco Bay that juts out to where it narrows the entry to the bay, creating a smaller enclave known as Manzanillo Bay.

Looking west across Acapulco Bay to the high rise beachfront in the older city area

The poorest barrios lie on the north side of the mountains that embrace the bay. Here you see the typical ramshackle neighborhoods with dirt or gravel streets and few city services. Hundreds of thousands of people are living in this new area totally removed from the coastline. These barrios are home to the menial workers or unemployed newcomers drawn to the city in hopes of bettering their lives. And it is in these areas that the drug cartels find fertile ground for exploitation.

The climate of Acapulco is tropical, but with a distinct wet and dry regime. The winter months are prime tourist season with mild temperatures, lower humidity and strings of bright, sunny days. The summer season is hot, humid and has almost daily convectional rain showers. And hurricanes develop along this coastline, often bringing havoc to Acapulco and cities farther north along the Pacific coast. With steep hillsides and many poor barrios high up along the slopes it is not uncommon for deluges to wash down whole areas, bringing mud, debris and houses down into the city center. These avalanches destroy infrastructure year after year, literally causing havoc.

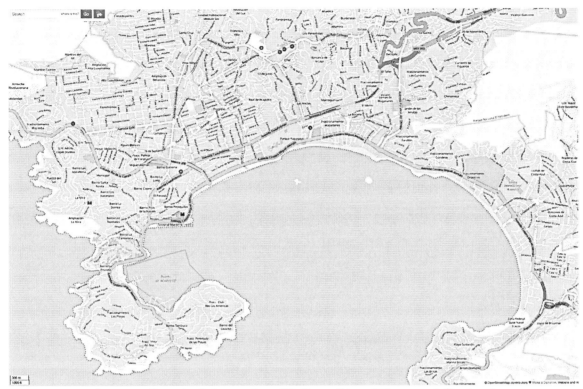

A map of central Acapulco, (© OpenStreetMap contributors)

The old downtown, situated to the southwest of the high rises along the Costera Miguel Alemán consists of narrow streets with an atmosphere of decrepitude, making this a non-attractive neighborhood for visitors. The Costera stretching northeast around the bay, however, is lined with a multitude of beachfront high rise hotels, condominiums, fashionable shopping plazas, restaurants and nightclubs. This is the heart of tourist activity that developed in the early 20th century and made Acapulco famous. Despite the luxury found along the Costera, none of the hotels by law can lay claim to the beach, which is public property. This leads to one harassing feature of the Acapulco beach – the myriad of vendors peddling everything from sunscreen to food to clothing and souvenirs. And they are as pesky as proverbial flies.

Overlooking both the eastern and western ends of the bay are the wealthier suburbs. The Las Playas Peninsula protrudes into the bay, guarding its western shore. It is here that many of the mid 20th century homes of film stars and other celebrity figures are located. At the northern end of the peninsula is the Hotel Mirador Acapulco. It overlooks a small cove on the Pacific shore where the high cliffs have become famous for the young men who dive into the churning waters of the cove as a means of performance for the guests. Those watching from the hotel terrace are then asked for donations to support the divers.

Today this peninsula has lost some of its luster, but still is home to many fine small hotels and the vacation properties of many wealthy citizens and visitors alike. Today the more fashionable properties overlooking the bay are found around the eastern end with fantastic views back toward the older heart of the city.

The eastern headlands guarding the bay have a commanding view of the whole city. And it is in these hills that several famous hotels have been built. The Las Brisas Acapulco is the most noted, its pink buildings being a predominant landmark. From here the main highway rounds the bay and climbs high above Puerto Marques Bay, a newly developing area growing out of an old fishing village. Once out on the flat coastal plain, the main highway enters the Zona Diamante, the newest addition to the city. The most elegant and noted beachfront hotel is the Fairmont Acapulco Princess, the city's jewel in the crown of hotel properties. The remainder of this flat plain presents a mix of shopping malls, small hotels, apartments and condominium developments in a rather unplanned manner.

The Costera Miguel Aleman along the city center backed up by middle income
neighborhoods and the poor barrios high above

ACAPULCO'S FASCINATING HISTORY: To understand this major city that has until recently been on every itinerary for ships making the Panama Canal transit, it is first important to review briefly the history of Acapulco. Unlike the new beach resorts on your itinerary, this is a city with a long history as a major port for the country dating back to early Spanish colonial times.

Older wealthy class homes on the Las Playas Peninsula

Long before the Spanish came, the Olmec, Aztec and Maya had influenced the area. The Aztec actually built a small outpost city north of present day Acapulco at Tehuacalco, an excavation that is now a current shore excursion for the more luxury oriented cruise lines because it is still not widely recognized as a major archaeological site. It is one of the oldest ruins in the entire greater Acapulco region.

The city of Acapulco dates to either 1523 or 1526, depending upon which historical reference one uses. The city was either explored from overland by one of Hernán Cortés' officers or it was scouted from the sea. None of the historic sources can agree, but suffice it to say that Acapulco is an exceptionally old city and played a major role in trade during the Spanish colonial period.

By 1531, the small port of Acapulco was established and it was linked to Ciudad de México by road. What put the city on the map was the development of a trade route to the Spanish Philippines. The annual Manila-Acapulco route would bring silks, spices and other luxury goods from the Philippines in exchange for Mexican gold. This trade continued until the time of the Mexican Revolution in 1921. To protect the route from English and Dutch marauders, the Fuerte San Diego was built overlooking Acapulco Bay. Despite the presence of the fort, the Dutch attacked in 1615, and ultimately the fort was destroyed by an earthquake in 1776. It was quickly rebuilt but never saw another siege. It still stands today as a tourist attraction directly across the street from the cruise terminal and is the only significant historic site that cruise passengers can reach on foot from their ship.

The luxury condominiums on the eastern side of Acapulco Bay near the Hotel Las Brisas

During the Mexican Revolution, the city was attacked and much of it burned down. It was the revolution that ended the Manila-Acapulco galleon traffic. But by the 1850's, Acapulco became an important provisioning stop on the route from Panama or around South America to San Francisco during the gold rush era. But as steam ships brought greater speed it became less necessary for the provisioning stop and Acapulco saw a decline in traffic.

The early 20th century role of Acapulco as an international resort was given a massive boost when Edward, Prince of Wales visited in 1920 and was captivated by the beauty of the bay. On his recommendation many of Europe's nobility and royalty ventured to Acapulco at the same time the Hollywood royals began their patronage. If you recall your British history, this was the same Prince of Wales who later married the American twice divorced woman named Wallace Simpson and he had to give up the throne to do so.

This catering to the rich and famous lasted well into the 1970's but travel to Acapulco became augmented by less expensive flights and moderately priced hotels once the jet travel age became commonplace. The end result was to turn Acapulco into a resort for the masses so the super-rich began to look for other locations, and Puerto Vallarta was soon discovered because of its remoteness. There are now few coastal resorts in México that are for the sole exclusive occupancy of the super wealthy crowd. Acapulco still has several hotels that do cater to a very upmarket clientele but this also holds true for Puerto Vallarta.

Fuerte San Diego has commanding views over the bay

What brought Mexican tourists was the completion in the 1990's of the Ruta del Sol, the toll highway from Ciudad de México to Acapulco that now enables visitors to come in mass for weekend getaways. It only takes about three to four hours by car from the capital.

Unfortunately since 2000 Acapulco has become the major way station on the route from Bolivia and Colombia for drugs heading north into the United States. Rival drug cartels have been battling it out for control of the state of Guerrero in which Acapulco is the major city. There have been several shootouts between drug gangs and the police, and many brutal atrocities have been committed in the past few years. The police maintain a strong presence, especially along the Costera Miguel Alemán where the cruise ship terminal is located.

The question you are no doubt asking now is whether it is safe to leave the ship. And the answer is a qualified yes. But to play safe you should only go out while on an excursion offered by your cruise line. If you wish to simply walk, do it with a small group of people along the Costera Miguel Alemán, but only to the right of the cruise terminal. Dress modestly and do not wear jewelry even when going on a group tour. Acapulco is a big and crowded city and if you were to become separated from your group, you would not want to stand out in a crowd. Also be careful with your camera bags or purses with regard to pickpockets.

SIGHTSEEING IN ACAPULCO: Acapulco is a large city with traffic congestion and its sidewalks can also be quite crowded. There are various options for exploring this city, and for each option I present both the pro and con factors to help you best decide what you will do with regard to getting out and seeing the sights.

In the historic old downtown of Acapulco

* OPTIONS FOR GETTING AROUND: There are several ways to see Acapulco and each is detailed below:

** Ship sponsored tours – Your cruise line will offer a variety of motor coach tours and quite possibly a walking tour. This is your best option for safety at the best price. But even on a group tour, it is your responsibility to not stray from the crowd, especially in any area where you feel less than comfortable. The tour guides are quite competent and will explain many aspects of what you are viewing. The drawback is that you are part of a group and do not have the flexibility to explore what interests you the most. Some call group tours nothing more than sheep being herded about, but I think that is a bit too harsh. The group tour is for those who do not feel comfortable venturing out privately.

** Private car and driver/guide – Your cruise line will contract with operators in Acapulco that can provide a private car with a driver and/or guide where you set the itinerary or have allow them to take you on a predetermined route. You have flexibility and your time is your own to linger as long as you wish. However, this option is far more expensive in a major city such as Acapulco. You may also wish to check out Viatour at _www.viatour.com_ and enter Acapulco as your destination. This is a very reliable company that works quite closely with Trip Advisor.

** There are no hop on hop off bus tours operating in Acapulco at the time of this publication being prepared. Given the rather exaggerated linear layout of the city and the fact that there are not that many distinctive venues for visitors, this service has not been viable.

** Taxi tours are available by prior booking through reputable companies. But I urge you not to simply negotiate a for a taxi outside of the cruise terminal or on the street, as there are many less than reputable operators and you could end up in a dangerous situation. If you wish to prearrange a taxi tour, I refer you to Tour Guides in Acapulco. Check their web page at _www.tourguidesinacapulco.com_ for further information and booking arrangements.

** Walking is not recommended as a means of touring because without both a good knowledge of Spanish and some understanding of the city's geography it would be easy to get yourself into a situation that could be dicey. A walk along the Costera Miguel Alemán going east from the cruise terminal is safe during daylight hours.

* SIGHTS TO SEE: Here is my list of important sights worthy of a visit. Some may be incorporated into various tours, or you may have your own car and driver and then be able to select what you wish to see. I have listed my recommendations alphabetically:

** Cathedral of Acapulco – Located in the old downtown area, the city's main cathedral is a rather modern structure, but built in a more traditional manner. Normally motor coach tours will simply drive by and point it out, but with your own car and driver you can actually visit. The cathedral is open to the public during daylight hours.

** Divers at La Quebrada – This is one of the major attractions in Acapulco and has been for decades. The young men who dive off the high cliffs are risking their lives to entertain you, so when the basket is passed around, please be generous. You can reach the open air viewing deck at the Hotel Mirador on most city tours or with your own car and driver. This is a spectacle to remember. Divers perform between 9 AM and 6:30 PM weekdays and between 9 AM and 3 PM on Saturday.

** Downtown Old Acapulco – The many narrow streets and the public market of the old downtown area are fascinating, but are not generally on the motor coach itinerary. You can visit with your own car and driver, but make certain the driver accompanies you. Although it is close to the cruise terminal, do not go on your own.

** Drive along the Costera Miguel Alemán – Here you have a chance to see the extent of the hotels, apartments and condominiums along with the fashionable shops and restaurants that have made Acapulco famous. Most tours will include this drive, and with your own car and driver you can also ask to park and walk a portion of the street.

** Fuerte San Diego – This ancient fort overlooks the Costera and is located across from the cruise terminal and is connected by a pedestrian bridge. If your group tour does not include the fort, you can visit on your own, as it is safe to do so. The fort and museum are open Tuesday thru Sunday from 9 AM to 6 PM.

** Zona Diamante – A visit to the Zona Diamante shows you the effort being put into recapturing the grandeur of Acapulco. Most of the motor coach tours do include a drive out to visit this new area, but often no stop is made for photographs or walking. It is quite a distance and your best access is on a group motor coach tour. You can also visit with your own car and driver, and if you do so I would recommend you include lunch at the Acapulco Princess Hotel.

The divers at La Quebrada

* TOURING OUTSIDE THE CITY: There are no significant sights to see in the immediate vicinity of Acapulco. The city is surrounded essentially by scrub woodland with few satellite communities. It is also too far from Ciudad de México for any cruise line to offer a one day visit to the national capital.

** Tehuacalco: The only major site to visit is Tehuacalco, a new national park about 90 minutes northeast of the city via the new Ruta del Sol, the main autoroute to Ciudad de México. Tehuacalco is a small Aztec community that was essentially an outpost during the period of empire. It was recently excavated and proved quite remarkable. There is an outstanding ball court and several small pyramids and former government buildings. Each year further excavations reveal more that is added to the list of sights. There is also a nice on site museum. Not all cruise lines offer this excursion, but if your cruise line does offer it and you are interested in Aztec culture, I highly recommend it. This new national park is open Tuesday thru Sunday from 9 AM to 6 PM. Also the drive there is quite interesting, as you start off on the main express highway to the national capital and end up for the last few kilometers or miles on an unsealed back road.

The excavated well preserved ball court at Tehuacalco National Park

DINING OUT: Most ship guests will only be dining out on a prearranged basis if you are on a tour that happens to be for the full day with lunch included. But the majority of tours are generally four hours or less, which means you will return to the ship after a morning tour or not be leaving until after lunch.

I am recommending four excellent restaurants for those who will be out in the city with their own car and driver because it is just not practical for you to leave the ship on foot to reach one of the recommended dining establishments. And calling a taxi that has not been prearranged to take you to lunch and return you is simply not practical or advisable.

My four lunch recommendations have been chosen carefully with cleanliness and food safety as a primary concern. These are outstanding restaurants featuring the finest in Mexican cuisine. My choices are shown alphabetically:

* La Finca Acapulco – Located at Boulevard las Naciones # 1300, this is a traditional Mexican and Latin American restaurant that has a broad menu and offers a great variety of dishes many who know Mexican cuisine may not have even heard of. The cuisine, service and ambiance are all first class and you will find this to be a dining experience. They are open from 8 AM to 10 PM daily. A reservation is advised. Have your private driver call them at 744 433 4262 to book your table.

There are many moderate price cafes along Costera Miguel Alemán but you need to exercise caution with regard to food safety and cleanliness

* Mariscos el Sirenito – On Camino Viejo # 1, this is a popular seafood restaurant with all their fresh fish and shellfish prepared a true Mexican traditional manner. The atmosphere is casual and friendly and the freshness of the seafood is what has made this a local favorite. It is open from 11 AM to 7:30 PM and reservations are not necessary.

* Paititi del Mar Restaurante – Located at Ignacio Zaragosa # 6, this is a superb restaurant featuring fine quality Mexican cuisine served in a relaxed atmosphere with excellent service. All dishes are expertly prepared and served in a warm, friendly atmosphere. Their menu is also heavily weighted toward fresh seafood locally caught and they also offer vegetarian dishes. They are open daily from 8:30 AM to 7 PM. You can have your driver call to book a table at 744 480 0031 but it is not required.

* Restaurante la Concha – Located at Calle Pedro Andres Sufrend # 33, this fine Mexican restaurant offers a variety of menu items including local favorites, a broad array of Latin American favorites and fresh seafood. They also are vegetarian friendly. Their cuisine and service are outstanding. Hours of service are from 1 to 7 PM daily. Have your driver call for reservations at 744 189 4755.

SHOPPING: Many visitors to Acapulco look forward to shopping in the more upscale boutiques and shops along the Costera Miguel Alemán. The emphasis is upon high fashion in sportswear, bathing suits, costume jewelry and evening ware along with perfumes and colognes. There are also very fashionable men's shops as well, so the guys are not left out. However, much of what you can buy here is also available at high end shops in your home city as well. Many do believe that there are good bargains in cologne and jewelry because of little or no excise tax or import duty. But you need to be wary because less reputable shops often cut perfume to water it down and jewelry is not always what it appears to be.

In the area of traditional crafts you will find dozens of street vendors and the public marketplace in the old historic downtown. But without a guide who speaks fluent Spanish it is difficult to know if you are getting a genuine item or one made in China. In the old historic downtown the merchants are expecting you to bargain, but here is where an accompanying driver/guide makes the difference. And also keep in mind that without a driver/guide you are vulnerable to pickpockets or muggers.

Here are my recommendations for reputable shops in the genre of traditional crafts shown in alphabetical order:

* Casa de la Cultura – On Avenida Costera Miguel Alemán at # 4834, in the main shopping area, this small shop does offer high quality arts and crafts of traditional origin. It is open daily form 9 AM to 9 PM.

* Mercado de Artesanias – Located on Avenida Cinco de Mayo in the old downtown, this is the best place to buy traditional Mexican crafts. Most of the shop and stall owners expect you to bargain on the price. It is part of the whole act of buying. However, do not walk in this marketplace on your own. It is open daily from 9 AM to 6 PM.

* Mercado Municipal – Located on Calle Diego Jurtado de Mendoza at the corner of Avenida Constituyentes – This is a large flea market indoors that is comprised of individual vendors. They sell everything from "junk" to good quality. You need to have a guide with you first of all to visit this part of the city and secondly to help you make wise purchases. The Mercado is open from 6 AM to 6 PM daily and can be a unique experience.

FINAL WORDS: I trust that all of my warnings about being careful in Acapulco do not cause you to simply remain on board the ship. It is worth taking at least one half day tour at a minimum to see this massive and crowded city that has such a famous and now notorious image. Acapulco is still a worthy place to at least get an overview of at the very least. But unfortunately I would not be acting in good faith if I had not mentioned the potential dangers that do plague Acapulco.

IXTAPA AND ZIHUATANEJO

A map of Ixtapa and Zihuatanejo, (© OpenStreetMap contributors)

Located 260 kilometers or 162 miles northwest of Acapulco along the coast of the state of Guerrero, the twin cities of Ixtapa and Zihuatanejo have become quite popular tourist destinations. Unlike the crowded and somewhat seedy city of Acapulco, these are both small communities with a combined population of only 113,000 residents. And they are somewhat isolated from the mainstream of the country's main highway system, which gives them a degree of protection from all of the drug violence seen in so many other important resort communities. This area has been relatively safe, but that is not to say that the occasional kidnapping of a wealthy Mexican citizen or shootout between police and the cartels has not happened. Ixtapa is exclusively a resort community with a young history. There are no residential barrios and the entire urban landscape is composed of luxury hotels and expensive homes. Zihuatanejo is separated from Ixtapa by a range of hills, yet it is only ten minutes away by automobile. It has a much longer history as a fishing village and it is also far larger, containing the bulk of the combined population. And Zihuatanejo does have a mix between rich, middle class and poor neighborhoods.

There is no dock in Zihuatanejo capable of handling even a small cruise ship. Therefore all ships that put into this port of call must tender their guests ashore, and the small bay has many swift currents often creating a relatively bumpy ride even though the distance is just a few kilometers or miles. But for those cruise ships that do offer this stop, it gives their guests a chance to see the quiet side of Mexican resort life and is generally appreciated by everyone as a chance to see the "real" México.

THE LANDSCAPE: The twin towns are separated by a low set of hills with only a single road connection. And they are totally different in the urban landscape and lifestyle they present. Ixtapa is a resort with no other outside activities. And all of its residents are financially very well off. Zihuatanejo is a small city that serves many functions and has a long and rich history.

A view over residential Ixtapa with the high rise hotel shoreline

The countryside is one of low hills that extend inland to meet the foothills of the higher Sierra Madre Sur, the chain of mountains that runs south from the transverse volcanic range that extends across the width of the country. Ixtapa developed on a more open bay that is incapable of providing any anchorage for ships. It is a new, planned beach resort and has no docking facilities or anchorage. Zihuatanejo is built at the head of a small bay and is encircled by hills with only its small central core being on level ground.

The landscape is one of tropical wet/dry forest with summer having the heaviest rainfall in more of a series of daily monsoonal downpours. The temperatures are always in the mid to upper 20's Celsius or upper 80's Fahrenheit. But cooling breezes off the Pacific keep the immediate shoreline quite comfortable.

A BRIEF HISTORY: The earliest explorations of the area date to the 1520's when the Spanish were scouring the land looking for gold. After discovering the small bay at Zihuatanejo, the Spanish used it as a staging area, building two ships capable of sailing across the Pacific to the Philippines. This was to be the precursor to the Manila-Acapulco trade route that would last for three centuries. However, one of the first of the two ships initially built was lost and the second failed to ultimately return from the Philippines to Spain. In the end, the bay was abandoned and further development took place at Acapulco, which became the major Pacific port.

Settlement in the area was very minimal. The area around what is now Ixtapa became an encomienda, but there were so few indigenous people in the region and thus Spanish peasants worked the land raising cotton, cacao and maize. There was minor lumbering with hardwood species such as oak and walnut dominating the market. Zihuatanejo ultimately developed as a minor fishing port and supply center for the few haciendas in the hinterland. To the bureaucrats in the capital this area was seen as a backwater.

During the Mexican Revolution against Spain this area saw no military action. But during the 1911 war to free the country from the rule of Dictator Porfirio Díaz, the people of Zihuatanejo joined in the fighting and thus incurred some reprisals from the government.

Into the first half of the 20th century this area remained on the fringe of development, as México was showing signs of modernization. Ultimately it was the federal government that brought vitality to the area by deciding to develop a tourist resort. With money from the Bank of México, secured by a loan from the World Bank, the master plan was developed for Ixtapa. The resort you see now is a totally planned community with all of its streets laid out in advance and the land use patterns all predetermined. The other totally planned resort under government auspices is Cancún on the Caribbean coast of Yucatan. Ixtapa has been quite successful, but it has never been able to compete with the more dynamic development of Puerto Vallarta farther north on the coast of Jalisco.

SIGHTSEEIN IN IXTAPA AND ZIHUATANEJO: Each cruise line that stops in Zihuatanejo will offer a varied number of excursions, but most tend to follow the same trend. There are tours of the twin cities, a tour into the surrounding countryside to visit a rural village and/or fishing community, a tour of a cacao plantation and a variety of waterborne activities from the beaches of either Ixtapa or Zihuatanejo.

Most cruise lines can make a car and driver/guide available for those who wish to tour in a less structures and more private manner. However, I must honestly say that what the area offers hardly merits the added expense of private touring.

There are local taxis available in Zihuatanejo but I advise using extreme caution when booking one for any private touring or to transfer between the main town and Ixtapa. I do not feel comfortable personally endorsing any of the three companies.

* LOCAL SIGHTS TO SEE: Depending upon your cruise line, the number and diversity of cruises will vary. Most cruise lines offer a half day motor coach tour around Ixtapa and Zihuatanejo. This is a relaxed tour with time to walk on the beach and visit the shops in Ixtapa. Tours into the surrounding countryside are few in number, as there are no significant historic sites within close proximity. There are tours to the local fishing villages, a cocoa

plantation or to where terra cotta bricks and tiles and still made by hand. Some cruise lines will offer the opportunity to Playa Manzanillo where one can enjoy snorkeling and swimming in the crystal waters.

A view of the Zihuatanejo waterfront from a ship's tender coming on shore

Many guests will simply tender into Zihuatanejo and enjoy the local color and possibly sample the local cuisine. The city center extends several blocks from the waterfront Paseo del Pescador, or fisherman's path, which follows the curvature of the bay. It is lined with quaint cafes and cantinas, affording that genuine Mexican atmosphere guests expect.

* LOCAL SIGHTS TO SEE: There are only a handful of local sights worth attempting to visit on your own, but if you go on a local tour most will be included. The local sights to see are (listed alphabetically):

** El Museo Arqueológico de la Costa Grande – Located at the south end of the Paseo de los Pescadores, it has many artifacts representing the archaeology and history of Guerrero, but also from the Aztec, Toltec and Olmec civilizations. It is open daily from 9 AM to 5 PM.

** Mercado Municipal Campesino – This is the colorful public market of Zihuatanejo that is quite genuine and not there to entertain visitors. You will have a chance to see how local people do their daily shopping and dining. It is located at Calle Mangos # 10 in the heart of Zihuatanejo. It is open daily from 6 AM to 6 PM.

** Parroquia de Santa Maria de Guadalupe – This is an attractive church with a great degree of local charm that is important to the community. It is found at Avenida Cinco de Mayo in the heart of Zihuatanejo. The church is open during daylight hours.

On one of the main streets in Zihuatanejo

* SIGHTS OUTSIDE OF TOWN: As noted previously, some cruise lines may offer a tour, usually for half a day, out into the surrounding countryside. If your cruise line does offer such a tour, it may be a nice way to see some of the back country that you might not otherwise get to experience in México. My favorite tour, which only two more upmarket cruise lines offer is the one that takes you to a traditional village off in the real backwoods where they make terra cotta roof and floor tiles by hand. The tour also includes a stop for a refreshing drink in the tiny coastal fishing village of La Soledad as well as a brief stop at a cacao plantation. If you have arranged for a car and driver/guide you may be able to duplicate this type of excursion by letting the booking agent know that you want to get away from the resort cities and do a bit of real exploring.

DINING OUT: Most guests who wish to dine out for lunch will do so in Zihuatanejo because the tours into Ixtapa are prior to lunchtime. And personally I have never found a restaurant in Ixtapa that was consistently up to the standards I feel merit my making a recommendation. My few good restaurant listings, however, do include both cities and are shown alphabetically:

* Carmelita's Café – This is a very popular local restaurant located a fair walk from the waterfront at Calle Heroica Colegio Militar . Here you will find genuine Mexican cuisine

with a local accent. Fresh seafood is featured along with great tamales, tacos and soups. And the restaurant is also known for its classic moles. The restaurant is open Monday thru Saturday from 8 AM to 4:30 PM and Sunday from 8 AM to 3 PM.

A lone fisherman brings in his net in the village of La Soledad

* La Terracita – Located in the heart of Zihuatanejo at Calle Adelita # 6 and open for breakfast and early lunch from 8 AM to Noon daily, this is a good place to have a traditional Mexican breakfast.

* Lety's Restaurante – Located just west of the Paseo de Pescador at Calle de Noria # 12, this is an excellent choice for seafood prepared in true Mexican style. One of their popular dishes is coconut shrimp that draws guests back. They are open from 1 to 10 PM Monday thru Saturday and from 1 to 9 PM Sunday.

* Restaurante el Arrayan – Located on Calle Adelitas just north of the waterfront in Zihuatanejo, this popular dining spot offers very fresh local seafood, much of it grilled in front of you. The menu is essentially traditional Mexican but with the emphasis upon the sea. They make excellent fish tacos as one sought after dish. They are open Monday thru Saturday from 8:30 AM to 9:30 PM and will accept reservations. To book a table call then at 755 112 1193.

SHOPPING: The central downtown core in Zihuatanejo is filled with small shops and stalls that serve the local needs but there are also those that sell souvenirs and arts and craft

items, strictly catering to visitors. These merchants do expect you to bargain before making a purchase, so do not be hesitant. Always express a willingness to pay half of what is being asked to start with and allow the dialogue to progress from that point. And if you slowly start to walk away and feign disinterest, it may work in your favor.

The souvenir and craft market area in Zihuatanejo

Among the art and handcraft items, you will find some nice woven pieces, but not as fine a quality as seen in Guatemala. Local pottery, lacquer wares and wood carvings are also widely seen. And when it comes to eatables remember that Mexican chocolate laced with cinnamon is very good for baking. Among the alcoholic offerings you will find fine quality tequila and Mexican coffee liquor under the famous brand name of Kahlua.

There are no shops of any special note in Zihuatanejo, as most tend to sell pretty much the same array of merchandise. The shops in Ixtapa tend to be more oriented toward resort ware clothing, jewelry and other fine quality merchandise at relatively high prices.

FINAL WORDS: Although your port of call to Ixtapa and Zihuatanejo may not be your favorite, it is a relaxing stop away from the major tourist crowds. And it offers a more serene glimpse into Mexican culture in contrast to the frenetic energy of Acapulco. If you are cruising north, the next potential ports of call such as Manzanillo, Puerto Vallarta and Cabo San Lucas have become very major destinations, but from these ports there is more opportunity for longer tours into the interior.

MANZANILLO

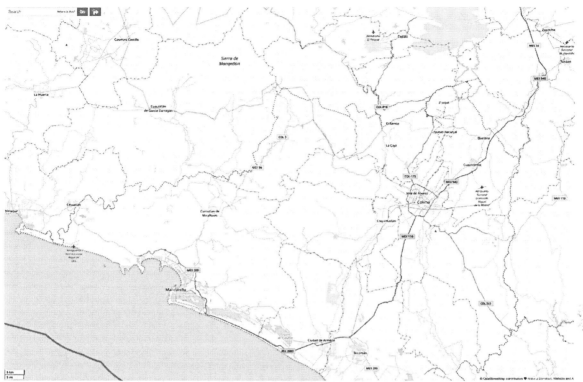

A map the state of Colima and Manzanillo, (© OpenStreetMap contributors)

Manzanillo in the small state of Colima is not a common port of call on Panama Canal itineraries, nor for that matter on Mexican Riviera cruises out of southern California. Only a handful of cruise ships call in at this port, which is a relatively busy container port because it has good road access to Guadalajara, Ciudad de México and other interior urban centers. This city with 100,000 residents has also become a tourist destination for those seeking beautiful beaches and less congestion than the major resorts on the Pacific Coast. Over the past two decades, a few distinctive hotels have been developed, giving Manzanillo this dual role of being a working port and a beach resort.

THE LANDSCAPE: Manzanillo is located 442 kilometers or 275 miles northwest of Zihuatanejo. It is 272 kilometers or 169 miles southeast of Puerto Vallarta. The capital and major city of the state of Colima, also having the same name, is only 107 kilometers or 66 miles to the interior on the main highway to Guadalajara.

The most dominant geographic feature of the entire state of Colima is Pico de Colima, a magnificent volcanic mountain standing 3,820 meters or 12,533 feet high. It rises up as an almost perfect cone similar to Japan's Mt. Fuji, and like the venerable Japanese peak, it is covered in snow much of the year. But apart from its landscape beauty, there is a sinister side. Pico de Colima is the most active volcano in México with major eruptions occurring as many times as three in a calendar year. Fortunately with as many eruptions as the mountain produces, this helps keep the internal pressures under control and precludes the potential for a catastrophic event. But in the realm of geology, one can never totally rule that out.

The magnificent Pico de Colima in mild eruption, (Work of Comición Mexicana de Filmaciones, CC BY SA 2.0, Wikimedia.org)

The coastal margins of Colima are very rugged with mountains seeming to rise out of the sea. There is little lowland fringing the Pacific and the Bay of Manzanillo is so vital being the only sheltered harbor on the entire coast. Beyond the coastal mountains, the remainder of this small state is comprised primarily of rugged mountainous terrain with a few intervening valleys. And Pico de Colima is the most dominant of all the peaks within the state, towering above the landscape.

Colima has a tropical wet and dry woodland with a mix of shorter trees and open grasslands. The great stands of tropical rainforest were mainly destroyed by the Spanish for their fine quality in the making of furniture, and today much of what was once forest cover has been set to farming and ranching. Temperatures are generally in the upper 20's Celsius or high 80's Fahrenheit in the coastal margin with high humidity. But in the cooler mountain valleys the climate is far more equitable.

A BRIEF HISTORY: There is a relatively long history dating back to 1527 when Alvaro de Saavedra first landed in Manzanillo Bay. This protected anchorage became one more Pacific shipbuilding port for the trade across the ocean to The Philippines along with Acapulco and Zihuatanejo. All during the Spanish colonial period there was a plague of Portuguese, French and British pirates attempting to siphon off their share of the riches in gold and exotic spices. Having a port like Manzanillo gave the added advantage of another place in which ships could take shelter.

The historic San Miguel Arcángel Mission in Comala is a classic example of the long Spanish occupancy in the state of Colima

After Mexican independence, the present day port known as Manzanillo began to develop even further as an important Pacific access point to the interior, which is the heart of the nation. And by 1889, the city had become an official port of entry with immigration and customs facilities.

All through the first half of the 20th century, Manzanillo was a favorite with sport fishermen, but its development of luxury resort hotels did not begin until the opening of the Las Hadas resort in 1972. It will be remembered as the background location for the famous Hollywood movie "10" starring Bo Derek. Unfortunately it is today a faded gem, overshadowed by newer and far more elegant properties.

VISITING MANZANILLO: When cruise ships dock in Manzanillo, the harbor is
far to the east of the tourist area of the city. Most major cruise lines will provide shuttle service to the beaches on Manzanillo Bay, as the older historic part of the city does not offer much other than its Spanish architecture much of which has not been maintained. But Manzanillo is one of the safest Pacific beachfront cities in México. Violent crime against tourists is virtually unheard of and even pickpockets are few in number. And drug related violence is also exceptionally rare. Why? I am sure you are asking that question. The answer

is quite simple. Manzanillo has both a Mexican Army and Mexican Navy Base in the city. In addition, Manzanillo is a regional headquarters from the Policia Federal Preventiva, the country's most important national police agency.

* WAYS TO GET AROUND: There are a few options for sightseeing while your ship is in the port of Manzanillo. These options include:

A map of Manzanillo Bay and Santiago Peninsula areas of Manzanillo,
(© OpenStreetMap contributors)

** Ship sponsored tours – Most] cruise lines offer at least one city tour that usually lasts three to four hours, as well as a variety of water sports activities for those still young and energetic enough to partake. The more up market cruise lines do offer either a half day or full day tour inland to the state capital city of Colima or the old historic town of Comala. And those cruise lines that do incorporate energetic nature oriented tours will offer one to Pico de Colima so long as the mountain is in a quiescent state, given that it is the most volatile volcano in the country.

** Private car and driver/guide – For those who do not want to participate in group motor coach tours, most cruise tour offices can arrange a private car and driver/guide to either duplicate an existing tour or customize activities to your own taste. This has always been my preferred option. And in the state of Colima there is the combination of beautiful scenery and Spanish colonial flavor. There is one private tour company known as Danitours that is very reliable and reasonably priced. Check out their web pages for further information as to what they can offer by going to *www.danitours.mex*

The center of old Manzanillo seen from the water, (Work of Jack Borno, CC BY SA 3.0, Wikimedia.org)

** There is no reliable hop on hop off bus service in Manzanillo. There are three taxi services, but I personally have never used them. I have, however, been assured that they are reliable and definitely safe in contrast to other Mexican ports. Those that are allowed at the cruise dock are considered the most responsible. If you choose to use a taxi for either sightseeing or transport, be sure to negotiate and settle upon a price before starting off.

* IMPORTANT SIGHTS TO SEE IN MANZANILLO: There are only a few actual venues worthy of your attention in Manzanillo. Most ship passengers will simply spend the day on the beach, sign up for one of the more adventurous water oriented activities or just take a walk through the old historic quarter. Depending upon your cruise line, there may be one or more trips out of Manzanillo to the state capital or the volcano. Here are in alphabetical order the few actual sights to see in Manzanillo;

** Centro Manzanillo – Many cruise lines will offer a short walking tour down the Malecón, the waterfront promenade in the heart of the city, as this is where your ship will dock. The major sight is the big sailfish statue, which is the symbol of Manzanillo. The old city center does have many historic buildings of interest and the usual tourist oriented souvenir and handcraft shops. Given the high safety factor of Manzanillo, this is a chance to explore an old historic quarter without the usual worry of becoming a victim of crime. If your cruise line does not offer such a tour, you can feel comfortable walking on your own because this is a city that is very safe for visitors.

The beautiful beach surrounding the Santiago Peninsula in Manzanillo, (Work of Yaomautzin Ohtokani Olivera Lara, CC BY SA 3.0, Wikimedia.org)

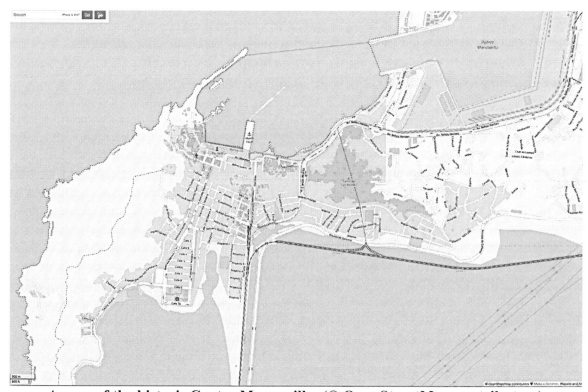

A map of the historic Centro Manzanillo, (© OpenStreetMap contributors)

** Peninsula Santiago: The popular and most photographed beach areas are alongside the Santiago Peninsula, which is located well to the west of the port area. Some cruise lines may offer a shuttle to one of the major hotels on the peninsula. It is here that the Karmina Palace and Las Hadas Hotels are located and this is where the majority of visitors stay when in Manzanillo.

** Playa la Audencia – Located to the west side of the Santiago Peninsula, this is one of the most beautiful of the beaches in Manzanillo. It is essentially a small beach that is tucked into a cove and represents the classic scene one expects along the Pacific Coast in a resort city. It is usually visited on the motor coach tour, or of course with your own car and driver you can linger here as long as you wish. A good taxi driver who knows the city can also bring you here, but do not dismiss the taxi, as it may be hard to find one to return you to Centro.

The Karmina Palace Hotel with Las Hadas in the background on the Santiago Peninsula,
(Work of Jack Borno, CC BY SA 3.0, Wikimedia.org)

* IMPORTANT SIGHTS OUTSIDE OF MANZANILLO: If you wish to really appreciate the state of Colima, I highly suggest one of the all day tours getting you away from the beach and into the heartland of this small, but interesting state. You will still have plenty of opportunity to enjoy the beach in other resorts both north or south of Manzanillo depending upon the direction of your itinerary. Here are my recommendations for unique travel in Colima that is hard to duplicate elsewhere:

** City of Colima – Only 1.5 hours by car or motor coach away from Manzanillo lies the state capital of Colima, Ciudad Colima. This is an historic city that dates to 1523, making it among the oldest of Mexican cities. It is rich in its architectural heritage and is a delightful place to visit if you are appreciative of the rich colonial heritage that Spain brought to México. Ciudad Colima has only 150,000 residents and it occupies a valley in the shadow of Pico de Colima, the mountain forming a dramatic backdrop to the colonial skyline. There are numerous churches plus the beautiful Basilica Menor adjacent to the Palacio del Gobierno, or state capitol building. Some cruise lines will offer a half day tour to the city while others may combine a brief visit as part of a full day tour to the volcano.

The sailfish is the symbol of Manzanillo, (Work of I. Tatehuari, CC BY SA 3.0, Wikimedia.org)

** Pico de Colima – This towering volcanic peak is hard to miss on the horizon, as it is the focal landmark of the state, snow covered for at least half of the year. It is the most active volcano in México and you have more than a 50 percent chance of seeing it either putting forth clouds of steam, ash or in full eruption, which is something you will never forget. The journey to and from Pico de Colima also gives you a chance to enjoy the overall landscape of the state. Likewise, the only way to the volcano is through the state capital city, which is rich in its historic architecture.

** Comala – This small colonial town just outside of Ciudad Colima dates to the 1550's and was once the hub of spiritual and cultural activity for several large haciendas where the ruling families once dominated the countryside. The historic mission church on the town plaza is a classic example of Spanish baroque architecture and is a source of inspiration to photographers seeking out quintessential images of México. Motor coach tours to Ciudad Colima or to Pico de Colima will often include a brief stop in Comala. If you have your own car and driver you can linger in this delightful town for much longer.

In the heart of the city of Colima, rich in Spanish heritage

DINING OUT: There are many restaurants in Manzanillo, but the majority are to be found in the beach area around the Santiago Peninsula and they are highly tourist oriented. Unless your ship has a shuttle bus to one of the major hotels or you have a private car and driver the only way to get to the beach or peninsula area would be by arranging for a taxi. If this is your option, be sure and set a return time and do not pay for the taxi until you are returned to the ship.

I have listed my three favorite restaurants for lunch in Manzanillo, including one in the Centro Manzanillo area, which is close to the ship. I have only given you three choices because for the majority of restaurants in Manzanillo the overall reviews, including my own, are mixed except for the three I give you. I also list three great choices in Ciudad Colima.

The Basilica and Palacio del Gobierno in Ciudad Colima, (Work of Wiper México, CC BY SA 3.0, Wikimedia.org)

Manzanillo:

* **Chantilly** – Located in Centro on Avenida Juarez y Madero, and quite popular. The only flaw is that if they are very busy, service can be quite slow. I recommend not going at the height of lunch hour. Their menu is essentially traditional to Mexican tastes and everything is nicely prepared. They do offer breakfast and also sandwiches during the afternoon along with hot entrees. They are open Sunday thru Friday from 7:30 AM to 10 PM and reservations are not needed.

* **Mariscos Carlos** – This very popular restaurant is located half way between the Centro Manzanillo area and the Santiago Peninsula. You will need a private car or pre-arranged taxi to dine here. It is located at the corner of Calle Atún and Leon Marino in the Colonia Oceno district. The emphasis is upon fresh local seafood prepared in strict Mexican traditional recipes. Meals are beautifully presented and the service is excellent. Just to play safe it is best to book a table by calling 314 336 5458.They are open from Noon to 7 PM every day of the week except Tuesday.

* **Pacifica del Mar** – This seafood restaurant serves in a rather elegant manner and has nice ocean views. It is located at Avenida del Mar # 1506 in Colonia Las Brisas. You will need a private car and driver or pre-arranged taxi to dine here. If you come by taxi, remember to arrange a pick up time and do not pay until you are retrieved. The menu at Pacifica del Mar is international and although seafood is a specialty, meat and poultry are on the menu and

the restaurant is also vegetarian friendly. It is open daily from 8 AM to 11:30 PM. If you wish to book a table, call them at 314 333 6353.

Ciudad Colima:

* Chepe Parilla de Bario – This restaurant has a decidedly Argentine flavor and meat is definitely the specialty. The grilled meats and accompanying dishes are beautifully prepared and nicely presented. It offers a nice change of taste from the traditional local cuisine and at night it is quite lively. It is located on Calle Amado Nervo #726. They are open Monday thru Saturday from 2 to 11:30 PM and Sunday from 2 to 5 PM. You can book a table by calling 312 313 9989.

* La Buena Vida – This is an excellent restaurant located at Calle 27 de Septeimbre # 1402. The menu is Mexican with recipes being traditional to this region. Everything is well prepared and nicely served in a warm and friendly atmosphere. It is not that well known by tourists, which gives it a genuine quality. They are open Tuesday thru Sunday from 8:30 AM to 1 PM and reservations are not needed.

* La Tostada y la Guayaba – A very distinctive local restaurant serving beautifully prepared meals in the traditional manner typical to Colima. Seafood plays a major role in the menu, but they restaurant is also vegetarian friendly. Their tacos and tostadas are outstanding just to mention two items. Hours of service are Tuesday and Wednesday 1:30 to 6:30 PM, Thursday thru Saturday from 1:30 to 11:45 PM and Sunday 1:30 to 6:30 PM. Reservations are not needed.

SHOPPING: You will find the same types of souvenirs and handcraft items to buy in Manzanillo as you saw in other ports along the Mexican coast. Shops not selling souvenir items or handcrafts are primarily attempting to interest the visitor in resort clothing, jewelry and liquor.

* Mercado 5 de Mayo – Located on Calle 5 de Mayo you will find the public market. There are numerous souvenir stores around the market, but I do not recommend any of them as being special. However, the main market is interesting to stroll through and see what food products are available to local shoppers in Manzanillo.

FINAL WORDS: It is a shame that the only dock for cruise ships is located along the shore of Centro, the older and historic part of Manzanillo. Yes there are several nice colonial buildings, but the overall ambiance of Centro does not compare to that of Puerto Vallarta. The beautiful beach areas around the Santiago Peninsula are several kilometers or miles to the west. Unless your ship offers a tour of Manzanillo or has a shuttle bus to one of the major hotels you will not be able to enjoy the resort area that is what visitors who come on holiday will experience. If, however, you have a car and driver or find a taxi driver with whom you feel comfortable, then you can enjoy the true meaning of Manzanillo as a resort city.

If the beach and seeing resort hotels is not something you are enthused about, I would highly recommend your ship tours into the interior to visit Pico de Colima or Ciudad Colima. The natural landscapes and the historic flavor of the capital are definitely worthy of your time. And if by chance Pico de Colima is in a moderate to mild state of eruption, you will find the experience most exciting. And who knows, you might just be in Manzanillo when Pico de Colima decides to put on a truly spectacular major eruption.

Pico de Colima in a major 2016 eruption, (Work of Dhatier, CC BY SA 4.0, Wikimedia.org)

PUERTO VALLARTA

A map of greater Puerto Vallarta, (© OpenStreetMap contributors)

In 1964, when a Hollywood studio decided to film the Tennessee Williams play, *A Night of the Iguana* in Puerto Vallarta, few in the United States had heard of this obscure village on the west coast of the Mexican state of Jalisco. The film, starring Richard Burton, Ava Gardner and Deborah Kerr, was dazzling even though it was shot in black and white. The exotic setting of this small Mexican town nestled against thickly forested hills was captivating to audiences. And many people wanted to try and visit this sleepy and remote town. Today more than half a century later, Puerto Vallarta is connected by air to major cities in the United States and Canada. Its shoreline is now home to modern high rise hotels and condominiums and it is an international destination. Some call it the new Acapulco in that it has become the most fashionable and favored of all the Pacific beach resorts. With a population of 255,000 residents, it has become the second largest city in the state of Jalisco after the capital city of Guadalajara. This population does not include the spill over into Nuevo Vallarta with over 115,000 residents. It is not part of the metropolitan population figures because it is across the border in the neighboring state of Nayarit. Thus if you include Nuevo Vallarta, the entire metropolitan population is 370,000 residents.

THE SETTING: Puerto Vallarta occupies a narrow coastal plain beneath the Sierra Madre Occidental, that wall of mountains that runs along the west coast of the country to where it intersects the transverse range south of Puerto Vallarta. The city of Puerto Vallarta just narrowly escapes being in the highly volcanic and tectonic zone that lies just to the south in the state of Colima. However, small earthquakes can and do occur in the area of Puerto

230

Vallarta and the potential for feeling the shockwaves from any major earthquakes in Colima is quite high.

A map of the historic old parts of Puerto Vallarta, (© OpenStreetMap contributors)

An aerial view of the main hotel district of Puerto Vallarta north of the historic old city

The climate is definitely tropical. The coastal plain and the lower foothills of the Sierra Madre Occidental are richly covered in tropical rainforest. The daily temperatures are in the mid to upper 20's Celsius or mid to upper 80's Fahrenheit. There is a distinct summer rainy season with the added impact of occasional hurricane strikes. Winter is somewhat drier and this is the height of the tourist season.

The mountains act as a barrier between the coast and the interior. It is 332 kilometers or 206 miles to Guadalajara over breathtaking winding road first to Tepic, capital city of Nayarit and then via Federal Highway 15 to Guadalajara. The major means of travel for those who can afford it is to fly between the two major cities of the state. And on a clear day, that can be a very spectacular journey.

* THE LAYOUT OF PUERTO VALLARTA: Today Puerto Vallarta is a sprawling urban center that consists of several distinctive zones that are strung together by the main highway that essentially follows the curve of the shoreline for a distance of 16 kilometers or ten miles. At no point is the built up area deeper than six kilometers or four miles extending inland from the sea. There is no cohesive urban landscape, but rather distinct nodes of development. Thus it is hard to appreciate the true size and population from visual appearances. And remember that this urban zone extends over two different states – Jalisco and Nayarit.

The major zones of greater Puerto Vallarta include:

** Zona Historico – This is the small old city located at the southern edge of the urbanized zone where the hills come so close to the shore that this area is very hilly. The old historic zone encompasses the original Spanish colonial town and the streets here are narrow, many of them cobbled. The architecture is especially beautiful with its colonial flavor. Today this historic heart of the city is really no longer the functional core. It is a very narrow zone sandwiched between the sea and the hills that rise rather abruptly. But it offers the flavor of the city that has been so famous through the years because of its charming architecture, which is in an excellent state of preservation.

* Zona Romantica – South of the historic old city and the Rio Cuale is one of the most beautiful parts of Puerto Vallarta. It is a very hilly district and contains many of the earliest vacation homes built after the discovery of the area, this following the Hollywood movie that first introduced Puerto Vallarta to the world. It is the area that first saw the arrival of wealthy visitors who chose to build vacation homes rather than stay in what at that early period were quaint hotels. It is important to note that foreign visitors can buy or build a home in México, but they must lease the land on a long term basis since foreigners cannot own land.

* Hotel Zone – This is the waterfront area north of the historic old city where high rise development is now crowding along the shoreline in the same way that Acapulco developed during the mid 20th century. But here the buildings are taller, much more modern in their appearance and are surrounded by lush landscaping unlike the way in Acapulco developed. This area is also quite close to the airport and it is also where cruise ships dock in the manmade harbor that is primarily for pleasure craft.

* Residential Zone – Behind the Hotel Zone is an extensive residential area that occupies the largest segment of level coastal plain and extends into the foothills. This is a mixed zone of middle income and lower income housing. There are very few homes in this part of the city that could be classed as substandard, something not true to so many Mexican cities.

In historic old Puerto Vallarta, (Work of Stan Shebs, CC BY SA 3.0, Wikimedia.org)

* Nuevo Vallarta – North of the airport and across the Ameca River into the state of Nayarit is the newest area to be developing. This is simply a northward expansion of a combination of elegant hotels, resort condominiums and private homes. But it just so happens that the state boundary between Jalisco and Nayarit is present, now making greater Puerto Vallarta an interstate metropolitan region, something rather rare in México.

A BRIEF HISTORY: A fair percentage of visitors that come to Puerto Vallarta confine their stay to the Hotel Zone, seeing a very modern, clean and vibrant city not realizing that Puerto Vallarta has a rich colonial heritage. Long before tourism, Puerto Vallarta was an active fishing village and service center for farmers living in the Ameca River Valley as well as for miners working claims in the Sierra Madre Occidental to the east of the coast.

As far back as 15,24, Hernán Cortés explored the Ameca River and battled the indigenous tribes that defended it. The bay into which the river flows is named Bahia Banderas for the colorful banners that the native people carried into battle. The bay was charted and mariners knew that in times of bad weather they could take refuge here. Yet all during this period there was no major settlement by colonists. During the 18th century the small village known as Las Peñas served as a smuggling port for goods destined inland to the mining and agricultural towns of San Sebastian del Oeste and Mascota. By 1859, the government had sold large tracts of land to the Camarena Brothers from Guadalajara to develop the area into a major agricultural and fishing region to better serve the many mines of the interior. The town grew steadily and in 1918, it officially became a municipality and was given the name Puerto Vallarta in honor of a former governor of the state of Jalisco.

The Zona Romantica, (Work of Cintyafloars, CC BY SA 4.0, Wikimedia.org)

What initially slowed the development of the region was that the land was all in the hands of one family and they would only sell to small farmers at inflated values. But in 1921, under new land reforms a large segment was given ejido status, which meant the farmers would own it cooperatively but could not sell it in the future. It took a local uprising in the late 1920's to ultimately bring about changes in the land ownership policies. As mining in the interior began to decline, many former miners sought agricultural land and slowly drifted into the Ameca River region looking to settle as farmers.

Until the early 1940's, the Puerto Vallarta area remained isolated, accessible only by air, sea or by torturous roads from the interior. The roads were hardly negotiable by automobile, only by mule or horse. And this stymied any modern development. To this day, the drive from Puerto Vallarta to Tepic, Nayarit is still somewhat difficult. However, those few tourists seeking out hidden places to relax would come by local small plane air service. After the filming of *The Night of the Iguana* the region rapidly developed. The film acted as a catalyst to the growth of the region. Part of the exposure given to Puerto Vallarta was generated by the press who descended upon the town because of the torrid relationship between its main star Richard Burton and Elizabeth Taylor, who was not his co-star at this time. Ava Gardner, another hot and sensual Hollywood star, was Burton's co-star.

After the success of the movie in generating interest, the government recognized the potential for development and invested heavily in the expansion of the airport, highway improvement and other city infrastructure. It did not take long for tourism to develop and it has not stopped since. Access by air to American and Canadian cities has made Puerto Vallarta one of the most favored of Mexican beach resorts. Today the city is crowded with five-star hotel properties, condominiums, apartments and smaller resorts catering to a wide range of tastes. And the cruise ship industry has also discovered Puerto Vallarta, making it a prime stop on Mexican Riviera and Panama Canal cruises.

Old historic Puerto Vallarta from the air

The resort's ongoing popularity maintains a high demand for tourist services, including the more menial janitorial and housekeeping jobs. This keeps the unemployment rate very low by national standards. In spring 2019, the rate was only 4.7 percent. As a result there is a low incidence of street crime such as pickpocketing and residential or auto burglary. However, because there is some degree of drug violence, the homicide rate in Puerto Vallarta is comparable to that of major American cities such as Miami.

SIGHTSEEING IN PUERTO VALLARTA: Cruise ships always spend a minimum of a full day in Puerto Vallarta. And many itineraries call for an overnight stay, which enables the offering of a full day's air excursion to Guadalajara. The majority of cruise lines will offer shuttle bus service to any number of locations either in the Hotel Zone or in the old historic city. All cruise lines offer extensive full day or half day tours of the city and surrounding sights. For those who do not wish to participate in a ship sponsored motor coach tour, there are alternatives, which include:

* Hiring a private car and driver/guide can be accomplished through your cruise line, but generally the cost is quite high unless you share the expense with another party. You should also check on line with Puerto Vallarta Tours at *www.puertovallartatours.net* for details regarding their private offerings, which are highly praised by guests.

* There are numerous taxi companies operating in Puerto Vallarta, and the port authority will only allow those fully licensed into the dock area. You can try to negotiate a full or half day of sightseeing, but do not pay up front for service. Negotiate a fixed rate and only pay a deposit. The only company I recommend you check out on line is one that mainly handles transfers but they can do tours. Visit Discovery Vallarta at *www.discoverpvr.com* for full details.

* There is no hop on hop off bus in Puerto Vallarta. However, Puerto Vallarta Tours does offer motor coach tours around the city and into the surrounding countryside. They are reputable so I recommend you visit them at *www.puertovallartatours.net* to see what they offer or can tailor to your needs.

* SIGHTS TO SEE IN PUERTO VALLARTA: There are not a great number of specific sights to see in Puerto Vallarta. This is a resort and most visitors who come to stay in one of its many hotels prefer the relaxation of the beach, the sea, a spa or they want to enjoy water sports such as parasailing or deep sea fishing. This is my listing of the must see sights, many of them will be covered by ship sponsored tours. I have listed them alphabetically to avoid any personal bias:

** Church of Our Lady of Guadalupe – In the old historic downtown at the top of Calle Hidalgo, this beautiful with its filigree crown atop the main spire is the epitome of colonial Puerto Vallarta. It is normally open all day and visitors are welcome, but asked to be respectful.

** El Centro – Also called the Zona Historica, this is the old main shopping area of Puerto Vallarta known for its cobblestone streets, historic architecture and overall delightful atmosphere both during the day and in the evening.

** El Malecón – This is the famous boardwalk that runs from the Zona Romantica all the way north to the Hotel Zone. It is lined with beautiful palm trees, many sculptures and has the ocean to the west. It is the place to promenade, see and be seen.

In the historic downtown at night with the bell tower of the Church of Our Lady of Guadalupe on the skyline, (Work of Adam Jones, CC BY SA 2.0, Wikimedia.org)

** Los Muertos Pier – This main fishing pier off the Malecón at the end of Calle Francisco Rodriguez offers great skyline views of the old historic district and north to the skyscrapers of the hotel zone. And the beach on either side of the pier is a favorite with locals for sunbathing or swimming. It is known simply as Playa los Muertos.

** Mirador de la Cruz- This observation point marked by a large cross offers the best high altitude view over the city. It is normally a stop on most city tours. It is located above the old historic downtown at the eastern end of Calle Abasolo.

** Playa los Gemelos – Located about 20 minutes by car south of the Zona Romantica, this is one of the most beautiful beaches in Puerto Vallarta and worthy of a visit just to enjoy the views. And if you are into sunbathing, it is a great destination. If you take a taxi on your own, be sure to negotiate both a price and a return pickup. Do not pay more than a small deposit until the driver returns for you. The garden is open Tuesday thru Sunday from 9 AM to 6 PM and is a beautiful retreat from the city.

** Vallarta Botanical Gardens – This 65 acre garden situated in the hills at an elevation of 1,300 feet offers you the lush and magnificent vegetation of this tropical coast combined with incredible views out over the countryside. It is located off Federal Highway 200 south of the city and then inland from Boca de Tomatlan. You will need a car and driver, as I would not trust a taxi to drop you off and return unless you are having the driver wait.

The modern skyline of the Hotel Zone of Puerto Vallarta

** Zona Romantica – Just across the Rio Cuales is the first district to develop as a tourist destination during the 1960's and 70's. You can follow the Malecón south of the river and it will bring you into this attractive district with its distinctive charm, loads of shops and bistros. Even if you do not wish to shop or dine, just walk through the streets and soak up the flavor of this delightful district.

* SIGHTS TO SEE OUTSIDE OF THE CITY: The more upmarket cruise lines may offer you either a visit to the colonial village of San Sebastian or a chance to visit Guadalajara by air. These are very special tours that I highly recommend to anyone who gets tired of visiting beach resorts. If you want to experience México in an entirely different way, then you should consider either of these tours, if offered by your cruise line.

** Guadalajara – If your cruise line offers a day in Guadalajara, I would highly recommend it as an experience to remember. Only the more high end cruise lines will offer such a trip because of the cost and logistics involved. Guadalajara can only be reached by air on a single day excursion. The cruise line will coordinate a motor coach or van to take a limited number of guests from the ship to the airport and then have a motor coach or van with a dedicated guide waiting at the airport in Guadalajara. Of the five major cities in México, I consider Guadalajara to be the jewel in the crown. It is the second largest city in the country with a metropolitan population of approximately 6,000,000. The city is located in the central plateau region of México, east of the Sierra Madre Occidental at an elevation of 1,870 meters or 6,131 feet above sea level. The city dates back to 1542, and its Centro is filled with monumental colonial buildings, making it one of the most majestic cities in all of Latin America. On a one day visit you will only be able to see a small portion of this massive city, but it will sharpen your appreciation of the rich history of México and the architectural legacy it has left behind.

In the historic heart of Guadalajara

The highlights of a visit to Guadalajara are a walking tour around the very heart of the city where the great cathedral is surrounded by four plazas. In this UNESSCO World Heritage Site you will find the magnificent Opera House and the Palacio del Estado or state capitol. It is noted for its famous revolutionary murals by the great Mexican artist Orosco. You will also visit the suburb of Tlaquepaque, noted for its many artists workshops and studios. This historic suburb with its colonial flavor is usually where you are taken to lunch. And finally you will visit Zapopan, the modern suburb with glitzy high rise buildings and elegant shopping malls.

** San Sebastian del Oeste – Located in the Sierra Madre Occidental 67 kilometers or 42 miles inland from Puerto Vallarta. By motor coach it will take approximately two hours to reach this former mining town that once had 20,000 residents. This is a quintessential mining town dating back to 1608 when it produced quantities of gold, silver and lead for the coffers of the Spanish Crown. It is an architectural gem and much of it has been well preserved. A visit is a step back in time to a different era. The tour occupies a full day and lunch is always provided. This is a totally different side of México that you can never see by staying on the coast in the beach resorts.

DINING OUT: As a major resort city you can expect to find a wide array of restaurants in Puerto Vallarta that range from fast food stalls to sumptuous and elegant dining establishments. Mexican and international fare can be found throughout the Hotel Zone, the Zona Historica and Zona Romantica. Of all the ports in this book, I have found selecting an array of my favorite restaurants to represent Puerto Vallarta quite difficult because there are so many. I have concentrated on those restaurants serving fresh seafood, having a strong Mexican tradition and have also mixed in casual, upmarket and very elegant to give you a good assortment. The biggest problem you will have unless you have arranged for a car and driver is transportation since Puerto Vallarta is quite spread out.

The village of San Sebastian del Oeste, (Work of Intersofia, CC BY SA 3.0, Wikimedia.org)

* Bravos Restaurant Bar – Located on Calle Francisco I Madero # 263 in the Zona Romantica close to the Rio Cuale, this is an exceptionally popular restaurant with a loyal following. The menu here has an Italian flavor with great pasta and seafood dishes that makes you think you are in the Mediterranean. The atmosphere is very refined with that added touch of elegance and the service is outstanding. Hours of service are Tuesday thru Sunday from 5 to 10:30 PM for dinner only. Call to book a table at 322 222 0339.

* Café des Artistes – Located on Calle Guadalupe Sánchez # 170 in the historic center, this is a very delightful restaurant. The atmosphere is rather elegant and gives you the feeling of being in a tropical garden. The menu is quite continental and diverse. Dinner is a multi-course experience. The restaurant only serves dinner between 5:30 and 11 PM and you need to book in advance. Call 322 226 7200 to book a table.

* El Dorado Restaurante – Located in the Zona Romantica at Calle Pulpito # 102, this restaurant specializes in very fresh seafood dishes served in a Mexican tradition along with dishes served in the manner of other Latin American tastes. They also offer vegetarian dishes. The atmosphere is casual and most tables have a great view out over the beach and the sea. Service is friendly and efficient. They are open daily from 8:30 AM to 11:30 PM and reservations are accepted. To book a table call 322 223 5568.

* Emiliano Restaurant at Casa Velas Resort – Casa Velas is easy to reach from the cruise ship on foot if necessary. It is about 1.6 kilometers or one mile away, located at Fraccionamento Marina Vallarta on Calle Pelicanos # 311. This highly acclaimed restaurant offers an International menu with a wide array of elegantly prepared dishes that include seafood, meat and poultry. Vegetarian dishes are also offered. Dining options include indoor or poolside. Reservations are essential. Call 322 226 6688 to book a table. They serve from 8 AM to 11 PM daily.

* La Palapa – At Pulpito # 105-3 in Playa Los Muertos and open from 8:30 AM to 11:30 PM daily, this is an excellent traditional Mexican restaurant that features a definite emphasis upon the cooking style of Jalisco. A reservation is suggested by calling 322 222 5225 to book a table.

* Layla's Restaurante – This popular restaurant is located at Calle Venezuela # 137, at 5 de Diciembre and open daily from Noon to 11 PM. The location is about 2.5 kilometers or 1.6 miles north of the heart of the old city center where most shuttle bus drops offs are located. You can take a taxi or enjoy a walk along the Malecón. Layla's features traditional Mexican recipes, especially those of Jalisco and serves the freshest seafood.

* Le Kliff – This elegant and spectacular restaurant is located south of Puerto Vallarta on the main road at Kilometer 17.5. You will need a car and driver or a pre-arranged taxi with a guaranteed return. It perches high up on a cliff with an incredible view. And likewise the magnificent setting is only part of the experience, as the gourmet menu and impeccable experience will make this a visit to remember. The menu offers a mix of Mexican and International dishes with an emphasis upon freshness and delicate preparation. Reservations are a must. Call to book a table for lunch or dinner between 1 and 9 PM daily. Their phone number is 322 228 0300.

* Planeta Vegetariano – Yes indeed a fine quality vegetarian restaurant that still features Mexican flavors. This is a popular, lite and refreshing option in the warm climate of Puerto Vallarta. Located at Calle Iturbide # 270 in the heart of the old historic city, the restaurant is open daily from 8 AM to 10 PM. Reservations are not essential.

* Salud Super Food – In the Zona Romantica at Calle Olas Atlas # 534, this is a very popular and consistently great restaurant for those who want to eat healthy. Their salads, wraps and sandwiches are made with the freshest ingredients and you will know you are eating well. They also make an awesome breakfast burrito and vege burgers. This is a great place for casual light dining. They are open Monday thru Friday from 9 AM to 5 PM and Saturday from 9 AM to 2 PM. Reservations are not necessary.

* Vista Grill – Located at Pulpito # 102 in the Zona Romantica and open daily from 8:30 AM to 11:30 PM, this restaurant offers excellent cuisine in the Mexican tradition. And fresh seafood figures prominently. Reservations are advised. Call 322 223 5568 to book a table.

SHOPPING: There are many smart boutiques and shops in Puerto Vallarta with an emphasis upon resort clothing and fine jewelry. And there are plenty of souvenir shops and those selling fine quality arts and crafts. The state of Jalisco is famous for its fine lacquered wood products, usually black with bold floral designs. And you will also find very fine quality woven ware and colorful blown glassware.

I am listing those shops that I feel offer you the best quality in traditional Mexican crafts and I also list the major shopping mall in the event you are looking for stylish clothing or jewelry.

* BBVA Bancomer Plaza Carocol – This is the major shopping mall located in the Hotel Zone along Boulevard Francisco Medina Ascencio opposite the major hotel strip. This is a large indoor mall comparable to those found in American and Canadian cities. Shops in the mall open at 8:30 AM and close at 4 PM Monday thru Friday. Saturday hours are 9 AM to 2:30 PM.

* Lucy's CuCu Cabana – In the historic old city as Calle Basilio Badillo # 295 and open from 10 AM to 6 PM daily, this shop specializes in a wide variety of handmade traditional art objects, especially colorful figurines and dolls.

* Mundo de Cristal – Located at Calles Esquina de Insurgentes and Basillo Badillo in the historic old city, this is a shop that specializes in handmade Mexican glassware. But they also offer fine quality lacquered wood products.

* Old Town Farmer's Market – Located in Lazaro Cardenas Park in the city center and open daily from 9:30 AM to 2 PM, this is a great open air bazaar with all types of craft items and foods for sale.

* Señor Talavera – In the Zona romantica at Calle Encino # 275, this shop specializes in the well-known and beautiful Talavera pottery. It is Monday thru Saturday from 10 AM to 8 PM and on Sunday from 10 AM to 4 PM.

FINAL WORDS: Over the years Puerto Vallarta has become a major city that now offers all the trappings of any major Mexican city but without the extreme crowding, air pollution or poverty you find in the large inland cities. As a resort city, Puerto Vallarta is essentially very clean and refreshing. It brings back the vibe that once made Acapulco famous. But like all major resort cities, there is the underlying drug factor, but without the extreme violence seen in Acapulco, especially at night. Puerto Vallarta is still relaxed and relatively safe for visitors.

If you have had your fill of beach resorts, and if your cruise line is offering an all day tour either to Guadalajara or San Sebastian, you might want to consider the opportunity to savor some of what I call the "real" México. San Sebastian is quaint, isolated and is like taking a step back in time. Guadalajara is also a wonderful place to visit even though it is a massive city. The historic district and Tlaquepaque offer you the richness and vibe that many visitors to México fail to see.

A view of one of the resorts in Nueva Vallarta, Nayarit

CABO SAN LUCAS

**A map of Los Cabos at the southern tip of the Baja Peninsula,
(© OpenStreetMap contributors)**

A stop in Cabo San Lucas will be either your last port of call or your first depending upon the direction of travel. Cruises that are traveling westbound from Fort Lauderdale or Miami will reach Los Cabos, as it is known, two days prior to arriving in Los Angeles. If your cruise is eastbound, you will arrive in Los Cabos two days after setting sail. The name Los Cabos refers to the two resort communities that are eventually growing together with a string of resorts spanning the 33 kilometers or 21 miles between Cabo San Lucas and San José del Cabo, both in the state of Baja California Sur. The total distance from Los Angeles to the tip of the Baja Peninsula at Cabo San Lucas is 1,843 kilometers or 1,145 miles.

Many ship passengers consider Los Cabos to be their most favored stop within México because it is very clean, modern and exceptionally safe. There is very little real poverty here since both Cabo San Lucas and San José del Cabo live to service tourism and jobs are plentiful. This then precludes the grinding poverty and the barrios you see in so many Mexican cities. Another reason for the lack of barrios or major crime is the isolation of these two resorts from the border of the United States and also from the rest of México by the Gulf of California, known to the Mexicans as the Mar de Cortés. The physical isolation makes this logistically an awkward place for the drug cartels with regard to bringing in drugs or then transporting them to the United States. When you read the section on the landscape you will come to see why the Baja Peninsula presents such a barrier to easy travel.

Los Cabos today is so strikingly beautiful and so peaceful that many Americans and Canadians have invested in vacation properties. In many ways you hardly feel like you are in México because of both the large number of expatriates living here combined with all of the visitors. English is the more dominant language than Spanish.

THE NATURAL LANDSCAPE: The 1,600 kilometer or 1,000 mile long Baja Peninsula is geographically very unique. It averages less than 160 kilometers or 100 miles wide with ocean on both sides, yet it is one of the most hostile desert regions on the continent. It is ribbed with high mountains that reach a maximum elevation of 3,096 meters or 10,157 feet and only on the very tops of these mountains will you see any traces of forest. The remainder of the land is covered in a rather distinctive desert flora that is home to many unique species, especially of large cacti that are only found here. Their close relatives, however, even taller are found in Arizona and the Mexican state of Sonora, known as the giant Saguaro.

The desert landscape of Los Cabos is so similar to that of Arizona with the seashore being the only visual difference, (Work of Stan Shebs, CC BY SA 3.0, Wikimedia.org)

The Baja Peninsula is separated from the mainland by the Gulf of California because underneath lies the great San Andreas Fault, a plate boundary between the Pacific and North American Plates. In this area major earthquakes are to be expected, and minor events occur with regularity.

The reason for the arid conditions of the Baja Peninsula are the very cold ocean current upwelling in the sea combined with stable descending air out of the great Pacific High Pressure Zone. These factors in combination create a very arid environment. However, occasional winter storms coming off the northern Pacific will brush the top end of the peninsula and summer monsoonal showers occur at the southern margins. And every few years a tropical Pacific hurricane may sweep into the Gulf of California bringing havoc in its wake to Los Cabos and on occasion as far north as Arizona. Temperatures are mild during the winter but reach rather high levels in summer, tempered along the immediate shoreline by ocean breezes. Temperatures in the Baja California interior can soar to over 38 degrees Celsius or 100 Fahrenheit and beyond. During winter it is not uncommon for the desert mornings to have temperatures below freezing.

Land's End – the southern tip of the Baja Peninsula

The peninsula is divided into two Mexican states. Baja California represents the northern half of the peninsula and is quite heavily populated along the United States border. Tijuana, the largest city, has a population in excess of 1,400,000 and the state capital of Mexicali has just over 1,000,000 residents. It is located in the Imperial Valley, which extends south from California to the top end of the Gulf of California and is a rich irrigated agricultural region. Tijuana is a popular tourist center for day trips, but to the south just over 100 kilometers or 60 miles is the former fishing town of Ensenada, a popular port of call for Mexican Riviera cruises.

The southern half of the peninsula is within the state of Baja California Sur, isolated by the mostly unsettled tracts of desert extending to the southern tip. The state population is just under 715,000 with over 215,000 living in the state capital city of La Paz and 287,000 residing in Los Cabos. Baja California Sur is more arid than its northern counterpart, yet more vulnerable to hurricanes as occurred in Los Cabos in late summer 2014.

A BRIEF AREA HISTORY: Prior to the coming of the Spanish, the native inhabitants of the peninsula were primarily primitive hunters and gatherers. The famous Hernán Cortés explored and actually named the Gulf of California in 1535, but found the area totally unworthy of development. He did name the gulf as Mar de Cortés, a somewhat egotistical gesture. Today all Mexican maps show it with that name.

Prior to the first missions being built, pirates, including the notorious British privateer Sir Francis Drake used the waters of Los Cabos to loot Spanish ships en route to or from The Philippines. Spanish missionaries established a few missions along the gulf coast to the north, and in 1730, two priests established a mission at what is today San José del Cabo. The town was established in 1820 near the end of the Acapulco-Manila trade as a resupply station.

The mission church at San José del Cabo beautifully preserved today

During the Mexican-American War and later during the 1911 Revolution only minor skirmishes took place in the remote southern portions of the peninsula. During much of the 20th century, this area remained a backwater. There was not even a completed road between Cabo San Lucas and San José del Cabo until 1970. It was intervention by the Mexican government that helped in the development of a tourist infrastructure, kick starting the concept of Los Cabos as a resort area. The progress has been phenomenal. Today this is one of the most popular destinations in the country. Direct air services link Los Cabos to many cities in both the United States and Canada. The fully sealed road now connects Los Cabos to La Paz and northward to Mexicali and Tijuana. Few people make the long drive, as there are still few services along the route. But the road does make it easier for the hotels to receive provisions and supplies.

The beachfront hotels of Cabo San Lucas

Los Cabos has become a popular destination year around despite the extreme desert heat during summer. With air conditioning and the cooling breezes blowing off the surrounding waters, summer is actually quite comfortable. Many expatriates have chosen to retire in Los Cabos, as it now offers all the major amenities North Americans in particular could want. There are elegant shopping malls, major supermarkets and adequate medical facilities. And given its physical isolation from the rest of México and distance from the United States border, Los Cabos has not become a major location for drug smuggling activities or illegal immigration. Therefore it has remained relatively free of violence. The normal street crime found on the Mexican mainland is also not a significant factor here because of the high degree of employment.

One major factor of concern with the development of tourism is the lack of significant environmental protection. The deserts of the Baja Peninsula are fragile despite their formidable appearance. The Mexican government has been slow to respond to environmental concerns raised from outside of the country. There is a need for safeguards to protect the desert from being overly exploited by developers in the Los Cabos region and elsewhere on the peninsula where visitors are congregating.

SIGHTSEEING IN LOS CABOS: Los Cabos is known for its stunning beaches, its surfing, sailing, sport fishing and whale watching. Water plays the major role in the activities people come for. Cabo San Lucas is relatively modern and has little if any historic features. San José del Cabo has developed its old town core along historic lines since it at least dates back to the late colonial era. There are few significant historic monuments, buts plaza and church along with a few surrounding buildings do give the city a degree of Mexican authenticity.

The historic old town area of San José del Cabo

There are no port facilities in San José del Cabo. And in Cabo San Lucas there is only a small harbor for pleasure craft. All cruise ships must anchor in the open sea off the coast of the small harbor and tender guests to the shore. And for large cruise ships this can be a very lengthy process.

* SIGHTSEEING OPTIONS AROUND LOS CABOS: All cruise ships that stop in Cabo San Lucas offer a variety of motor coach tours, either to tour the small city itself or to take guests over to San José del Cabo for additional sightseeing. Many guests choose simply to tender to the shore and spend the day walking around in Cabo San Lucas or going to the beach for relaxation in the sun and to splash in the sea.

** Local Boat Tours – At the Cabo San Lucas small craft harbor there are numerous operators who offer sailing or motorized cruises around the rocks of Land's End or out into the sea for whale watching. Some cruise lines contract with these operators for exclusive tours while other cruise lines leave it to their guests to make their own arrangements. There are also small craft tours out to remote beaches among the rocks of Land's End that some guests choose to engage. You may also go out on a deep sea fishing trip if you can fit it into your ship's hours in port, as there are several local operators ready to assist you at the port. There are also special operators that offer small private group sailing adventures. I recommend a company called Get Your Guide. You can check their web page at *www.getyourguide.com* for details.

The onshore tender site in Cabo San Lucas

** Private cars and drivers can be arranged through the ship's tour office, but as in other ports this can be quite costly. And frankly there is not much to see that would be different than what the standard motor coach tour to San José del Cabo would offer. You should also check Cabo San Lucas Tours at *www.cabosanlucastours.net* for information and rates on hiring a private car and driver on your own.

** There is no hop on hop off bus service in Los Cabos. Again I recommend checking with Cabo San Lucas Tours at *www.cabosanlucastours.net* to see what they offer by way of small group tours.

** Taxi tours – There are so many different taxis in Cabo San Lucas outside of the small craft port area. Most drivers do speak English. And the taxi services are well supervised for safety, so that is not a concern. You can negotiate with a driver for sightseeing by the hour or for the day. Their rates are relatively high and you will not be likely to get a bargain especially of more than one ship is anchored offshore. Prices are quoted in Mexican Pesos, so you must make sure the driver will also accept American Dollars or other currencies. And tipping is not expected.

* SIGHTS IN LOS CABOS: There are few historic or cultural sites to see in either Cabo San Lucas or San José del Cabo. This is such a relatively new resort area that apart from a few buildings surrounding the historic plaza in San José del Cabo, the Los Cabos region has little to offer. I have listed below what I consider the must see venues and you will find that most are beaches or scenic locales. Here are my recommendations shown alphabetically

** Beaches of Los Cabos – The majority of the beaches are open to the public, but to enjoy any services you need to check the hotels adjacent to a beach that appeals to your taste if you wish to have any washrooms, cabanas, towels or food service. Some do offer special day packages. Many of the beaches are totally wild in that there are no services available. Some cruise lines will offer a day at the beach as a tour for small groups. The various beaches are too numerous to name, and the names would be meaningless. If you wish to spend a day at the beach without the need for a car and driver or a taxi, the main beach adjacent to the small craft harbor is ideal, as there are hotels and eateries opposite the sand.

*** Playa el Médano is the most popular, but it is crowded and filled with vendors, convenient with regard to facilities, but not very peaceful. If you go to Playa el Médano, move to the right and go down the beach until you reach the quiet areas where you can enjoy the sand in peace.

Part of the extensive beachfront in Cabo San Lucas seen from the sea

** Desert Park Natural Reserve – This small reserve is located just north of Cabo San Lucas at Kilometer 19.5 on Federal Highway One. Here is a chance to explore a piece of Baja Peninsula desert either on a walking tour, or by camel and have a chance to also get good views out into the Pacific Ocean, great during the late winter when Humpback wales are to be seen. The park is open daily from 9 AM to 5 PM and can be reached on your own with a private car or taxi.

** Los Arcos – These are the rock formations that are the absolute tip of Land's End and you will see them from the deck of your ship or close up from almost any motorboat or launch tour out of the private craft harbor.

**Lover's Beach – For those who want to spend time enjoying a very spectacular and also romantic time on the sand, you can take a small group or private launch to Lover's Beach. It is a strip of sand sandwiched between the rocks of Land's End with one side facing the open Pacific Ocean and the other side facing the Gulf of California. Some cruise lines will offer a small group tour to Lover's Beach.

The absolute peaceful beauty of Lover's Beach

** Old Town San José del Cabo – The drive to and from San José del Cabo either by private car or motor coach is in itself quite scenic. Once in town, you will have time to walk around the plaza, visit the old mission church and then enjoy the shops and cafes of this most historic part of all of Los Cabos.

** Playa Hotelera – This is the public beach in San José del Cabo that is lined with the beautiful hotels of this resort. Spending time on the beach is free for all since most beaches in the country are public. But to use any of the facilities at the various hotels will require either a day fee (if offered) or having a meal on the property. At high tide the surf can be a bit wild, but at low tide it is nice to walk along the beach since there are many small tide pools that are filled with sea creates temporarily stranded until the next high tide. You will need either a private car and driver or a taxi to reach this beautiful beach.

** San José Estuary and Bird Sanctuary – Located off Paseo San José in San José del Cabo, this beautiful bird sanctuary set amid the waters of a calm estuary is one of the interesting wildlife locales you can see on the Baja Peninsula. Many cruise lines do offer this venue as part of their overall Los Cabos tour or the more upmarket cruise lines make this special in depth nature tour. You can also go by private car or taxi. The site is somewhat primitive, but there are passable walkways for you to follow. It is truly a desert oasis. The estuary is open daily from dawn to dusk.

The rugged Pacific Ocean shoreline of Cabo San Lucas

** Wirikuta Botanical Park – This is a special place for anyone who loves the desert flora and wants to stroll amid a massive and beautifully presented array of cacti. It has over one million plants, a botanical labyrinth and you can also order cactus for your own garden or indoor pots at home. It is offered as a stop on some tours offered by the cruise lines, but can be reached with a private car or taxi. The park is open daily during daylight hours.

DINING OUT: The Los Cabos region is filled with hundreds of restaurants that range in price from the fast food take out type to gourmet establishments where you can dine in style. You will only be in Los Cabos for a few hours and either on a group or private tour or on your own. Any group tour that lasts more than six hours will often include lunch, but without any choice on your part. If you have a private car and driver or have arranged for an all-day taxi tour you will most likely want lunch. I am recommending my favorite restaurants in Los Cabos, which are all in the category of excellent to outstanding, ignoring the fast food or take out variety. I have also left out several good possible choices because of more recent negative reviews. Thus unlike the mass market guides, my recommendations are personalized and will steer you in the right direction. My listings are alphabetical and include both Cabo San Lucas and San José del Cabo

There is a greener and more elegant atmosphere to San José del Cabo

** Cabo Blue – Just off the harbor at Boulevard Marina # 30, a short walk from the ship tender dock and open daily from 10 AM to 2 AM, this is a very popular restaurant and bar that visitors seem to enjoy congregating in, especially on days ships are in port. It has a large indoor/outdoor bar noted for its drinks. But despite the reputation as a bar, it is also a very good Mexican style restaurant featuring traditional recipes that are well prepared. A great lunch spot.

** La Chatita Restaurant & Bar – Located on the pleasure craft harbor on the opposite side of where ship's tenders arrive, this is a very well-known and popular lunch spot with a menu that combines Mexican favorites with a variety of international dishes. And fresh seafood figures prominently on the menu. Cuisine and service are excellent. Their hours are from 7 AM to 10 PM daily.

** Lolita Café – On Calle Manuel Doblado # 24, this is a Mexican restaurant that also aims to give its foreign guests non spicy options such as delicious sandwiches, vegetarian dishes and numerous fresh seafood choices. It is open Tuesday thru Sunday from 9 AM to 4 PM.

** Mariscos la Palmita – Located at Calle 16 de Septiembre north of the main city center, a bit far to walk, so you are safe to take a taxi. This is a very special seafood restaurant serving local fresh fish and shrimp prepared in true Mexican style or simply grilled if that is your choice. It is very popular with locals. It is open Tuesday thru Saturday from 11 AM to 9 PM.

** Pan di Bacco – In Cabo San Lucas at Lazaro Cardenas at the corner of Boulevard Marina facing Playa Médano, this is a very popular Italian restaurant featuring pizza, pastas, sandwiches, salads and it is also vegetarian friendly. They are open daily from 9 Am to 11 PM. The atmosphere is casual, but the food is good, especially suited to the beachfront atmosphere.

** Sand Bar – On Playa Médano, this is one of the most popular casual restaurants on the beach for very fresh seafood. Most dishes are prepared with zest in the Mexican style, and they also do offer vegetarian entrees and salads. They are open daily from 8 AM to 10 PM.

** Sardinia Café – In San José del Cabo at kilometer 29.5 on the Careterra Transpeninsular as you enter town, this is a delightful restaurant serving fresh seafood, salads and soups in a Mexican tradition. Everything is fresh, using the finest ingredients and beautifully presented. Vegetarian dishes are also available. They are open daily from 8:30 AM to 10 PM.

** Sea Grill – In San José del Cabo at kilometer 19.5 on the Careterra Transpeninsular, this is an very delightful restaurant serving on a beautiful indoor/outdoor deck overlooking the sea. The cuisine is a combination of Mexican and International styles served with a definite elegant flair. They are open daily from 11:30 AM to 10 PM and reservations are advised. Call them at 624 144 2800 to book a table.

SHOPPING: Cabo San Lucas and San José del Cabo offer excellent shopping for both handcraft items with genuine Mexican flavor and also fine quality Mexican furniture that can be shipped to your home by very reliable dealers. And in Cabo San Lucas there is a major shopping mall that features numerous exquisite shops for clothing and jewelry. Here are my recommendations for quality Mexican products shown alphabetically:

* Arte de Origin – In Cabo San Lucas at Puerto Paraiso Mall, Store 3 $6, this is an excellent store for handmade works of art and traditional Mexican home furnishings. It is open daily from 10 AM to 7 PM.

* Paquime Gallery – Located in San José del Cabo at Calle Alvaro Obregon # 17, this small shop features traditional pottery, woodcarvings and a variety of handmade treasures from all across México by popular artisans. There are so many excellent treasures that you would be hard pressed not to find something you want to buy. They are open daily from 9 AM to 8 PM.

* Paquime Gallery - In San José del Cabo at Calle Alvaro Obregon #17, this small shop features traditional pottery, woodcarvings and a variety of handmade treasures that are sure to please. Open 9 AM to 5 PM daily.

* Puerto Paraiso Mall – Located at the small craft harbor, this is a magnificent mall containing a large selection of upmarket shops

* Vitrofusion Glass Blowing Factory – In Cabo San Lucas a short distance from the pleasure craft harbor, this glass blowing workshop uses recycled glass to make incredibly beautiful vases, figurines and larger art objects. They will also customize anything you request and then ship it to you. Tours are given daily from 9 AM to 2 PM. They are located on Boulevard Lázaro Cárdenas just north of the Puerto Paraiso Mall. Its main anchor store is Liverpool Department Store, one of the two finest department stores in all of México. It is open daily from 9 AM to 10 PM.

There are many colorful shops on the main shopping street of San José del Cabo

FINAL NOTES: I personally find Los Cabos to overly Americanized to really present the true flavor of México to enable a visitor to get a true picture of the country. But looking at it from a visitor's perspective, the absence of any significant historic sites, rather depressing barrios, numerous pesky street vendors or significant drug violence combine to make one feel comfortable. And for people on a cruise who are looking for enjoyment when they go ashore, this is a great port of call. It is us purists who want to feel the authenticity of a country that find a place like Los Cabos too incipit. I must give credit to the cleanliness and safety factor and the rather exotic desert surroundings that combine to make Los Cabos quite enjoyable for the majority of those who visit.

Modernity and cleanliness are quite dominant as here on the promenade in
Cabo San Lucas

ABOUT THE AUTHOR

Dr. Lew Deitch

I am a dual Canadian-American and a semi-retired professor of geography with over 46 years of teaching experience. During my distinguished career, I directed the Honors Program at Northern Arizona University and developed many programs relating to the study of contemporary world affairs. I am an honors graduate of The University of California, Los Angeles, earned my Master of Arts at The University of Arizona and completed my doctorate in geography at The University of New England in Australia. I am a globetrotter, having visited 97 countries on all continents except Antarctica. My primary focus is upon human landscapes, especially such topics as local architecture, foods, clothing and folk music. I am also a student of world politics and conflict.

I enjoy being in front of an audience, and have spoken to thousands of people at civic and professional organizations. I have been lecturing on board ships for Silversea Cruises since 2008. I love to introduce people to exciting new places both by means of presenting vividly illustrated talks and through serving as a tour consultant for ports of call. I am also an avid writer, and for years I have written my own text books used in my university classes. Now I have turned my attention to writing travel companions, books that will introduce you to the country you are visiting, but not serving as a touring book like the major guides you find in all of the bookstores.

I was raised in California, have lived in Canada and Australia. Arizona has been his permanent home since 1974. One exciting aspect of my life was the ten-year period during which I volunteered my time as an Arizona Highway Patrol reserve trooper, working out on the streets and highways and also developing new safety and enforcement programs for use statewide. I presently live just outside of Phoenix in the beautiful resort city of Scottsdale and still offer a few courses for the local community colleges when I am at home.

**TO CONTACT ME, PLEASE CHECK OUT MY WEB PAGE
FOR MORE INFORMATION AT:**
http://www.doctorlew.com

Made in United States
Orlando, FL
09 February 2022

14618733R00141